Corporate Information Systems Management
The Issues Facing Senior Executives

Corporate Information Systems Management
The Issues Facing Senior Executives

James I. Cash, Jr.

F. Warren McFarlan

James L. McKenney

All of the
Graduate School of Business Administration
Harvard University

Third Edition
1992

IRWIN
Homewood, Illinois   60430
Boston, Massachusetts   02116

© RICHARD D. IRWIN, INC., 1983, 1988, and 1992

Senior sponsoring editor: Larry E. Alexander
Project editor: Karen Murphy
Production manager: Bob Lange
Designer: Larry J. Cope
Compositor: Carlisle Communications, Ltd.
Typeface: 10/12 Century Schoolbook
Printer: R.R. Donnelley & Sons Company

Library of Congress Cataloging-in-Publication Data

Cash, James I.
    Corporate information systems management : the issues facing
senior executives / James I. Cash. Jr., F. Warren McFarlan, James L.
McKenney,—3rd ed.
        p.   cm.
    Includes index.
    ISBN 0-256-09008-4
    1. Management information systems.   I. McFarlan. F. Warren
(Franklin Warren)   II. McKenney, James L.   III. Title.
T58.6.C367   1992
658.4'038'011—dc20   91–39976

Printed in the United States of America
1 2 3 4 5 6 7 8 9 0 DOC 9 8 7 6 5 4 3 2

To Clemmie, Karen, and Mary

Preface

Corporate Information Systems Management, Third Edition, is written for students and managers who desire an overview of contemporary information systems technology (IT)—computer, telecommunications, and office systems—management. It explains the relevant issues of effective management of information services activities and highlights the areas of greatest potential application of the technology. No assumptions are made concerning the reader's experience in IT technology, but it is assumed that the reader has some course work or work experience in administration or management.

Our purpose is to provide perspective on the business management implications of the information explosion—as evidenced by the doubling of the number of volumes in the Library of Congress between 1933 and 1966, another doubling between 1967 and 1979, and yet another doubling by 1987. Huge leaps in the growth of scientific knowledge have stimulated a dramatic increase in the number of new products based on new information technologies. Ranging from the sophisticated super computer to the humble, ubiquitous facsimile machine, these products have impacted the very heart of a corporation's operations and will continue to do so. In many cases, the firm's competitiveness and its very survival are at stake. This growth, coupled with the increasing international nature of business, puts an enormous burden on the individual and the organization to keep abreast of events and to make intelligent decisions and plans. The broad objective of this book is to help individuals and their organizations to better adapt new technologies to their circumstances and thus to compete in their industry segments more effectively.

Since the first and second editions of this book appeared in 1983 and 1988, IT has continued to evolve. This Third Edition addresses this evolution by giving particular attention to the technology-enabled changes in corporation organization, control, response times, and costs. Its treatment of organizational issues as they relate to the development of IT resources has also been modified to deal with the new challenges posed by technologies. This book will help present and future managers to recognize and implement effective information services management.

Corporate Information Systems Management, Third Edition, is organized around a management audit of the information services activity. This management audit details all the questions that should be asked in identifying whether a firm is appropriately using and controlling IT. The book's text, examples, tables, and figures convey and illustrate key conceptual frameworks. Chapter 1 presents an overview of the key questions to ask in assessing the effectiveness of an IT activity. Chapter 2 then presents frameworks we have found useful for analyzing and structuring problems in the field. Subsequent chapters show how information technology can best be applied and how the IT activity can best be organized, planned, and controlled.

The material in this book is the outgrowth of directed field-based research we have conducted at the Harvard Business School since the early 1970s. We thank Dean John H. McArthur for making the time available for this work.

We are particularly indebted to the many firms and government organizations that provided us with much time and insight during the course of our research. All of the examples and concepts in this book are based on observation of actual practice. Without the cooperation of these organizations, it would have been impossible to prepare this Third Edition.

We are especially grateful for the many valuable suggestions and insights provided us by our Harvard Business School colleagues Lynda Applegate, Nancy Balaguer, Bill Bruns, Benn Konsynski, Jane Linder, John Sviokla, and Shoshana Zuboff as well as Associate Professor Eric Clemens of the Wharton School. In addition, we acknowledge the valuable work of doctoral students Jim McGee, Poppy McLeod, Charley Osborn, Keri Ostrofski, Donna Stoddard, Jeff Smith, Arthur Warbelow, and Kathleen Curley. Lynn Salerno and Bernard Avishai, in their editorial capacity at the *Harvard Business Review,* provided valuable assistance. We would also like to express our appreciation to Judith Tully, Maureen Donovan, and Nancy Hayes, who typed and edited numerous versions of the work.

James I. Cash, Jr.
F. Warren McFarlan
James L. McKenney

Contents

Chapter 1

The Challenge of Information Systems Technology

INTRODUCTION TO IT MANAGEMENT

Over the past 30 years, a major set of managerial challenges has been created by the rapid evolution and spread of information systems technology (IT), which in this book is defined to include the technologies of computers, telecommunications, and office automation. To deal with these challenges, new departments have been created, massive recruiting of new types of staff has occurred, major investments have been made in computer hardware and software, and systems have been installed that have profoundly affected how firms operate and compete. IT's impact has not been confined to large corporations; in its current form, it influences mid-size and very small (that is, under $1 million in sales) firms as well. Further, its influence in large corporations has been pervasive, reaching into the smallest departments and into managerial decision-making processes to an extent not even visualized 10 years ago.

Dealing with these challenges is complex because many members of corporate senior management received their education and early work experience before the wide-scale introduction of computer technology or in environments where the capabilities of information technologies were widely different from what they are today. Consequently, many of these people feel somewhat uneasy about the subject (legitimately so) and lack sufficient grasp of the issues to provide appropriate managerial direction. Many IT managers face similar problems, since their initial and technical experience was with technologies so different from those of the 1990s that their early experience is of little practical value. Understanding the programming challenges caused by the rotational delay of the drum on an IBM 650 (a popular machine in the late 1950s) has no value in dealing with the challenges posed by the sophisticated computer operating systems, local area networks, computer-assisted software-engineering tools, and other technologies of the 1990s.

Further, the identification of what makes effective management practice in the IT field has changed dramatically since 1976, when the personal computer first appeared and AT&T was reorganized. Virtually all major, currently accepted conceptual frameworks for theories of management in this field have been developed since 1976. Therefore, a special burden has been placed on IT management, not just for meeting day-to-day operating problems and new technologies but for assimilating and implementing quite different methods for managing the activity. IT managers who are not committed to continuing self-renewal very quickly become obsolete.

This book is aimed at two quite different corporate audiences. The first is corporate general managers who are collectively responsible for providing general guidance for all activities, including IT. For these readers, this book offers frameworks for evaluating the IT activity in their firm, defines policies that must be executed, and provides insights on the specific challenges of execution. It will help them to integrate IT and its management challenge with the overall activities of the firm.

The book's second audience is senior IT management. For these readers, this book provides an integrated view of the totality of IT management issues for the 1990s. Key patterns that organize and make sense out of a bewildering cluster of operational detail are identified. The focus for these senior managers is to move from analysis of "bark composition" of individual "trees" to an overall perspective of the IT "forest" and its management challenge. The book thus integrates the needs of two quite different—though operationally interdependent—audiences and provides them with a set of common perspectives and a language system for communicating with each other.

It would be a serious mistake, of course, to think of the problems of IT management as totally different from those found in other management settings. While the authors freely admit to having spent most of their professional lives dealing with IT technical and managerial issues, their thinking has been shaped by literature dealing with general business. The issues of IT organization, for example, are best thought of as special applications of the work on integration and differentiation begun by the behaviorists Paul Lawrence and Jay Lorsch. Issues of IT strategy formulation are influenced on the one hand by the work of Michael Porter and Alfred Chandler in business policy and on the other hand by that of Kirby Warren and Richard Vancil in the area of planning. Notions of budgeting, zero-based budgeting, transfer pricing, profit centers, and so forth, from the general field of management control are relevant here. The work of Richard Rosenbloom, Robert Hayes, Kim Clark, and Steve Wheelwright in the areas of management of technology has shed light on how the computer operations function can be better managed.

Concepts of IT Management

Many individual aspects of IT management challenges thus are not unique. What *is* unique is the peculiar *confluence* of these challenges, which must be resolved if an organization is to be effectively supported by IT in the long term. In thinking about this, the authors have sometimes found it useful to regard IT as a business within a business. Integrating the IT "business" into the rest of the firm poses many organizational and strategy-formulating challenges. Four concepts that permeate this book relate to how this kind of integrated IT business can be better managed. They are explained here.

Strategic Relevance.   The strategic impact of the IT activity varies among industries and firms and, over time, within an individual firm. Further, it is more significant to some operating units and functions within a company than to others. This notion of differing strategic relevance is critical in understanding the wide diversity of potential practices that can be used to manage and integrate IT within a firm.

Corporate Culture.   *Within a business* corporate culture is a phrase that must be stressed when attempting to identify how the IT business should be managed. The values of a firm's senior management, the firm's approach to corporate planning, its philosophy of control, and the speed of technological change in its core products all influence how the IT business should be managed. Of course, there are also generic tools such as databases, management systems for example, that should permeate all environments. Combining these generic tools with the values, culture, and processes of a particular firm is the art of management. A combination that works in one corporate environment can fail abysmally in another.

Contingency.   IT management in the 1990s is much more influenced by notions of contingency than it was in the 1970s and 1980s. In the 1970s IT management systems were implemented in settings where sheer chaos had existed. Consequently, simplistic and mechanistic approaches to work organization, management control, and planning were a great improvement over what was there before. As these new approaches and tools were assimilated into the firm, the initial surge of value from their introduction gave way to frustration in many cases because of their inherent rigidity. They answered some types of challenges very well and others not at all. For example, the emergence of PCs in the 1980s freed up constraints by permitting new types of networking possibilities, which in turn posed challenges to previously installed tools and structures. These factors combined to require more complexity and flexibility in the management approaches and tools to enable them to better fit the needs of a complex, changing environment. As we face the challenge of managing the diffusion, particularly of intelligent terminals with mainframe power, the situation will become more important.

Technology Transfer.   The diffusion of information technology can and must be managed. If it is poorly managed, IT will evolve not into a well-functioning system but, instead, into a collection of disjointed islands of technology that pass data between each other only with great difficulty. Since IT can now change the very infrastructure of how an organization functions, the implementation problems are very difficult. Success only comes when people are able to change their old habits and thinking processes. Hence we must think of IT as an "intellectual technology." Without concomitant change in thinking when a new system is installed, technical success is likely to be accompanied by administrative failure.

CHALLENGES IN IT MANAGEMENT

A number of other factors make the assimilation of IT a particularly challenging task. An understanding of these factors is essential if a sensible IT management strategy is to be developed. The more important of these factors are enumerated here.

A Young Technology

At least in its modern form (with high-speed computers), IT has had a very short life; its earliest commercial application occurred in 1952. Forty years is a very short time for the distilled outline of a new management profession to develop. Fields like management policy, accounting, finance, and production had thriving bodies of literature and know-how in place by 1930. Incredible amounts of knowledge and changes in thinking have occurred in these fields in this century, but they could be assimilated within an organized field of thought. Evolution, not revolution, has been the challenge in these fields. The challenge in IT, conversely, has been that of developing from a zero base during a period when its applications have grown from narrow and specialized to broad and integrated—with budgets and staffs that have been exploding in size.

Not surprisingly, the half-life of administrative knowledge in this environment has been quite short. No framework or avenue of thinking in this book predates 1973 in a published form, and most currently useful theories were developed in the late 1970s or later. Indeed, this Third Edition differs markedly from its predecessor, which was published only four years earlier. (The authors are under no illusion that this edition will be the last word on the subject and hope to contribute to better insights through further research.)

Technological Growth

Another source of administrative challenge lies in the fact that the field has undergone sustained and dramatic growth in the cost performance of its technologies. Over a billionfold improvement in processing and storage capacity has occurred since 1953, and the rate of change is expected to continue through the 1990s and early 21st century. (As with all technologies, a point of maturity will be reached, but we are not yet there.) Further complicating this, some core technologies—such as CPU size and speed—have grown explosively, while others such as software development tools have grown much more slowly.

This technical explosion has continuously cast up new families of profitable applications and permitted old ones to be done in new ways. One painful aspect of this has been that yesterday's strategic coup (a dramatic set of new customer service tools) may be today's high-overhead, inefficient liability (outperformed by those that followed and improved on the design). The natural tendency to utilize a particular approach too long has been exacerbated by the prevailing accounting practice of writing off software expense as it is incurred, rather than capitalizing it and amortizing it over a period of years. These practices conceal two facts: (1) that the organization has an asset, and (2) that it is an aging and often very inefficient asset.

IT—User Coordination

The complexities associated with developing IT systems have forced the creation of departments filled with specialists that continue to persist although many of the reasons for their existence have disappeared. Today data center consolidation, distributing development staff, and out-sourcing dominate debate on the organization of IT resources. Very often these specialist departments with their specialized vocabularies have created strained relationships with the users of their service. This has been an enduring headache from the start of IT. While the proliferation of desktop PCs, local area networks, and departmental minicomputers has changed the nature of the dialogue, there is probably no better example of C. P. Snow's technocrat-versus-generalist problem in the 1990s than the relationship between IT staff and general management.

IT has specialized in order to harness the various technical skills necessary for accomplishing its tasks, and not surprisingly, the specialists have developed their own language systems. To communicate among each other, they use words such as *bits, bytes, DOS, CICS,* and so on, which are totally opaque to general managers. General managers, conversely, have a quite different language that includes such terms as *sales growth, return on investment,* and *productivity,* terms that are opaque to the IT specialists. While it is clear that some of the newer technologies (such as object-oriented programming languages and spreadsheet programming languages) have helped IT specialist–user communication, substantial problems remain. A long-term need will exist for continually developing new integrating devices within firms to help handle the problem.

For numerous reasons, education will continue to address the technical versus generalist gap only partially. The experiences college and high-school students have in writing one-time, problem-solving programs and using PC-based word-processing packages, while useful and confidence expanding, develop a very different set of skills than those skills necessary to generate programs for processing business transactions reliably on a day-in, day-out basis. Similarly, experience in preparing spreadsheet programs as a staff analyst or in working with a word-processing package do not provide necessary perspective on the issues involved in large-transaction processing and data-base management systems. Unfortunately, education often fails to acknowledge these differences and produces graduates who are ill-trained for these tasks, do not know they are ill-trained, and thus have excessive self-confidence. Another educational issue is that some general managers are cognitively better equipped to deal with information technology issues than others. One of our colleagues describes the world's people as being equally divided into "poets" and "engineers." This split seems to prevail in general management as well.

Specialization

The increased complexity of contemporary technology has created a number of subspecialties. This explosion of skills needed for staffing IT has posed a fourth major managerial challenge. As IT has evolved, it has proliferated languages, data-base management systems, tele-communications issues, and operating systems support staff. All of this has increased the complexity of staff coordination within the organization.

Shift in Focus

A fifth challenge is the significant shift in the types of applications being developed. Early applications were heavily focused on highly structured problems, such as transaction processing for payroll and order processing, in which one could be quite precise about the potential stream of benefits and the nature of the end outputs. These applications automated clerical and operational control functions, such as inventory management, airline seat reservations, and credit extension. In the case of airline seat reservations, the shift led to a level of structure and decision rules not previously present and it sharply increased customer service.

Increasingly, today's applications are providing new types of decision support information for both management control and strategic planning. Evaluation of the payout of these expenditures on an objective basis before, during, or after they are expended is extraordinarily difficult and judgmental. Individuals may have opinions about these values, but meaningful quantification is very elusive.

Additionally, the development of these decision support applications differs from that of the transaction-driven systems. The detailed systems study, with its documentation and controls prior to programming, is often too rigid and fails to build the end-user commitment necessary for success. For these decision support systems, prototyping or doing it "rough and dirty" is proving to be the best approach. In short, new applications are forcing shifts in the ways projects are evaluated and in the ways they are developed. This is not an argument for a more permissive approach to system design and evaluation but, rather, a cry to be tough-minded in a positive way.

In combination, these factors create a very complex and challenging managerial environment. They form the backdrop for the discussions of specific managerial approaches in the succeeding chapters.

QUESTIONS FROM SENIOR MANAGEMENT

In viewing the health of an organization's IT activity, our research indicated that six critical questions repeatedly emerge in senior management's minds. We will not argue at this stage that these are the questions that *should* be raised but, rather, note that they are the questions that *are* raised. Four of these questions are essentially diagnostic in nature, whereas the remaining two are clearly action oriented.

1. Is my firm being affected *competitively* either by omissions in IT work being done or by poor execution of this work? Am I missing bets that, if properly executed, would give me a competitive edge? Conversely, maybe I am not doing so well in IT, but I don't have to do well in IT in my industry to be a success. Failure to do well in a competitively important area is a significant problem. Failure to perform well in a nonstrategic area is something that should be dealt with more calmly.

2. Is my development portfolio *effective*? Am I spending the right amount of money, and is it focused at the appropriate applications? This question is one that is often inappropriately raised. Scenario: An industry survey calculating IT expenditures as a percent of something or other for 15 industry competitors is circulated among the firm's senior management. On one dimension or another, it is observed that their firm is distinctly different from the others, which causes great excitement (normally, when their firm's figures are on the high side). After much investigation, one of two findings often emerges: (a) Our company uses a different accounting system for IT than our competitors use, and therefore the numbers are not directly comparable, or (b) Our company has a different strategy, geographical location, and/or mix of management strengths and weaknesses than our competitors, and therefore, what competitors are or are not doing with IT is not directly comparable.

   Raising the question of effectiveness is appropriate, in our judgment, but attempting to answer it simplistically through industry surveys of competitors' expenditures is not. Similarly, rules of thumb on expenditure levels a decade ago are virtually useless in today's environment, where very different technology labor cost tradeoffs are possible. For example, a fast-food chain is now exploring a set of technologies that would eliminate the need for up to 90 percent of its staff in a store. The approach was not viable even three years ago.

3. Is my firm spending *efficiently*? Maybe I have the right expenditure level, but am I getting the productivity out of my hardware and staff resources that I should get? This is a particularly relevant question in the 1990s, a decade that will be dominated both by extreme levels of professional staff shortages and by intensified international competition.

4. Is my firm's IT activity sufficiently insulated against the *risks* of a major *operational disaster*? There is no general-purpose answer as

to what an appropriate level of protection is. Rather, it varies by organization, relating to the current dependence on the smooth operation of existing systems. In general, however, firms are *much* more operationally dependent on IT's smooth performance than their general managers believe.

5. Is the *leadership* of IT activity being exercised appropriately for the role it now plays in our organization and for the special challenges it now faces? Historically, senior general management has used change of IT management as its main tool in dealing with frustrating IT performance shortfalls. (This high turnover has continued unabated into the 1990s.) One key reason for this is that it represents the quickest and apparently easiest step for senior management when it is uneasy about departmental performance. Also, as we note in Chapter 2, the nature of the job and its requisite skills tend to evolve over time, and the set of leadership skills and perspectives for one point in time may not be appropriate for another. Further, in many situations the problem is compounded by a lack of suitable explicit performance-measurement standards (metrics) and data for assessing performance objectively. As will be discussed in subsequent chapters, we believe the development and installation of these metrics is absolutely vital. In the absence of these metrics a 50 percent improvement in the firm's ability to meet service schedules, for example, may be totally overlooked by the end users. Their articulated concerns about remaining problems are simply amplified, so the managerial situation is judged not to have changed.

6. Are the IT resources *appropriately* placed in the firm? Organizational issues such as where the IT resource should report, how development and hardware resources should be distributed within the company, what activities, if any, should be out-sourced, and the existence and potential role of an executive steering committee are examples of topics of intense interest to senior management. Easily actionable, they are similar in breadth to decisions made by general managers in other aspects of the firm's operations.

These questions are intuitive from the viewpoint of general managers and flow naturally from their perspective and experience in dealing with other areas of the firm. We have not found them, as stated, to be easily researchable or answerable in specific situations and have consequently neither selected them as the basic framework for this book nor attempted to describe specifically how each can be answered. Rather, we selected a complementary set of questions that form the outline for the book and whose answers will give insight into these six questions. The next section briefly summarizes these questions and relates them to the content of this book.

ISSUES IN INFORMATION TECHNOLOGY

The IT Environment

Chapters 2, 3, 4, 5, and 6 define a role for IT in the 1990s that is very different from its uses in the 1970s. One way of describing this new role is illustrated in the chart in Figure 1–1. The chart explains the changing environment by focusing on three items: the administrative framework for facilitating and controlling the assimilation of information technology, the primary target of IT applications, and the way IT applications have been justified.

Era I.   From the 1950s to the early 1970s the manager of data processing was the single source of computing cycles and technology expertise. To use an industrial analogy, IT operated as a "regulated monopoly." If someone wanted access to computing cycles and technology expertise, he or she had to go to the data processing manager. There was no alternative. The primary focus of applications was organization-wide (payroll, accounting, production scheduling, order entry). New applications were justified on either a cost-elimination or cost-displacement basis. We call this IT management environment *ERA I.*

Era II.   Era II began with the introduction of minicomputers and time-sharing in the early 1970s. It was dramatically accelerated in the late 1970s by the personal computer. Suddenly a wide range of new channels was introduced for users to acquire technology expertise, processing cycles, and software. This introduced a "free market" (at least, relatively; users no longer had to go to the IT manager to gain access to computer and communications technology). Today's M.B.A. graduates often enter a company bringing with them a computer that has 20 times the capability of an early computer at 0.5 percent the price. In Era II's free-market arena, the rigid top-down controls developed and implemented in Era I were no longer applicable. At this point for many applications, the individual was the primary decision maker and had sufficient discretionary resources to reinforce that independence, and not deal with the central IT function unless they wanted to.

During this period a dramatic shift occurred in project justification. Individual and corporate *effectiveness* became the key justification measure. Era-I applications and their administrative systems could not and did not disappear. Rather, the IT management environment was made more complex with the additional challenge of managing easily accessible, individually exploited technology concurrently with Era-I technology.

Era III.   In what we designate the third era of information technology, management again did not preempt prior applications, although it

FIGURE 1–1   The IT Environment

	Administrative framework	Primary target	Justification/ Purpose
Era I	Regulated monopoly	Organizational	Productivity/ Efficiency
Era II	Free market	Individual	Effectiveness
Era III	Regulated free market	Business process/ Interorganizational	Strategic/ Competitive

forced important changes in administrative processes. Era III is best distinguished on the basis of the justification/purpose column in Figure 1–1. A growing number of companies have used IT to cause significant shifts in market share, competitive positioning, and organizational restructuring. As we examine the administrative framework for these companies, it becomes clear they are not at one end of the regulated versus free-market spectrum or the other. They have attempted to create a "regulated free-market environment" where the primary objective is exploiting the awareness, knowledge, and expertise generated during Era II to innovate and create dramatically different approaches to the conduct of business based on the capability of IT. Frequently these uses of technology transcend traditional company or industry boundaries and/or facilitate restructuring internal organizations and functions. Dealing with these issues makes IT strategy, on balance, much more important than it was a decade ago.

Organization

Chapters 7 and 8 are most closely aligned to the senior management questions 5 and 6 listed earlier in this chapter relating to the leadership and organization of the IT activity. Several main themes are addressed in those chapters. First and foremost, what is an appropriate way to think about the architecture of the distribution of hardware networks, software development resources, and data bases within the corporation? The issues of patterns of distributed resources have been well studied, and appropriate ways of thinking about them continue to be developed as new technology capabilities emerge. These issues go well beyond the technology itself and are heavily contingent on such influences as corporate organization, corporate culture, leadership style of the chief executive officer (CEO), importance of IT to achievement of corporate goals, and current sophistication of IT management. Surrounding the selected architecture of distributed and networked resources, there is need for central administrative policies to ensure that suitable overall direction is being maintained. The nature, intensity, and criticality of this direction varies widely among settings.

A second theme is ensuring that IT is broadly enough defined and that the converging and increasingly integrated technologies of computing, telecommunications, and word processing are in fact being adequately integrated. International coordination issues are much more complicated than those in the domestic arena. **Chapter 12** is devoted to discussing the coordination issues posed by different national infrastructures: staff availability, level of telecommunications sophistication, specific vendor support, great geographic distance, different spoken languages, transborder data flows, national culture and sensitivity, and so forth.

Finally, issues of organization reporting chains, level of reporting, IT leadership style, and other coordinating processes are also of concern. We believe there are better ways to think about these issues in the 1990s than there were a decade ago. Although common questions and methods of analysis exist, very different answers will emerge in different organizational settings.

Appropriate controls over daily IT operations as described in **Chapter 11** ensure that both cost efficiency and operations reliability are being achieved. The IT operations activity represents a very specialized form of manufacturing environment with some unique problems. First, operations have moved from primarily a batch, job-shop style to a continuous-process manufacturing or utility style. Not only has this changed the way these tasks can best be organized, but it has dramatically altered the types of controls that are appropriate. Second, in a number of firms, the IT activity has embedded itself so deeply in the heart of the firm's operations that unevenness in its performance causes immediate operating problems. These firms need significantly greater controls and back-up arrangements than firms with less dependence on IT.

The performance of operations can be measured on a number of dimensions. Cost control, ability to meet batch report deadlines, peak-load response time, and speed of response to complaints or unexpected requests are examples of these dimensions. To optimize all of these simultaneously is impossible. Each firm needs a clear identification and prioritization of these items before it can come up with a coherent operations strategy. Different firms will have quite different priorities; hence, a search for a universal IT operations strategy and set of management tools represents a fruitless quest.

Management Control

The questions of efficiency and, to a lesser degree, those of effectiveness are best addressed by ensuring that an appropriate IT management-control structure and process, as discussed in **Chapter 9**, are in place. Planning's role is to ensure that long-term direction is spelled out and that steps are taken to acquire the necessary hardware/staff resources to implement it. The role of management control is to ensure that the appropriate short-term resource-allocation decisions are made and that acquired resources are being utilized efficiently. The key issues in this field include the following:

1. Establishing an appropriate balance between user and IT responsibility for costs. Establishment of IT as a managed cost center, profit center, and so on, is a critical strategic decision for an organization, as is the election of an appropriate IT transfer-pricing policy to go along with it. Again, not only does this policy appropriately change over time, but it varies by type of organization as well.
2. Identification of an appropriate budgeting policy for IT. While many components of the IT budget are either fixed or transaction-driven, others are discretionary. These discretionary components need to be examined to ensure both that they are still being allocated to essential missions and that an appropriate balance is struck between the needs of many legitimate end users. This balance is necessary in a world where financial resources for projects are limited and where project benefits in many cases are not easily quantifiable.
3. A need for a regular weekly and monthly performance reporting. Reporting should reflect performance against goals and also against objective standards wherever possible. Unfortunately, the move of IT operations from primarily a batch activity to an on-line or networked activity not only reduces the territory for objective standard setting, but has made many of the older approaches obsolete.

Project Management

The questions of efficiency and effectiveness are also addressed through analysis of the project management process in **Chapter 10**. The 1980s generated a plethora of so-called project management processes and methodologies that have helped to rationalize a formerly very diverse area. The installation of these methodologies, an obvious improvement, has created a new set of opportunities.

The first opportunity lies in the area of implementation risk. The advocates of these methodologies have implied that by utilizing their approach, implementation risk will be eliminated. A careful examination of the long list of partial and major project fiascoes in the past decade suggests clearly that this is not the case. As described in Chapter 10, our contention is that project implementation risk not only exists but can be measured, and a decision can be made regarding its acceptability long before the majority of funds must be committed to a project development effort. In the same vein, it is possible and appropriate to talk about the aggregate-implementation-risk profile of the development and maintenance portfolio of projects. Not only does implementation-risk information provide a better language between general management, user management, and IT management during the project planning phase (where many options can be considered), but it provides a firmer and more valid context for after-the-fact performance assessment.

The second opportunity exists in the recognition that different types of projects are best attacked by quite different management methodologies. A single methodology is usually an improvement over the anarchy and chaos that often precede its introduction. Several years of its use, however, can create a straitjacket environment. A single approach may fit one kind of project very well and others considerably less well. Organization structure within a project team, types of user interfaces, leadership skill, and planning and control approaches legitimately differ by type of project. Today it is clear that the most appropriate management approach for any project should flow out of the project's innate characteristics. (That is, tell me something about the project, and then we can select an appropriate management approach.)

IT Strategy

"Is my firm competitive and effectively focused on the right questions?" We believe this question is best answered by looking carefully at the IT strategy formulation process covered in **Chapter 13**. The design and evolution of this process has turned out to be much more complicated than anticipated in the early 1980s, when some fairly prescriptive ways of dealing with it were identified. Elements creating this complexity can be classified in three general categories.

1. The first is an increased recognition that, at any time, IT plays very different strategic roles in different companies. These strategic roles significantly influence both the structure of the planning process (who should be involved, the level of time and financial resources to be devoted to it, and so on) and its interconnection to the corporate strategy and formulation processes. Where new developments are critical to the introduction of new products and to achievement of major operating efficiencies or speeded-up compet-

itive response times, firms must devote significantly more senior management time to this direction setting than in firms where this is not the case.

2. The second category of issues relates to IT and user familiarity with the nuances of the specific technologies being examined. Applications of technologies with which both IT and user staffs have extensive experience can be planned in considerable detail and with great confidence. To IT and/or the users, the newer technologies pose very different problems, both as to why planning is being done and how it can best be done. In any given year, a company will be dealing with a mix of older and newer technologies that complicates the strategy formulation task tremendously.

3. The third category of issues relates to the matter of the specific corporate culture. The nature of the corporate planning process, formality versus informality of organizational decision making and planning, and geographic and organizational distance of IT management from senior management all influence how IT planning can best be done. These issues suggest that, as important as IT planning is, it must be evolutionary and highly individualistic to fit the specific corporation.

The IT Business

Chapter 14, the last chapter, integrates this discussion by considering the challenge of managing IT development and diffusion from the perspective of a business within a business. In that chapter, we emphasize the present marketing posture of the IT business.

We see the early years of IT as unavoidably captured by the term *R&D:* "Can it work, and can we learn to make it work?" Subsequent years were characterized by start-up production: "Can large projects be managed in a way that will create useful, reliable services in a period of rapid growth when technology is new and changing?" We learned to manage a service organization with a rapidly evolving technology, and applications proliferated. Today's environment is characterized by focused marketing. The challenge is to blend, in a thoughtful manner, new product opportunities posed by new technologies with new customers.

CONCLUSION

This chapter has identified, from a managerial viewpoint, the key forces shaping the IT environment, senior management's most frequent questions in assessing the activity, and the questions that we think are most useful in diagnosing the situation and taking corrective action. In this final section, we would like to leave you with a set of questions that we believe both IT management and general management should ask on a periodic basis—every six months or so. They are a distillation of the previous analysis and, we believe, a useful managerial shorthand.

1. Do the perspective and skills of my IT and general management team fit the firm's changing applications thrust, operations challenges, user environment, and often shift in strategic relevance? There are no absolute, for-all-time answers to these questions, only transitional ones.

2. Is the firm organized to identify, evaluate, and assimilate new information technologies? In this fast-moving field an internally focused, low-quality staff can generate severe problems. Unprofitable, unwitting obsolescence (from which it is hard to recover) is terribly easy here. There is no need for a firm to adopt leading-edge technology (indeed, many are ill equipped to do so), but it is inexcusable not to be aware of what the possibilities are.

3. Are the three main management systems for integrating the IT environment to the firm as a whole in place and implemented? These are the strategic planning system, the management control system, and the project management system.

4. Are the security, priority-setting, manufacturing-procedure, and change-control systems in the IT operations function appropriate for the role it now plays in my firm?

5. Are organization structures and linking mechanisms in place that will ensure informed senior-management guidance of IT-informed user innovation and appropriate insertion of IT realities?

To help you answer these questions, this book presents a framework for analysis that encompasses four organizing concepts: strategic relevance, corporate culture, contingent action planning, and managed IT technology transfer. In each of the areas of organization—strategic planning, management control, project management, and operations—we will be examining the concepts' implications for action. Realistically, we are moving today in a complicated milieu of people, differing organization strategies, different cultures, and changing technologies. We have taken up the task of identifying a sequence of frameworks that can allow better analysis of the problems and issues facing organizations in relation to IT. We rely upon readers to apply this discussion to their own business situations in formulating realistic action plans.

Chapter 2

Manageable Trends

UNDERLYING THEMES

In the first chapter, we identified key issues that make the assimilation of information technology (IT) challenging. We then discussed four implications of these issues for management practice. This book is designed to provide a comprehensive treatment of these key issues. (An analysis of these areas for a firm, complete with appropriate recommendations, is referred to as an *IT management audit.*) Underlying our treatment of each issue are six themes that reflect current insight into management practice and guidance for administrative action. This chapter discusses the nature and implications of each theme. These themes also provide the organizational basis for the chapters that follow, because they represent what we believe to be the most useful ways to think about the forces that are driving transition in the use and management of IT in the mid-1990s. Our expectation, as mentioned in Chapter 1, is that additional experience, research, and evolving technology will inevitably produce new formulation of these and other themes in subsequent years.

1. IT impacts different industries and firms within them in different ways strategically. In many settings this has great strategic importance. The thrust of the impact strongly influences which IT management tools and approaches are appropriate for a firm.
2. Office technology, telecommunications technology, and information-processing technologies are evolving and will continue to evolve dramatically. This evolution will continue to destabilize existing systems and offer new types of IT application opportunities.
3. Organizational learning about IT is a dominant fact of life and limits the practical speed of change. The type of management ap-

proaches appropriate for assimilating a specific technology must change sharply as the organization gains familiarity with it.

4. External industry pressures have shifted the balance of make-or-buy IT decisions in the direction of buy. Managing this is complex.

5. While all the elements of the system life cycle remain, the new technologies allow them to be executed in dramatically different ways for different types of applications in various settings.

6. Effective IT policy and control involve a partnership between general management, IT management, and user management. Managing the long-term evolution of this partnership is crucial as technologies and opportunities change.

THEME 1: STRATEGIC IMPACT

Increasingly, it is clear that different industries are being affected in fundamentally different ways by information technology. In many industries, IT has enabled massive transformation of the various operational aspects of the value chain. Embedding technology in the product, computer-aided design and manufacturing (CAD/CAM), automation of factories and inbound logistics, increased quality, and massive cost shocks have all profoundly changed many industries' standards of competition in producing goods and services, and industry leaders have put great pressure on competitors to meet new standards. Many of these changes have linked independent functions into integrated systems that allow ever faster delivery of new and more complex products.

In other industries, the new technology has more strongly affected marketing, sales, distribution, and service to meet ever more focused and differentiated markets. New channels of distribution have been set up, prior methods outmoded, new customer service features introduced, and new promotion and market research methods developed. In such areas as product formulation and service response time, both operational and marketing impacts have been achieved; this separation between operational and marketing impact permits us to make a useful distinction between the role of technology in different industry settings.

Table 2–1 presents a series of questions for managers who are trying to place their firm and industry in the marketing axis. If the answers to most of the questions are no, IT probably would play a rather limited role in transforming the marketing function. Conversely, if the answers to most are yes, technology has played or will play a major role in transforming the firm's marketing organization. Table 2–2 provides a similar series of questions for managers trying to place firms on the operational axis.

TABLE 2–1   Marketing Questions for Managers

- Does the business require a large number of routine interactions each day with vendors for ordering or requesting information?
- Is product choice complex?
- Do customers need to compare competitors' product/service/price configurations simultaneously?
- Is a quick customer decision necessary?
- Is accurate, quick customer confirmation essential?
- Would an increase in multiple ordering or service sites provide value to the customer?
- Are consumer tastes potentially volatile?
- Do significant possibilities exist for product customization?
- Is pricing volatile (can/should salesperson set price at point of sale)?
- Is the business heavily regulated?
- Can the product be surrounded by value-added information to the customer?
- Is the real customer two or more levels removed from the manufacturer?

TABLE 2–2   Production Questions for Managers

- Is there large geographic dispersion in sourcing?
- Is high technology embedded in the product?
- Does the product require a long, complex design process?
- Is the process of administering quality control standards complex?
- Is the design integration between customer and supplier across company boundaries complex?
- Are there large buffer inventories in the manufacturing process?
- Does the product require complex manufacturing schedule integration?
- Are time and cost savings possible?
- Is there potential for major inventories reductions?
- Are direct and indirect labor levels high?

Figure 2–1 shows how leaders in several industries have competitively used IT very differently. In the airline industry, for example, the reservation system, which heavily controls the travel agencies, has given leading developers American Airlines and United Airlines major marketing and operations advantages. It has been the foundation for better aircraft utilization and new services such as "frequent flyer" programs and has also allowed the development of joint incentive programs with hotels and car rental agencies. The ongoing operations of seat allocation, crew scheduling, maintenance, and so on, have also

FIGURE 2-1   IT Impact: Current Position of Industry Leaders

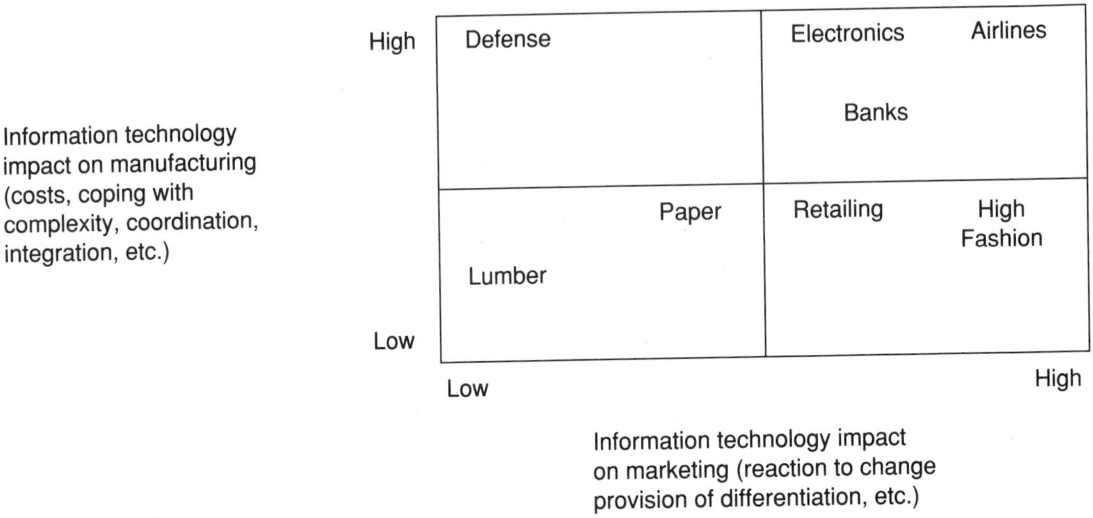

Information technology
impact on manufacturing
(costs, coping with
complexity, coordination,
integration, etc.)

High	Defense	Electronics	Airlines
		Banks	
	Paper	Retailing	High Fashion
	Lumber		
Low			

Low   High

Information technology impact
on marketing (reaction to change
provision of differentiation, etc.)

been profoundly impacted. When one of these systems fails, the overall operations of the airline are unfavorably affected almost immediately. As Figure 2–2 illustrates, however, second-tier airlines have invested much less and consequently have paid a significant penalty in terms of their ability to differentiate their services in the eyes of the buying public (marketing) and in their ability to coordinate and cost-effectively transform the delivery of their product (manufacturing). Indeed it has been cited as a leading cause for several failures.

A similar analysis of the banking industry shows, for example, that Bank-1, Citibank, and Chemical Bank have moved aggressively to distinguish their products and services through effective use of information technology. Other banks, however, have used it primarily to transform the back office and have been unable to significantly change the front office (to ultimate competitive disadvantage). The competitive problem is further complicated because some large players in industries such as banking and airlines have made major (and successful) investments that have created very high entry barriers for their successors, who are smaller and who find such investments prohibitive.

Figure 2–1 shows the impact of information technology for the leader in several other industries. Defense, for example, with CAD/ CAM robotics and embedded technology has been deeply affected by this technology on the manufacturing side. The marketing impact on defense, however, has been markedly less significant, partly because of the much lower transaction rate, but also because the much higher

FIGURE 2–2 IT Impact: Position of Key Players in Airlines and Banks

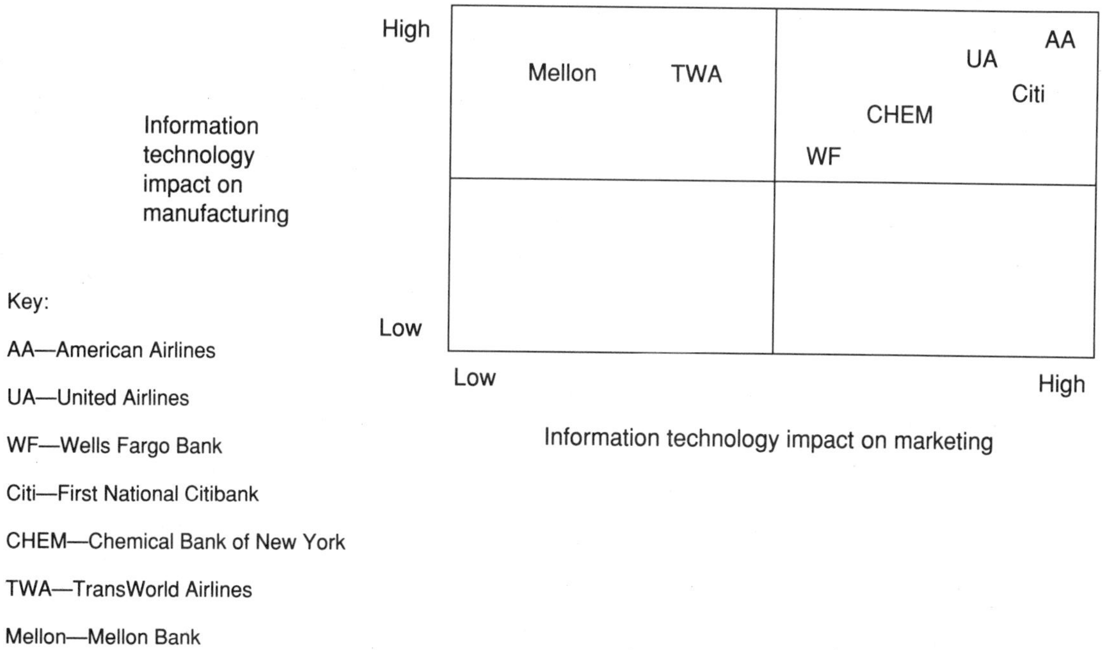
High
Low
Information technology impact on manufacturing
Mellon
TWA
AA
UA
Citi
CHEM
WF
Low
High
Information technology impact on marketing
Key:
AA—American Airlines
UA—United Airlines
WF—Wells Fargo Bank
Citi—First National Citibank
CHEM—Chemical Bank of New York
TWA—TransWorld Airlines
Mellon—Mellon Bank

value of transactions brings into play a very different set of marketing forces that are less sensitive to the technology's impact.

By comparison, retailing operations have been significantly altered by the technology (but not to the same extent as for the leading airlines or banks) through just-in-time ordering and cost-reduction programs. Similarly, display management, computer-assisted cosmetics analysis, and point-of-sale terminals have made important marketing contributions (but again, not in the same life-and-death fashion as in other industries).

Interestingly enough, significant impact for retailing operations has come from the effective use of IT by suppliers as they fight for space on the retailers' shelves. Twenty-four-hour delivery on key items, on-premise order entry, and other important features are now being demanded by retailers from their suppliers.

In the lumber and cement industries, on the other hand, the manufacturing and the marketing impacts of the technology have been relatively limited except for impacts on office work and order handling. Although there was great technology change in their production process control systems in the 1970s, their products remain commodities, which are purchased primarily on cost and timely delivery. Further, their core administration processes have been automated to a point that overhead is an insignificant aspect of cost due to links to customers, automatic ordering, and sophisticated production control processes. Consequently, the opportunity to use systems to change the nature of competition appears low for many firms in these industries.

Different IT challenges

Figure 2–3 identifies the competitive investment selections facing players in industries in which IT gives major transforming advantage in marketing, operations, or both. First are those firms that have already made dramatic transformations in the marketing and operations areas and are positioned strongly relative to the competition. They have normally been facilitated by leadership and structure. (At Bank 1 the CEO chairs the IT planning committee and is responsible for this technology; at Sears, Roebuck and Co. the chief information officer (CIO) sits on the company's executive committee.) The challenge is to *maintain advantage,* and current management approaches are usually adequate.

Another group of firms is in settings where the marketing component is relatively unimportant but where major investments are

---

FIGURE 2–3   Competitive Investment Selection: Task as compared with Industry Leader

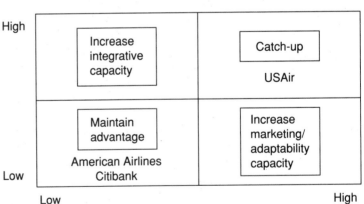

needed in operations to increase integration and to control costs and catch up with the industry leaders. Firms in industries such as aerospace, manufacturing, and petroleum often require work that cuts across many organizational boundaries and that cannot be easily implemented by a highly decentralized IT organization. Strong IT and senior-management linkage is needed to *increase the firm's integrative capacity.*

A third group of firms faces a primary challenge of catching up with industry leaders through better differentiating their products and services to meet the needs of ever more focused markets. Many of these firms need investments in IT research and development and new marketing analysis infrastructures for tracking trends and revising marketing strategies to meet competition. Items such as capturing point-of-sale (POS) data in order to analyze individual buyer habits and providing capacity for responding quickly to competitors' prices and product moves are often key. Similarly, the ability to use data and networks to move aspects of product decision making downward in the organization can increase responsiveness to local needs; the new systems at Frito-Lay illustrate this.

Finally, some firms are in a deep *catch-up* situation, having been outmaneuvered on both dimensions vis-à-vis the industry leader. Strong, coordinated efforts are needed by both the CEO and IT management of these firms to enable organizational adaptation to the new environment. The combination of being outmaneuvered by competitors in ways that really matter, the long lead times required to develop a competitive response, and the high capital investment costs of a new response has in some cases created a situation so serious that the survival of the corporation is at stake. (This is felt by many to be the primary cause of the demise of People's Express and Frontier Airlines.)

In short, information technology plays very different roles in various industry settings. In some industries it has played a predominantly operational role, while in others its impact has been primarily on marketing. In many of these settings, industry leaders have been so aggressive that they have transformed the rules of competition and put followers under great pressure. Leadership, structure, and other changes, as mentioned in the previous chapter, are all part of this adaptation.

Given this industry context, it is increasingly clear that good management of IT varies widely in different settings. For some organizations, IT activities have great strategic importance; for other organizations, they play and, appropriately, will continue to play a role that is cost-effective and useful but distinctly supportive in nature. Orga-

---

FIGURE 2–4   Categories of Strategic Relevance and Impact

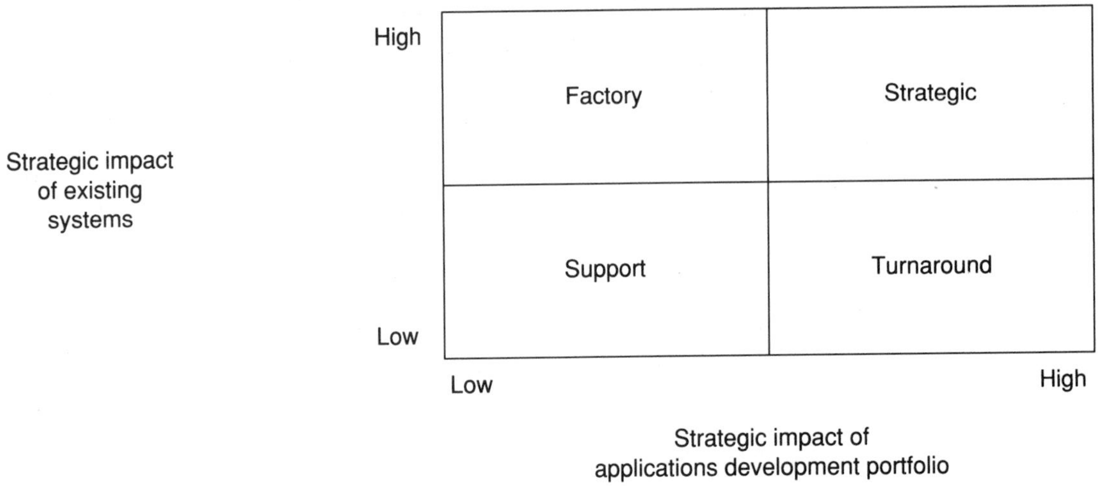

nizations of this latter type require less senior-management strategic thinking to be devoted to their IT organization.

IT Environments

As an individual firm approaches the management of IT, two aspects embedded in the previous discussion have profound importance. The first is that for some firms, the second-by-second, utterly reliable, zero-defect quality of its IT operations is crucial to its very survival. Even small interruptions in service or disruptions in quality may have profound impact. In other firms, significant disturbances in IT operations would have to occur over an extended period before the firm's overall operations would be severely impacted. The second aspect, discussed earlier, is that whereas new IT development initiatives are of great strategic importance for some firms, for other firms, what is under development is useful but not a matter of life or death. Understanding an organization's position on these two aspects is critical in trying to develop an appropriate IT management strategy. Figure 2–4 summarizes these points by identifying four quite different IT environments.

Strategic.   For some companies, smooth functioning of the IT activity is critical to their daily operation and applications under development are critical for their future competitive success. The IT strategy is the backbone of such firms' competitive success and receives considerable attention. Banks, insurance companies, and heavy-equipment manufacturing companies exemplify firms that frequently fall into this category. Appropriately managed, these firms require considerable IT planning, and the organizational relationship between IT and senior management is very close. In fact, in some of these firms the head of the IT function, broadly defined, sits on the board of directors.

Turnaround.   Some firms may receive considerable amounts of IT operational support, but the company is not absolutely dependent on the uninterrupted cost-effective functioning of this support in order to achieve its short-term or long-term objectives. The applications under development, however, are absolutely vital if the firm is to reach its strategic objectives. A good example of this is a manufacturing firm that was undergoing rapid growth. The information technology embedded in its factories and accounting processes, though important, was not absolutely vital to their effectiveness. However, the rapid growth of the firm's domestic and international installations in number of products, number of sites, number of staff, and so on, severely strained its management control systems and made their improvement of critical strategic interest to the company. Steps the company took to resolve the situation included enhanced IT leadership, new organizational placement of IT, and increased commitment to planning.

Another firm got into this quadrant by systematically stunting the IT development function over a period of years until the existing systems became dangerously obsolete. In fact, they were running on unique hardware platforms that their vendor was about to decommit on. Retrieving this situation through a crash systems rebuilding effort became a matter of high corporate priority.

Factory.   For smooth operations, some firms are heavily dependent on cost-effective, totally reliable IT operational support. Their applications portfolios, however, are dominated by maintenance work and applications that, though profitable and important in their own right, are not fundamental to the firm's ability to compete. Some manufacturing, service, and retailing firms fit into this category very nicely. In these organizations, even a one-hour disruption in service from existing systems has severe operational consequences on the performance of the business unit. In the 1990 AT&T long-distance collapse, one telemarketing firm had to send its 500 telephone representatives home, and that day's sales were irretrievably lost.

Support.   Some firms, some of them with very large IT budgets, are not fundamentally operationally dependent on the smooth functioning of the IT activity, nor are their applications portfolios critical to achieving strategic revenue and profit goals. For example, a large professional services firm is spending nearly $30 million per year on IT activities that involve more than 200 employees. Without a doubt, this sum is being well spent, and the firm is getting a good return on its investment. Nonetheless, the firm could operate, albeit unevenly, in the event of major operational difficulties, and the strategic impact of the application portfolio under development, viewed realistically, is quite limited. Consequently, their attention to the development and maintenance of an IT strategy is modest, although they keep abreast of new software products. (Their competitors are in much the same position.) IT appropriately is positioned at a significantly lower organizational level in this firm than in other settings, and the commitment to linking IT to business planning activities particularly at the senior-management level is essentially nonexistent. Our research has uncovered a surprisingly large number of companies still in this category, although over time the number has diminished somewhat.

In attempting to diagnose where a firm or business unit should be on the dimension of strategic impact of the applications development portfolio, careful analysis of the impact of IT on each part of the value chain is essential (as described in Chapter 3). In addition, competitors' use of IT must be analyzed periodically to ensure that major opportunities have not been missed. For example, ten years ago the retailing industry was considered to be *support*. Few competitors paid attention to what Wal-Mart was doing, and now most of them are trying to play catch-up in what is emerging as an industry in which IT is a strategic force. Subsequent chapters describe several widely used frameworks of competitive analysis and suggest how they can facilitate the identification of strategic IT applications when used effectively.

THEME 2: CHANGING TECHNOLOGIES

At the heart of the challenges lies the dramatic, sustained, long-term evolution of the cost performance of this technology. This means that applications undoable in 1985 would be state of the art by 1990 and distinctly unimaginative and obsolete by 1995. This theme above all has contributed to the complexity of managerial endeavor in this field.

The 1980s produced development of increasing electronic and storage capacities, which in turn supported an explosion of new types of software. As we enter the era of increasing chip density—jumps in excess of one million logic gates—new capabilities will exceed the installed base by several orders of magnitude. These changes will continue well on into the next century. The 64-million-bit chip is in development, and the next size is already in the research laboratory. This capacity will quickly add full-motion digital video, voice attachment to spreadsheets, new development procedures, and a cost of text communication approaching zero. Additionally, management of data processing or computing has long since ceased to be a useful concept around which to organize a program of management focus. Rather, the technologies of computing (DP), telecommunications (TP), and office support (OS) must be thought of as an intertwined cluster around which policies and management focus must be developed. When we refer to information technology departments or policies, we include all three technologies under this umbrella. At present, the coordination and, indeed, integrated management of these technologies have been accomplished in most firms, although the performance of these technologies continues to accelerate dramatically.

For at least two major reasons, the three technologies are viewed and managed (at least at a policy level) as a totality. The first reason is that an enormous number of physical interconnections must occur among the three. On-line inquiry systems, electronic mail, and end-user programming terminals exemplify the types of applications requiring the physical integration of two or more of the technologies. The second major reason is that, today, execution of all projects utilizing one or more of these technologies pose very similar management problems. Each technology involves large coordinated projects in terms of expenditures, rapidly changing technology, substantial disruptions to people's work styles, and often the development of complex computer programs.

Integration has been complicated by the facts that until about 1976 these technologies were not integrated and that they come from vastly different managerial traditions. The three technologies must be thought of as a totality at a policy-setting level and, in many settings, must have common line management, at least over architectural issues.

Since 1980 this integration has advanced from a largely speculative idea to one that is overwhelmingly embedded in management practice. Consequently, we will spend little time defending it and will focus rather on the managerial implications of this ongoing integration in a world of sustained rapid changes in the technology. Particularly we will attempt to distinguish between decisions that must be guided by central policies and decisions that are better left to end users.

THEME 3: ORGANIZATION LEARNING

Implementing a portfolio of IT systems projects built around continually evolving technologies is an extraordinarily complex endeavor. However, a range of concepts exists to assist the manager in managing technological diffusion. Key to most of these is early involvement of the users whose lives will be impacted by the design and adoption of the technology in their daily activities. Successful implementation of IT requires that individuals learn new ways of performing intellectual tasks. This learning process involves unscrambling old procedures and attitudes, moving to a new pattern, and then cementing this new process into the procedures of the individuals and groups. From a broader perspective, success demands that users be heavily involved in deciding how the systems can be designed to meet their needs and then in ensuring that the new system is actually assimilated into the key staff and managers' work routines instead of becoming an idle, expensive appendage.

Throughout the development of IT there has been an ongoing effort to understand the managerial issues associated with implementing and evolving automated systems in an organization. Starting with Thomas Whisler and Harold Leavitt's article[1] on the demise of middle management and going on to Dick Nolan and Cyrus Gibson's stages[2] and Chris Argyris's[3] espoused theory versus theories in actions, a range of concepts has been advanced for dealing with the problem of getting individuals to use automated systems appropriately. After field studies (many of them longitudinal) on 28 organizations over a decade, we have concluded that the managerial situation can be best framed as one of managing technological diffusion. Successful implementation of a technology requires that individuals learn new ways of performing intellectual tasks. As this learning takes place, changes occur in information flows as well as in individual roles. Often this has resulted in organization changes substantiating Leavitt and Whisler's conjecture and reinforcing Nolan and Gibson's original four stages.

We consider this process to be closely akin to the problems of organizational change identified by Kurt Lewin[4] and described in action form by Ed Schein[5] as unfreezing, moving, and then refreezing again. The process can best be summarized by rephrasing Nolan and Gibson's original four stages (called *phases* here) and considering the process as ongoing, with a new start for each new technology—be it database, local area networks, or new CAD workstations. This approach usefully

---

[1]Thomas L. Whisler and Harold J. Leavitt, "Management in the 1980s," *Harvard Business Review,* November–December 1958.

[2]Cyrus F. Gibson and Richard L. Nolan, "Managing the Four Stages of EDP Growth," *Harvard Business Review,* January–February 1974.

[3]Chris Argyris, "Double-Loop Learning on Organizations," *Harvard Business Review,* September–October 1977, p. 115.

[4]Kurt Lewin, "Group Decision and Social Change," in *Readings in Social Psychology,* ed. G. E. Swanson, T. M. Newcomb, and E. L. Hartley (New York: Holt Reinhart & Winston, 1952).

[5]Ed Schein, "Management Development as a Process of Influence," *Industrial Management Review,* Second Issue (1961), pp. 59–77.

emphasizes the continual tension between efficiency and effectiveness in the use of IT. At one time it is necessary to relax and let the organization search for effectiveness; at another it is necessary to focus on efficiency in order to control costs.

Phase 1. Technology Identification and Investment

The first phase involves identifying a technology of potential interest to the company and funding a pilot project, which may be considered akin to R&D. An alternative approach is to identify promising applications in the corporate strategic plan that seem amenable to systems innovations and then to provide funds for investigating whether this potential in fact exists. This approach is designed to attract product champions for systems innovations. The key outputs of the project should be seen as expertise on technical problems involved in using the technology and a first cut at identifying the types of applications where it might be most useful. It is generally inappropriate to demand any hard profit-and-loss payoff identification either before or after the implementation of this pilot project.

An important role of strategic planning is to encourage ongoing scanning for potentially relevant new technologies and to foster careful experimentation. In the past these were more often initiated by IT, but in recent time the user community is launching more pilot programs. For example, a major chemicals company recently authorized funds to investigate how to link overseas plants more closely. One pilot program connected similar U.S. plants to their European counterpart with a radio communications link and found they could quickly exchange process control innovations. This has led to an entirely new concept of distributing process control enhancements throughout the organization.

Phase 2. Technological Learning and Adaptation

The objective during the second phase is to take the newly identified technology of interest where a first level of technical expertise has been developed and to encourage user-oriented experimentation with it through a series of pilot projects. The primary purpose of these pilot projects is to develop user-oriented insights into the potential profitable applications of the technology and to stimulate user awareness of the existence of the technology. In the past, what key IT staff thought were going to be the practical implications of a technology have repeatedly turned out to be quite different in reality. As is true of Phase 1, there is a strong effectiveness thrust to Phase 2.

Phase 3. Rationalization/Management Control

Phase-3 technologies are those whose end applications are reasonably understood by both IT personnel and key user personnel. The basic challenge in this phase is to develop appropriate support systems and controls to ensure that the technologies are utilized efficiently as they spread across the organization. In earlier phases, basic concerns revolve around stimulating awareness and experimentation. In this phase, the primary attention turns to developing standards and controls to ensure that the applications are done economically and can be maintained over a long period of time. Formal standards for development and documentation, cost-benefit studies, and user charge-out mechanisms are all appropriate for technologies in this phase.

Phase 4. Maturity/Widespread Technology Transfer

Technologies in the fourth phase have essentially passed through the gauntlet of organizational learning with technological skills, user awareness, and management controls in place. A common pitfall in this phase is for the initiating staff to become bored because they want to move on to new technologies and to spend little energy transferring their expertise. If not managed, this phenomenon may sharply slow the process of adaption of the new technology.

This product life cycle of innovation, learning, rationalization, and maturity is now clearly understood within most well-managed firms. The framework is a useful base around which to develop a strategic view of diffusion of technology throughout the firm. As the experiments with a specific technology spread new by-product innovations should be encouraged in an organized fashion. Knowledgeable managers have proven to be better sources of new application ideas than either technology experts or single-minded product champions.

The key decision is how much to allocate to exploiting Phase-2 and Phase-3 technologies versus how much to allocate for Phase-1 technologies. There is no hard and fast guideline for making this decision, although clearly *strategic*-quadrant firms must do much more Phase-1 technology investment than *support*-quadrant firms.

The general theory on fostering innovation suggests waiting for a product champion to emerge and only then funding the product. Our thesis, however, is that an aggressively funded Phase-1 technology effort is a key precondition for generating these entrepreneurial product champions, who have been so important to successful IT innovation.

Technologies in all four phases exist simultaneously in an organization at any point in time. The art of management in the 1990s is to bring the appropriate perspectives to bear on each technology simultaneously; that is, support IT Phase-1 research, IT Phase-2 aggressive selling to the end user, and intensive IT Phase-3 generation of controls. This calls for a subtlety and flexibility from IT management and general management that too often they do not possess or see the need for. A monolithic IT management approach, however, will not do the job. This will be discussed further in Chapters 6 and 7.

THEME 4: SOURCING POLICIES FOR THE IT VALUE CHAIN

An issue of great tension and repositioning of IT in the 1980s was the acceleration of pressures pushing firms toward greater reliance on external sources for software and computing support. Outsourcing is one of the genuinely hot topics today. Escalating costs of large-system development, limited staff, availability of proprietary industry databases, and a dramatic increase in the number of potential applications have been some of the factors driving the trend to buy from outside sources rather than make systems internally. Increasingly, firms are also asking, "Do I really need to develop competence in running large computing centers, or can I delegate it to professionals and focus my energy more effectively on areas where I can get a real strategic edge?" These pressures will dramatically accelerate in the 1990s.

Make.   Key factors that favor the "make" decision include the following:
1.   Potential for the firm to develop a customized product that is totally responsive to its very specific needs. This is true for initial development as well as for necessary system enhancements and maintenance throughout its life. Further, one has the psychological comfort gained by having key elements of one's firm under one's supervision (the corollary of "not invented here").
2.   Ability to maintain confidentiality about data and type of business practices being implemented. This is particularly important in situations where IT services are at the core of how the firm chooses to compete.
3.   Ability to avoid vulnerability to the fluctuating business fortunes of outside software or data services suppliers.
4.   Increased ease in developing systems due to the growth of user-oriented programming languages, database management systems, on-line debugging aids, computer-assisted software engineering, and other user-oriented software. (It should be noted that the development and adoption of these tools has been slow.)
5.   Ease of adapting made software to rapidly changing business needs without having to coordinate the requirement with other firms.

6. Developing leading-edge competence that puts extraordinary pressure on competitors who do not have this competence. American Airlines and Wal-Mart are examples of firms that have excelled in this area.

Buy.   Key factors that favor the "buy" decision include the following:

1. Ability to gain access to specialized skills that cannot be retained or for which there is insufficient need to have continuously available. These include skills in end-use applications, programming and system construction, system operation, and system maintenance. Demographic trends (reduced work-force entrants) and increased end-use specialization needs are making this factor more important.

2. Cost. The ability to leverage a portion of the development cost over a number of firms can drive the costs down for everyone and make the in-house development alternative unattractive. This is particularly significant for standard accounting applications and database systems.

3. Staff utilization. Scarce in-house resources can be reserved for applications that are company-specific or so confidential that they cannot safely be subcontracted. Reserving these resources may involve buying into a set of systems specifications for the common applications that are less than optimal.

4. Ability to make a short-term commitment for IT processing support instead of having to make a major investment in staff recruitment and training.

5. Immediate access to the high standards of internal control and security offered by the large, well-run service organization. (A fee is charged for this of course.)

6. Proliferation in the types of information services that can be bought. Key categories include:

- Programmers (contract programmers, etc.)
- Proprietary databases.
- Service-bureau computer processing.
- Large-scale facilities-management firms.

The change in balance of these pressures in favor of the buy alternative has significantly impacted IT management practice as internally supplied services lose market share. Care must be taken to ensure that adequate management procedures are in place so that an appropriate balance exists. For example, the management control system must be checked to ensure that it is not, through excess charges, tilting the balance too much in favor of buy. Another example is that as software development is being outsourced, clear audit procedures must be developed to ensure that the suppliers have project-management systems that will enable them to deliver on their commitments. Implementation risk on a fixed-price contract is strongly related to vendor viability. A "good" price is not good if the supplier goes under before completing the project. For operational outsourcing this is critical, since 10 years is the normal length of these contracts.

THEME 5: APPLICATIONS DEVELOPMENT PROCESS

Traditionally, the activities necessary to produce and deliver a specific information service have been characterized as a series of steps:

1. Design.
2. Construct.
3. Implement.
4. Operate.
5. Maintain.

Since the First Edition of this book was published, the practical shape of this process has been dramatically impacted by the emergence of very different types of projects. At one extreme are the traditional projects that were once the mainstay of the industry. These projects are noted for being large, requiring extensive development periods (often well in excess of 18 months), changing the nature of work in several departments, being functionally complex, and involving at the outset unknown data structures and processing procedures. Production scheduling, airline reservation systems, and demand-deposit accounting systems are examples of projects that lie in this area. The traditional system life cycle described here continues to be appropriate for these projects, although one or more pieces may be done in parallel or overlapped in ways that make the old processes unrecognizable.

At the other extreme are projects that may involve the construction of a decision support system (DSS) on a department minicomputer or personal computer, perhaps using data from a central database. Here a heuristic approach (repeatedly cycling through the design and construction activities) using prototyping and other tools is most appropriate; the rigid sequencing of steps implied in the traditional development cycle is simply inappropriate. Further, a significant amount of software is often purchased for these types of projects. As a practical matter, the majority of firms' development dollars today are associated with this type of project. For all projects, however, design and implementation are essential.

The following paragraphs define the traditional components of the life cycle of the traditional project and also identify those aspects most likely to be mismanaged today in the development of decision support systems. A test of the appropriateness of an IT organization and its project management policies is how successful they are in encouraging and controlling each of the steps below for multiple large projects. While changing technology and improved managerial insights have significantly altered the way each of these steps can be implemented, their functions have remained relatively unchanged for a considerable period. With the increasing shift to buy (versus make) decisions, however, significant changes are needed in many of these steps, and IT management in many cases is becoming more like a broker.

Design

The objective of the design step is to produce a definition of the information service desired. This includes identification of the users, the initial tasks to be implemented, and the long-run service and support to be provided. Traditionally, the first step has been either a user request or a joint IT department–user proposal based on the IT plan. More and more, however, it is being initiated by a user request. The design step is a critical activity that demands careful attention to short- and long-term information service requirements as well as to ensuring the delivery of reliable service. Implementation of this step was traditionally dominated by the IT staff but is more and more being assumed by the user.

Design normally begins with an analysis to determine the feasibility and potential costs and benefits of the proposed system. If the results of the analysis are favorable, an explicit decision to proceed is made. This is followed by substantive collaborative work by the potential user and an IT professional to develop a working approach to a systems design. Depending on the systems scope, these design efforts may range from formal systematic analysis to informal discussions.

The end product of design is a definition of the desired service accompanied by an identification of the means (including in-house or purchased) for providing it. Prototyping is proving to be an indispensable tool today for speeding up the design process, improving the quality of the design, and reducing the possibility of major misunderstandings.

Construction

A highly specialized activity, construction involves the structuring of automatic procedures for performing a timely, errorless information service. IT combines art and logic. Professional judgment is needed in the areas of:

1. Selection of brand of equipment, firm, and/or service bureau.
2. Selection of programming system, database system, and so on.
3. Documentation of operating procedures and content of software.
4. Identification and implementation of appropriate testing procedures.
5. Review of adequacy or long-term viability of purchased software service.

Very technical in content, this work depends on good professional skills and good IT management skills. In the past it was very dependent upon good organization linkage to the users to ensure that design needs did not change. As more services are purchased, this phase is being eliminated entirely for many projects, although a portion often remains that involves modifying a standard system to the specific details of the situation. This phase, the design phase, and the implementation phase are often inextricably intertwined in the development of decision support systems.

Implementation

Implementation involves extensive user–IT coordination as the transition is made from the predominantly technical, IT-driven tasks of the construction step to its completed installation and operation in the user environment. Whether the system is bought or made, the implementation phase is very much a joint effort. Establishment and testing of necessary communication links between staff and departments, bringing new skills to the firm, and managing an assortment of intrusions into the normal habits of the organization are critical.

Operation

In most settings the operation of systems has received the least amount of attention during the systems development process. Consequently, enormous frustration and ill will have frequently occurred when a system is installed. Further, as more users become operators, the subtleties of operations shortfalls become familiar to all managers. A significant amount of the difficulty, as will be discussed later, stems from inadequate attention to clearly defining the critical performance specifications to be met by the new system and from failure to recognize the often inherent conflicts between specific service goals.

A part of the design phase is identification of the specific procedures that will be used to test the services. These usually include a formal procedure for approval by operations personnel, which serves to clearly separate responsibility for a service's construction from responsibility for its operation. This role separation is particularly important when the same department (or individual) is responsible for both constructing and operating a system. In addition, operations approval procedures are needed for system enhancements and maintenance.

After the system is built and installed, measures must be developed to assess the actual delivery of the service and its quality. This is a point of weakness in many user-designed decision support systems.

Many of them are so idiosyncratically designed that they cannot easily be transferred to another user when the initial user is promoted or easily be linked into the firm's networks and databases.

Maintenance

Ongoing design, construction, and implementation activities on existing services are components of maintenance. (The word *maintenance* is a complete misnomer because it implies an element of deferrability that does not exist in many situations. *Modernization* is a better term.) Much of the maintenance requirement stems from real-world changes in tax laws, organization shifts such as new offices or unit mergers, business changes such as new product line creation or elimination, acquisition of new technology, and so on. It can be as simple as changing a number in a database of depreciation rates or as complex as rewriting the tax portion of the payroll. Effective maintenance faces two serious problems:

1. Most professionals consider it to be dull and noncreative, because it involves working on systems created by someone else. Consequently, the work may be done by individuals of lesser talent.
2. Maintenance can be very complex, particularly for older systems. It requires highly competent professionals to safely perform necessary changes in a way that does not bring the system (or the firm) to its knees.

Newer systems permit users to develop their own adaptations by including report writers or editors. Because these complex systems require more CPU cycles, however, a cost accompanies the benefit. Managing maintenance continues to be a troublesome problem, but organization, planning, and management control all provide critical context to ensure that these issues are resolved appropriately. For the user-designed decision-support applications, this has been an area of particular concern.

Summary

This description of the systems life cycle helps to show the complexity of IT management. At any time an organization may have hundreds of systems, each at a different position along this life-cycle line. Of necessity, the IT department in the overwhelming majority of cases must be organized by IT functions (user programming, operations, etc.), rather than by a specific application system. This inevitably creates significant friction, because the IT organization forces the passing of responsibility for an application system from one unit to another as it passes through these steps. The user is often the only link (although changes often occur here also) as responsibility for the system is passed from one group of technical specialists to another.

To further complicate the situation, the execution of the life-cycle process (as well as the dividing line between the steps) varies widely from one type of application system to another. For example, a structured, transaction-oriented system requires an intensive, up-front design effort to arrive at firm specifications that can then be programmed. A decision support system as described in the last section, however, may involve a process of user learning. An appropriate methodology here may begin with a crude design followed by a simple program. Use of the program by the user leads to successively different and more comprehensive designs as its performance is analyzed and then to a series of new programs. This interactive sequence cycles through a number of times. Such a design process (pragmatically useful) flies in the face of many generally held nostrums about good development practices.

In Chapter 11 we deal with the issues of operations management and the impact of buy decisions on the systems life cycle.

THEME 6: PARTNERSHIP OF THREE CONSTITUENCIES

Much of the complexity of IT management problems stems from managing the conflicting pressures of three different and vitally concerned constituencies: IT management, user management, and the general management of the organization. The relationships between these groups around IT users quite appropriately varies over time as the organization's familiarity with different technologies evolves, as the strategic impact of IT shifts, and as the company's overall IT management skills grow. Chapters 7 through 11 are largely devoted to identifying the various aspects of managing this relationship.

IT Management

A number of forces have driven the creation of an IT department and ensured its existence. The IT department provides a pool of technical skills that can be developed and deployed to resolve complex problems facing the firm. Appropriately staffed, an important part of the department's mission is to scan leading-edge technologies and make sure that the organization is aware of their existence. The department is responsible for conveying knowledge of the existence of a technology, and of how to use it, to appropriate clusters of potential users. By virtue of its central location, IT can help identify where potential interconnection between the needs of different user groups exists and facilitate the development of the interconnection. In a world of changing and merging technologies, this unit is under continued pressure to modernize in order to remain relevant. Basically, the reason the unit exists is that its specialization permits the identification of new opportunities and the cost-efficient implementation of tasks, which often cross departmental boundaries.

As information technology has evolved, the problem has become more complex because IT staff members themselves have become important users of the system (to test and develop new systems, etc.). Further complicating the situation is the growing availability of user-friendly systems and experienced users who do not feel the need to call on IT for help. Unfortunately, inadequate involvement of IT skills in the development of new systems often comes at the peril of the organization. Great fiascoes can occur when user vision and excitement overlooks the realities of implementation and the ongoing operation of a system.

User Management

Specialization of the IT function has taken place at a cost: it has transferred some detailed operational tasks from the users to the IT department without relieving the users of the responsibility for ensuring that ultimately the tasks are well done. Obviously, this is a source of friction. Additionally, in the past, the often mysterious requirements of the technology appeared to disenfranchise users from some aspects of the design of services. These frictions, when coupled with a complicated charge-out system, further estranged the user from IT.

Also complicating matters is the aggressively marketed availability of outside services that go directly to the user. (The IT department is no longer the sole source provider.)

The term *user* often implies a narrower definition than exists in a real situation: the user may be many individuals at different levels scattered across several departments. Particularly in the early stages of a technology, the user is a specialist in living with the problem and not a specialist in the technologies that can be brought to solve the problem. As the user has become more sophisticated through experience with the older IT technologies, and as the newer technologies become more user friendly, some (not all) of the reasons for having a specialized IT organization disappear. User management, through increased experience with personal computing, is gaining more confidence (sometimes unwarranted) in its ability to manage all aspects of information systems development. (The same is true of general management; see the next discussion.) Appropriately, the division of service functions between the IT specialist department and the user is being reappraised continuously.

General Management

The task of general management is to ensure that the appropriate structure and management processes are in place for monitoring the balance between the user and IT to fulfill the overall needs of the organization. (This task is complicated for executive decision-support systems when general management becomes the user.) The ability and enthusiasm of executives for playing this role vary widely. This is both a function of their comfort with IT and their perception of its strategic importance to the firm as a whole. Since many have reached their positions with little exposure to IT issues early in their careers or with exposure to radically different types of IT issues, discomfort is often extreme. Much of this book is aimed at helping this group to feel more comfortable with this activity. It should be noted, however, that over the past decade general management has become more comfortable with this technology. Experience with personal computing and earlier encounters with different (now obsolete) IT technologies have generated confidence (often misplaced) in their ability to handle the policy issues implicit in information systems technology.

In brief, each group's perspective and confidence is evolving. Although these changes are solving some problems, they are also creating new ones.

SUMMARY

In this chapter we have identified the manageable trends that are intimate to all aspects of managing information services in the 1990s. Figure 2–5 maps the remaining chapters and identifies each chapter's emphasis in relation to these six organizing themes.

Chapter 3 describes how IT is changing the way companies compete. It provides a set of five diagnostic questions that can reveal the likely impact of technology in a firm. It then introduces value-chain analysis and shows how each element of the chain is permeated by information opportunities in different settings. The chapter concludes by identifying some strategic risks posed by this technology. Chapter 4 describes the types of strategic alliances that IT has enabled. Chapter 5 focuses on the role of interorganizational IT systems and how they have changed the boundaries of firms and industries. Chapter 6 identifies how IT is changing organization structure, management controls, and other aspects of the firm's infrastructure.

FIGURE 2–5 Map of Chapters and Themes

	Strategic Impact	DP/TP/OA	Organization Learning	Make/Buy Decisions	Life Cycle	Power Balance
Manageable Trends **Chapter 2**						
Effects of IT on Competition **Chapter 3**	•	•				
Interorganizational Systems **Chapter 4**	•	•				•
Organization and Control **Chapter 5**	•	•				•
Information-Enabled Alliances **Chapter 6**	•	•				•
IT Architectural Alternatives **Chapter 7**		•	•			•
IT Organizational Issues **Chapter 8**	•		•	•		•
IT Management Control **Chapter 9**	•		•	•		•
A Portfolio Approach to IT Development **Chapter 10**	•				•	•
Operations Management **Chapter 11**	•			•	•	•
Transnational IT Issues **Chapter 12**		•				•
IT Planning—A Contingent Focus **Chapter 13**	•		•			•
The IT Business **Chapter 14**	•		•	•		•

40

Chapter 7 describes the assimilation of new technology as an organizational learning problem that requires a series of contingent actions for managing the diffusion of technology effectively. It then proposes a new organizational unit for focusing on this need. Chapter 8 describes in depth the special management issues posed by the new, fast-moving evolution in technology and some essential modifications in the IT organization structure.

Chapter 9 explains the influence of corporate cultures on managerial roles and describes various management controls that can be used to integrate the IT services into the firm. Chapter 10, on project management, focuses on developing a set of contingent actions for IT, users, and general management for different types of projects and the inherent risks of different types of projects. Chapter 11 focuses on the special issues and challenges of delivering reliable day-to-day service. Chapter 12 extends the culture concept to include the range of complexities present in international situations. The planning discussion in Chapter 13 focuses on how planning is influenced by the strategic relevance of IT and on its potential impact on the organization. This includes both corporate culture and the type of contingent actions needed to assimilate the technology. Chapter 14 uses the marketing mix model to synthesize the overall issues in order to interface IT activity with the company as a whole.

Chapter 3

Effects of IT on Competition

To solve customer service problems, a major distributor installed an on-line network to its key customers so that they could enter orders into its computer directly. The computer was intended to cut order-entry costs, to speed processing time, and to provide more flexibility to customers in the order submission process. Although the company's expectations for the system were very modest initially, it yielded a large competitive advantage, adding value for customers and generating a substantial rise in the distributor's sales. Over a period of years new features were added, and the resulting increase in the company's market share forced a primary competitor into corporate reorganization and a massive systems-development effort to contain the damage, but these corrective actions were only partially successful. Only when the distributor stopped innovating because of internal cost pressures did its advantage deteriorate.

A regional airline testified before Congress that it had been badly hurt by the reservation system of a national carrier. It claimed that the larger airline, through access to the reservation levels on every one of the smaller line's flights, could pinpoint all mutually competitive routes where the regional was performing well and take competitive pricing and service action. Since the regional airline lacked access to the bigger carrier's data, it alleged, it was at a decided competitive disadvantage. Partly because of this, the airline ultimately failed.

A large aerospace company required major suppliers to acquire CAD (computer-aided design) equipment to link directly to its CAD installation. The company claims this has dramatically reduced the total cost and time of design changes, parts acquisition, and inventory, which has made it more competitive.

These examples capture the changing face of the IT applications world. With great speed the sharp reduction in the cost of information systems technology (IT) has allowed computer systems to move from back-office support to applications that offer significant competitive advantage. Particularly outstanding are systems that link customer and supplier (discussed at length in Chapter 4). As this chapter will explain, the evolution of such systems is usually extraordinarily expensive and extends over a number of years. The very competitive airline reservations systems, for example, have evolved over 30 years and they continue to evolve. To use a track analogy, the investment decisions in this area are more akin to the marathon than to the one-hundred-meter dash.

Though such initiatives offer an opportunity for a competitive edge, they also bring a risk of strategic vulnerability. In the case of the aerospace manufacturer, operating procedures have shown much improvement, but it has been at the cost of vastly greater dependence, since it is now much harder for the manufacturer to change suppliers.

In many cases the new technology has opened up new opportunities for a company to redeploy its assets and rethink its strategy. This gives the organization the potential for forging sharp new tools that can produce lasting gains in market share. Of course, such opportunities vary widely from one company to another, just as the intensity and the rules of competition vary widely from one industry to another. Similarly, a company's location, size, and basic product technology also shape potential IT applications. These opportunities are not restricted to the large firms; they affect even the smallest companies. Further, in different situations, a company may appropriately attempt to be either a leader or an alert follower. In many settings, what is a strategic advantage for the first investor becomes a necessity for the other firms in the industry as the rules of competition shift. The stakes can be so high, however, that this must be an explicit, well-planned decision.

ANALYZING IMPACT

Forces that Shape Strategy

The variety of potential competitive and strategic uses of IT is as broad and complex as the industries within which the uses have evolved. To facilitate planning for these uses, general managers need a comprehensive framework. This framework must view use of computer and communications technology from a strategic rather than a tactical perspective. Michael Porter's industry and competitive analysis (ICA) framework,[1] augmented with potential technological uses, has proven very effective in this respect.

Porter's work was directed at strategic business planners and general managers. He argued that many of the contemporary strategic

---

[1]Michael E. Porter, *Competitive Strategy: Techniques for Analyzing Industries and Competitors* (New York: The Free Press, 1980).

planning frameworks viewed competition too narrowly and pessimistically because they were primarily based on projections of market share and market growth. He asserted that the economic and competitive forces in an industry segment were the result of a broader range of factors than the strengths and weaknesses of established combatants in a particular industry. According to him, the state of competition in an industry depends on five basic forces: (1) bargaining power of suppliers, (2) bargaining power of buyers, (3) threat of new entrants into the industry segment, (4) threat of substitute products or services, and (5) positioning of traditional intraindustry rivals. Figure 3–1 shows the five competitive forces and illustrates the ICA framework.

Although Porter's initial work did not include information systems as part of the company's resource pool for ICA, it has proven very useful in considering the business and industry impact of IT. Table 3–1 puts the basic ICA model in the context of implications for industry and potential technology impact.

Column 1 lists the key competitive forces that shape competition in a given industry segment. In a specific industry, not all forces are of equal importance (Figure 3–2). Some industries are dominated by suppliers (for example, the impact of OPEC on the petroleum industry), while other industries are preoccupied with the threat of new entrants and/or substitute products (such as the banking and insurance industries).

Column 2 of Table 3–1 lists key implications of each competitive force. For example, when new entrants move into an established industry segment, they generally introduce significant additional capacity. They frequently have allocated substantial resources in order to establish a beachhead in the industry. The result of new entrants typically is reduced product prices or increased costs for incumbents.

FIGURE 3–1   Competitive Forces

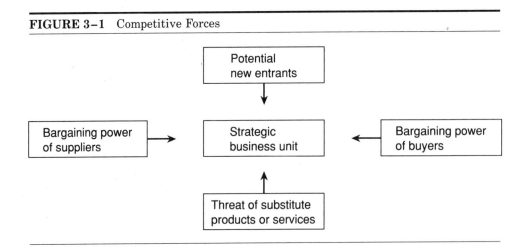

TABLE 3–1   Impact of Competitive Forces

Force	Implication	Potential Uses of IT to Combat Force

Threat of new entrants	New capacity
	Substantial resources
	Reduced prices or inflation
	  of incumbents' costs
		Provide entry barriers:
		  Economies of scale
		  Switching costs
		  Product differentiation
		  Access to distribution
		    channels

Buyers' bargaining power	Prices forced down High quality More services Competition encouraged	Buyer selection Switching costs Differentiation Entry barriers

Suppliers' bargaining power	Prices raised
	Reduced quality and
	  services (labor)
		Selection
		Threat of backward
		  integration

Threat of substitute products or services	Potential returns limited Ceiling on prices	Improve price/performance Redefine products and services

Traditional intraindustry rivals	Competition:
	  Price
	  Product
	  Distribution and service
		Cost-effectiveness
		Market access
		Differentiation:
		  Product
		  Services
		  Firm

Column 3 lists some examples of how IT can be used to combat the implications of the given competitive force. For example, the establishment of entry barriers can be implemented with IT that generates significant economies of scale, builds in switching costs that reduce the ability of suppliers and buyers to move to new entrants, differentiates product or company, or limits access to key markets or distribution channels.

Two basic types of competitive advantage, combined with the scope of activities for a firm seeking to achieve them, make for three *generic strategies* for achieving above-average performance in an industry: cost leadership, differentiation, and focus. (See Figure 3–3.) The focus strategy has two variants: cost advantage and differentiation.

Each generic strategy involves a fundamentally different route to competitive advantage, combining a choice about the type of competitive advantage sought with the scope of the strategic target in which

FIGURE 3–2   Elements of Industry Structure

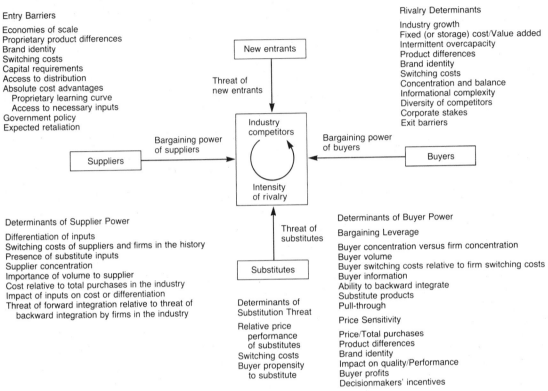

Entry Barriers

Economies of scale
Proprietary product differences
Brand identity
Switching costs
Capital requirements
Access to distribution
Absolute cost advantages
  Proprietary learning curve
  Access to necessary inputs
Government policy
Expected retaliation

Threat of
new entrants

New entrants

Industry
competitors

Intensity
of rivalry

Rivalry Determinants

Industry growth
Fixed (or storage) cost/Value added
Intermittent overcapacity
Product differences
Brand identity
Switching costs
Concentration and balance
Informational complexity
Diversity of competitors
Corporate stakes
Exit barriers

Bargaining power
of suppliers

Suppliers

Bargaining power
of buyers

Buyers

Determinants of Supplier Power

Differentiation of inputs
Switching costs of suppliers and firms in the history
Presence of substitute inputs
Supplier concentration
Importance of volume to supplier
Cost relative to total purchases in the industry
Impact of inputs on cost or differentiation
Threat of forward integration relative to threat of
  backward integration by firms in the industry

Threat of
substitutes

Substitutes

Determinants of
Substitution Threat

Relative price
  performance
  of substitutes
Switching costs
Buyer propensity
  to substitute

Determinants of Buyer Power

Bargaining Leverage

Buyer concentration versus firm concentration
Buyer volume
Buyer switching costs relative to firm switching costs
Buyer information
Ability to backward integrate
Substitute products
Pull-through

Price Sensitivity

Price/Total purchases
Product differences
Brand identity
Impact on quality/Performance
Buyer profits
Decisionmakers' incentives

competitive advantage is to be achieved. The cost leadership and differentiation strategies seek competitive advantage in a broad range of industry segments, while focus strategies aim at cost advantage (cost focus) or differentiation (differentiation focus) in a narrow segment. The specific actions required to implement each generic strategy vary widely from industry to industry, as do feasible generic strategies in a particular industry. Selecting and implementing the appropriate generic strategy is very difficult, but it lies at the heart of what a firm must do if it is to achieve long-term competitive advantage in an industry.

At the core of the concept of generic strategies are the notions that competitive advantage is the goal of any strategy and that to achieve competitive advantage a firm must define the type of competitive advantage it seeks to attain and the scope within which it will attain it. Being "all things to all people" is a recipe for strategic mediocrity and below-average performance, because it often means that a firm has no competitive advantage at all.

FIGURE 3–3 Three Generic Strategies Related to Competitive Advantage and Scope

Competitive Advantage

	Lower Cost	Differentiation
Broad Target	Cost leadership	Differentiation
Narrow Target	Cost focus	Differentiation focus

Competitive Scope

Search for Opportunity

To assess the ultimate impact of IT for planning purposes, companies should begin by addressing five questions. If the answer to one or more of these questions is yes, IT may be a strategic resource that requires attention at the highest level. These questions "operationalize" the competitive IT analysis implicit in the previous discussion.

Can IT Build Barriers to Entry?   In an example early in the chapter, a distributor was able to open up a new electronic channel to its customers. The move was highly successful for the company, and other companies found it very hard to replicate. Customers did not want devices from different vendors on their premises; for space, training, and ease of use purposes, they wanted one device from one supplier.

A successful entry barrier not only offers a new service that appeals to customers; it also offers features that keep the customers "hooked." The harder the service is to emulate, the higher the barrier is for the competition. An example of such a defensible barrier is the development of a complex software package that adds value and is capable of evolution and refinement. A large financial service firm used this approach to launch a different and highly attractive financial product that depended on sophisticated software. Because of the complexity of the concept and its software, it took competitors several years to develop similar features, which gave the firm valuable time to establish market position. Further, the firm did not sit on its laurels; it enhanced its original product significantly, thus making itself a moving target.

The payoff from value-added features that increase both sales and market share is particularly noteworthy for industries in which there are great economies of scale and where price is important to the customer. By being the first to move onto the learning curve, a company can gain a cost advantage that enables it to put great pressure on its competitors. In the airline industry, for example, where the software costs have run into the hundreds of millions of dollars, this has been particularly significant.

Electronic tools that increase the scope and speed of price quotes for salespeople represent another kind of barrier. The sophisticated financial-planning packages with embedded expert systems that are being used by sales forces of major insurance companies around the globe are building similar barriers, because they have raised the standards of service.

Conversely, while many of these projects require large capital investments, they also have uncertain ultimate benefits, which poses real risks. Further, in difficult economic times, investment in these electronic systems may create both serious cost rigidity and barriers against an orderly exit from the industry. It is difficult, for example, for a large airline to scale down its computing activity sharply in order to deal with reduced operations or great cost pressures.

Can IT Build in Switching Costs? Are there ways to encourage customer reliance on the supplier's electronic support, to build it into their operations so that increased operational dependence and normal human inertia make switching to a competitor unattractive? Ideally, the electronic support system is simple for the customer to adopt and contains a series of increasingly complex and useful procedures that gradually insinuate themselves into the customer's daily routines. Thus the customer will become so dependent on these value-added procedures that it will be reluctant to change suppliers. Electronic home banking is a good example of this. It is hoped that once customers have learned to use the system and have coded all their monthly creditors for the system, they will be very reluctant to change banks.

A manufacturer of heavy machines provides another example of electronic services and features that add value to and support a company's basic product line while increasing the switching cost. The company has attached electronic devices to its major machine installed on customer premises. In case of mechanical failure, the device signals over the telecom network to a computer program at corporate headquarters. The program analyzes the data, diagnoses the problem, and either suggests changes in the machine's control settings or pinpoints the cause of the failure and identifies the defective parts and, when appropriate, triggers the dispatching of a mechanic. Now installed around the globe, the system has dramatically improved service levels and significantly cemented customer loyalty. Attrition on service contracts has shrunk dramatically.

Can IT Change the Basis of Competition? In some industries dominated by cost-based competition, IT has permitted development of product features that are so different that they cause the basis of competition to change radically. For example, in the mid-1970s, a major distributor of magazines to newsstands and stores was in an industry segment that was dominated by cost-based competition. For years it had used electronic technology to drive costs down by developing cheaper methods of sorting and distributing magazines. Using less staff and lower inventory, it had achieved the position of low-cost producer.

In 1977 the distributor decided to build on the fact that its customers were small, unsophisticated, and unaware of their profit structures. By using its records of weekly shipments and returns from a newsstand, the distributor could identify what was selling on the newsstand. It developed programs that calculated profit per square foot for every magazine and compared these data with information from newsstands operating in economically and ethnically similar neighborhoods with varying mixes of merchandise. The distributor could thus tell each newsstand every month how it could improve the product mix. In addition to distributing magazines, the company used technology to offer a valuable inventory-management feature that changed the basis of competition from cost- to service-based differentiation, while raising its prices substantially.

Dramatic cost reduction can significantly alter the old ground rules of competition. In a cost-competitive environment, companies should look for a strategic IT opportunity. There may be an opportunity for sharp cost reduction, such as through staff reduction or the ability to grow without hiring staff, improved material use, increased machine efficiency through better scheduling or more cost-effective maintenance, or inventory reduction. Alternatively, there may be an opportunity to add value to the product that will permit the company to compete on the basis of product differentiation.

A large insurance carrier recently identified systems development as its biggest bottleneck in the introduction of new insurance products. It is, therefore, investing heavily in software packages and outside staff to complement its large (500-person) development organization. A cost-cutting activity in the 1960s and 1970s, the carrier's IT organization became vital to the implementation of a product-differentiation strategy in the 1980s. Though the company is cutting staff and financial expenditures overall, it is increasing IT expenditures and staff as a strategic investment.

Understanding when to move on these issues is particularly difficult and troublesome. For example, few people doubt that videotext and cable services will eventually become important in retailing, particularly in upscale markets, but *when* that will happen and in what *form* it will come remain very murky. In many cases, however, these changes could in a short time dramatically alter old processes and structures, to the extent that today's forms will be unrecognizable. No example is more striking than the situation confronting libraries. They have a 1,000-year-plus tradition of storing books made of parchment and wood pulp. Soaring materials costs, the advent of cheap microfiche and microfilm, expansion of computer databases, CD-ROM (compact disk read-only memory), and electronic links between libraries will make the research facility of the year 2000 utterly unrecognizable from that of today. The period of transition will be short, and the discontinuity with the past sharp. Those libraries that persist in spending 65 percent of their budget to keep aged wood pulp warm (and cool) will be irrelevant to the needs of their users.

Though in the early stages it is difficult to distinguish the intriguing (but ephemeral) from an important structural innovation, the consequences can be devastating if managers misread the issues in either direction.

Can IT Change the Balance of Power in Supplier Relationships?
The development of interorganizational systems has been a powerful asset in many settings for dealing with suppliers. For example, just-in-time delivery systems have drastically reduced inventory levels in the automotive and other industries, thus permitting big cost savings in holding costs, warehouse expenses, and so on. Since companies in these industries are uncertain about what they will need downstream or when they will be cut off from their suppliers, they used to keep enormous safety stocks of components and ready-to-ship subassemblies. Increasingly, they are taking up slack by using electronic links between suppliers and dealers; in essence, substituting information for surplus inventory, capital, and production facilities.

Similarly, electronic CAD links from one organization to another permit faster response, smaller inventory, and better service to the final consumer. In one case, a large retailer has linked its materials-ordering system electronically to its suppliers' order-entry systems. If 100 sofas are needed for a particular region, the retailer's computer automatically checks the order-entry systems of its primary sofa suppliers, and the one with the lowest cost gets the order.

Equally important, the retailer's computer continually monitors its suppliers' finished-goods inventories, factory scheduling, and commitments against its schedule to make sure enough inventory will be available to meet unexpected demand. If a supplier's inventories are inadequate, the retailer alerts the supplier. If any suppliers are unwilling to go along with this system, they may find their overall share of business dropping until they are replaced by others.

A major manufacturer proposed CAD/CAD links with a $100 million/year in sales pressed-powder metal parts manufacturer. Within 18 months this system shrunk what had been an eight-month product design cycle down to three months.

Such interorganizational systems can redistribute power between buyer and supplier. In the case of the aerospace manufacturer, the CAD/CAD systems increased dependence on an individual supplier, making it hard for the company to replace the supplier and leaving it vulnerable to major price increases. The retailer, on the other hand, was in a much stronger position to dictate the terms of its relationship with its suppliers.

Can IT Technology Generate New Products?   As described earlier, IT can lead to products that are of higher quality, can be delivered faster, or are cheaper. Similarly, at little extra cost, existing products can be tailored with special features to customers' needs. Some companies may be able to combine one or more of these advantages. They should ask themselves if they can attach an electronic support service to a product to increase the value of the total package in the consumer's eyes. This can often be done at little additional cost, as in the case of the on-line diagnostic system for machine failure described earlier.

In another example, credit card companies are voracious consumers of delinquent account receivable data from other firms. Indeed, there is a whole industry dedicated to the collection and organization of these data. Similarly, nonproprietary research data files often have significant value to third parties.

In some cases, a whole new industry has emerged. POS data in supermarkets is a case in point. The first firm in the industry began by purchasing data from a large supermarket chain. The chain was under great cost pressure (like most U.S. chains) and could not profitably use the data; the cost of developing a market research system for itself would have been too great. Consequently, they sold the data for cash and future access to it. These data have been organized by ZIP code into a research tool for retail chains, food suppliers, and others interested in consumer activity.

ANALYZING THE VALUE CHAIN FOR IT OPPORTUNITIES

An effective formal way to organize a search for effective IT opportunities is through a systematic analysis of a company's value chain—the series of interdependent activities that brings a product or service to the customer. Figure 3–4 shows a typical value chain, drawn from Michael Porter's analysis, and briefly defines the meaning of each of the company's activities. In different settings, IT can profoundly affect one or more of these activities, sometimes simply by improving effec-

---

FIGURE 3–4   The Value Chain

Support activities	Corporate infrastructure					
	Human resource management					
	Technology development					
	Procurement					
	Inbound logistics	Operations	Outbound logistics	Marketing and sales	Service	
	Primary activities					Margin

Activity	Definition*
Inbound logistics	Materials receiving, storing, and distribution to manufacturing premises.
Operations	Transforming inputs into finished products.
Outbound logistics	Storing and distributing products.
Marketing and sales	Promotion and sales force.
Service	Service to maintain or enhance product value.
Corporate infrastructure	Support of entire value chain, such as general management, planning, finance, accounting, legal services, government affairs, and quality management.
Human resource management	Recruiting, hiring, training, and development.
Technology development	Improving product and manufacturing process.
Procurement	Function or purchasing input.

*Abstracted from Michael E. Porter, *Competitive Advantage* (New York: Free Press, 1985), pp. 39–43.

Source: Michael E. Porter and Victor E. Millar, "How Information Gives You Competitive Advantage," *Harvard Business Review,* July–August 1985, p. 151.

---

tiveness, sometimes by fundamentally changing the activity, and sometimes by altering the relationship between activities. In the process, what a firm does may have a significant effect on the value chains of key customers and suppliers as well.

Inbound Logistics

As can be seen from the earlier examples, in many settings, IT has already had an important impact on expediting materials to the point of manufacture. One major distribution company, for example, has installed hundreds of terminals on supplier premises to permit implementation of just-in-time, on-line ordering. The company requires its suppliers to keep adequate inventory and to make their figures on available stock accessible to its computerized purchasing system.

This system has cut down on warehousing needs for incoming materials and has reduced disruptions due to inventory shortfalls. The need to maintain inventory safety stocks and the associated holding costs have been passed along to the suppliers. The purchaser's computer can also rapidly scan several suppliers' databases and order from the one offering the lowest price. This new efficiency has sharply eroded suppliers' margins. Because this distribution company has great purchasing power, it has reaped most of the system's benefits. Changing vendors, however, has become more difficult for the distributor.

A large department store chain is linked directly to several of its textile suppliers. This hookup has not only improved delivery and permitted inventory reduction; it has also provided the chain the flexibility to meet changing demand almost immediately. This in turn has offset price differentials by making it easier to deal with domestic suppliers than with remote foreign suppliers. In this cost-sensitive environment, this has been enormously important to U.S. textile manufacturers.

Operations and Product Structure

Information systems technologies affect a manufacturer's operations and its product offerings. In 1989 a manufacturer of thin transparent film completed a $30 million investment in new computer-controlled manufacturing facilities for one of its major product lines. This change slashed order response time from 10 weeks to 2 days and improved quality levels significantly.

When one financial services firm decided to go after more small private investors (with portfolios of about $25,000), it introduced a flexible financial instrument. It gave investors immediate on-line ability to move their funds among stocks or out of stocks, and it provided money market rates on idle funds as well as liquidity equal to that of a checking account. The company was the first to introduce this service and captured a huge initial market share. Continued product enhancement has ensured that investors have no incentive to switch services. In the first two years, this original provider achieved six times the volume of its nearest competitor. Five years later it still retained a 70 percent share of the market.

A videotext service company reconceptualized its business as essentially a bit-moving operation—that is, getting data from one place to another. This concept led it to offer a new line of financial services, such as instantaneous financial information (up-to-the-second foreign exchange rates, for example), and was the key to development of other new services. The company had to make no important changes in its technology, and its sales and profits soared.

A major insurance company thought of its business as a provider of diversified financial services and as a bit-moving company. It improved its services to policyholders by allowing them immediate on-line checking of status for claims and claims processing. The company also provided on-line access to new services and products. These included modeling packages that enabled corporate benefits officers to determine the costs of various benefit packages so as to tailor them to costs and employee requests. It further responded to clients' needs by selling either software for claims processing or claims-processing services to corporate clients who elect to self-insure. The company credits these information technology–enabled product initiatives with keeping it firmly in place at the top of its industry despite tremendous competition from other diversified financial services companies.

Outbound Logistics

IT has had a great impact on the way services and products are delivered to customers. As mentioned earlier, the reservations-system links to travel agents, provided chiefly by United Airlines and American Airlines, have affected their business relationships so profoundly that the smaller airlines that do not furnish this service have found it difficult to match. Indeed, in December 1984 the prominent placement on the screen of their flights, versus those of competition, was believed to so strongly influence purchasing behavior that the Civil Aeronautics Board issued a cease-and-desist order against the practice. Automatic teller machines allow cash and services to be rapidly and reliably delivered to outlying locations. Theater-ticket and airline-ticket machines are other examples. Obviously, each example just cited of inbound logistics for one company represents outbound logistics for the other partner.

Marketing and Sales

A large pharmaceutical company offers on-line order-entry services to pharmacies for itself and a consortium of allied, noncompeting companies. This service has increased its market share and derived sizable added revenues from its consortium partners. Some companies excluded from the bundle have threatened legal action because of damage to their market shares.

In the industrial air-conditioning industry a major corporation built a microcomputer-based modeling system to help architects model the heating and cooling system requirements for commercial properties, measurably reducing their design time. The system leads many architects to consider this company's products more favorably than others. A competing corporation subsequently made a similar model available to remote users via communications links, providing rapid support and allowing the architect to get detailed costs and parts listings quickly to complete the design. Because the system is on-line, this company was able to neutralize the damage produced by the competitor's earlier product.

An agricultural chemicals company has obtained similar results through a sophisticated on-line crop-planning service for its chief agricultural customers. From a personal computer, using a standard telephone connection, farmers can call up agricultural databases containing prices of various crops, necessary growing conditions, and the costs of various chemicals. They can then call up various models and decision support systems and tailor them to their fields' requirements, after which they can experiment with the models and examine the implications of various crop rotations and timing for planting. The model then helps the farmers to select fertilizer and chemical applications and to group their purchases to achieve maximum discounts. Finally, farmers can place orders for future delivery by hitting a few keys. Similar services have been offered by a major seed company and at least one state's Agricultural Extension Service.

Along a different vein, a major bank that is trying to strengthen its marketing of agricultural loans has offered a similar crop-planning service. Two previously noncompetitive companies are now competing in the same software arena. Marketing, the functional area most often bypassed in the first three decades of IT, is now the area of highest impact in a number of firms, and they are arming their sales forces with a wide array of handheld and laptop computers.

Over the past five years a major food company has assembled a national database that keeps track of daily sales of each of its products in each of the 300,000 stores they service. This database is now totally accessible through a wide-area network to market planners in their 21 regional districts. Combined with comparative data from market research companies, it has brought another order of precision and sophistication to their market research activities.

After-Sale Service

On its new line of elevators, an elevator company has installed flight-recording devices similar to those used by the airlines. It has done so because customers often place service calls without indicating how their elevators have malfunctioned. The service representative connects the recording device to the elevator company's computer, discovers the cause of the malfunction of two hours before, and then makes the necessary repairs on the spot. This reduces repair costs and increases customer satisfaction because the proper repairs are made on the first service call.

A large manufacturer of industrial machinery has installed an expert maintenance system in its home-office computer. When a machine failure occurs on a customer's premises, the machine is connected over a telephone line to the manufacturer's computer, which performs a fault analysis and issues instructions to the machine operator. Direct service visits are down by 50 percent, and customer satisfaction is up markedly.

Corporate Infrastructure

A large travel agency uses an on-line link to provide support to small, outlying offices. Because the travel industry still needs to deliver paper documents—passports, visas, tickets, itineraries—satellite or remote offices near big corporate customers are highly useful for pickup and delivery. These offices must have the full support capabilities of the home office. The on-line links have changed the organizational structure from that of one large, central office to many small, full-service offices. This change appears to have produced a 27 percent growth in sales. Chapter 6 will examine these organizational ramifications in far greater detail.

Management Control. A major financial services firm used to pay a sales commission on each product sold by its sales force. The result was that the sales force had maximum incentive to make the initial sale of a product and no incentive to make sure the customer was happy and did not take his money elsewhere (a matter of intense concern to the management of the financial services firm). With its new integrated customer database in place, the company has reduced the commissions it pays on initial sales of products and pays a new commission for maintaining and expanding the customer assets managed by the financial services firm. This approach, made possible by new technology, has aligned the company strategy and its sales incentive system much more effectively.

In some instances IT has dramatically enhanced coordination through fairly simple but powerful tools such as voice mail, electronic mail, videotext to update instructions to sales personnel in the field, and so on. These tools have dramatically accelerated the depth and breadth of communication. Other means of increasing coordination may involve much more extensive use of modern technologies including wide-area networks, local area networks, executive information packages, image processing, and so on. These tools, as discussed in greater detail in Chapter 6, both reduce staff costs and enhance effectiveness.

For example, at least one U.S. air carrier uses a network to monitor the location of all its aircraft. By knowing its airplanes' locations and passenger lists, the passengers' planned connections, and the connection schedules, it can instantaneously make decisions about speeding up late flights or delaying connecting departures. The opportunities for controlling fuel costs and preventing revenue loss (because many passengers must continue on competitors' flights if they miss their connections) amounts to tens of millions of dollars a year. Trucking companies and railroads use similar methods to track cargoes and optimize schedules.

Human Resources

The sophistication of human resources management has turned inside out. For example, an oil company has given desk terminals to all its corporate management committee members. Through these machines the committee has full on-line access to the detailed personnel files of the 400 most senior members in the corporation, complete with such data as five-year performance appraisals, photographs, and lists of positions each person is backing up. The company believes this capability has facilitated its important personnel decisions. Special government compliance reports, which used to take months to complete, can now be done in hours.

Technology Development

On-line access to large computing facilities inside and outside the company has allowed a heavy industrial manufacturer to increase technical productivity by more than half. Senior technical management now would not want to operate without this support.

To guide its drilling decisions, a large oil company processes large amounts of infrared data gathered from an overhead satellite. The company believes this information, which is used in all aspects of the search for petroleum deposits, is essential to its operations, from deciding on which tracts to bid to determining where to drill. Similarly, CAD/CAM (computer-aided design and manufacturing) technology has fundamentally changed the quality and speed with which the company can manufacture its drilling platforms.

A seed company notes its single most important technology expenditure is computer support for research. Modern genetic planning involving hundreds of thousands of plant variations and molecular simulation models—the keys to their future—are not possible without large-scale computing capacity. Their detailed data files repeatedly have allowed them to find appropriate germ plasms thousands of miles away to solve a problem in an Iowa cornfield.

Procurement

Procurement activities are also being transformed. For example, with a series of on-line electronic bulletin boards that make the latest spot prices instantly available around the country, a manufacturing company directs its nationwide purchasing effort. The boards have led to a tremendous improvement in purchasing price effectiveness, both in discovering and implementing new quantity pricing discount data as well as ensuring that the lowest prices are being achieved.

A retailer, by virtue of its large size, has succeeded in its demand for on-line access to the inventory files and production schedules of its suppliers. This access has permitted the company to manage its inventories more tightly than before and to pressure suppliers on price and product availability. This is another dimension of the earlier cited inbound logistics example.

In short, we have found systematic examination of a company's value chain to be an effective way to search for profitable IT applications. This analysis requires keen administrative insight, awareness of industry structure, and familiarity with the rules of competition in the particular setting. Companies need to understand their own value chains as well as those of key customers and suppliers in order to uncover potential new service areas. Similarly, understanding competitors' value chains provides insight on likely sources of competitive attack. Careful thought is needed in order to identify potential new entrants to an industry. These are companies whose value chains make expansion into a particular area attractive.

THE RISKS OF INFORMATION SYSTEMS SUCCESS[2]

A real and complex danger for developers of would-be strategic information systems is that they will succeed in the narrow technical sense but generate disastrous organizational and competitive consequences.

[2]Some of the material in this section has been adapted from Michael R. Vitale, "The Growing Risks of Information Systems Success," *MIS Quarterly*, December 1986.

Problems and Evaluations

This section discusses nine problems of information systems "success" and identifies management policies and procedures that help to ensure that potentially high-risk projects are appropriately evaluated. These risks focus on strategic vulnerabilities as opposed to the more-defined implementation issues covered in Chapter 10.

Systems that Change the Basis of Competition to a Company's Disadvantage.   Once information systems are used to gain competitive advantage in a given industry, in some settings their use not only may become obligatory for continued competitive viability, but significant additional resources may have to be expended to keep them viable. An organization that is not prepared to stay the course with continued investments in information systems may be better off not firing the first salvo.

This lesson was learned, through experience, by a U.S. manufacturer of commercial appliances. The company's products were typically purchased and installed by building contractors who worked from a set of technical specifications for size, capacity, and so on. Historically the company had offered contractors a mail-in consulting service that could translate specifications into products and instructions for the wiring, plumbing, and other site preparation work required.

The company initially built this consulting expertise into programs for a mainframe and an early-model microcomputer. Contractors could continue to send specifications by mail; the company would feed the requirements through the mainframe and mail back a neatly printed list of products and instructions. (As would be expected, most of the products were manufactured by the company itself.) The relatively few contractors who at that time owned that particular microcomputer could, using company-supplied software, enter their specifications onto a diskette and mail that instead of written data. The micro itself was not powerful enough to analyze the specifications, although it could check them for completeness and consistency.

Over time the appliance market evolved, as did the microcomputer industry. Having achieved success with its initial development, the company reaped a harvest of increased market share but carried out no further development. One of its competitors—larger, older, and equipped with a larger, more progressive information systems staff—developed a similar system. This system, however, ran on the more powerful and more readily available IBM personal computer. Software was provided to contractors at no charge, as were electronic connections to the company's mainframe. Analysis could be performed immediately, and the required products made almost exclusively by that system's owner could be ordered at the push of a key. As IBM began to dominate the business microcomputer market, the second company recaptured its lost market share and more.

By introducing customers and competitors to the use of information systems and then failing to track or adapt to changes in the technology, the first company turned an initial IT success into a competitive failure.

The moral: Once you have entered the game it is very hard to disengage.

Systems that Lower Entry Barriers.   As described earlier, information technology can be used to raise and/or maintain barriers to entry in many industries. In some situations an extensive investment in hardware and software has become necessary for all participants, increasing the investment required for entry. In other circumstances information systems have been used to capture distribution channels, again increasing the cost and difficulty of entrance.

On the other hand, by making information systems the major vehicle for producing, selling, distributing, or servicing its product, a company may in fact be encouraging competitors that have greater IT resources.

A major seller of health and casualty insurance faced this type of decision. The company does the majority of its business on a payroll-deduction basis with very small employers who do not offer insurance as a fringe benefit. These employers often do their payrolls by hand, making bookkeepers a major target for the insurer's sales force. The primary competition is not so much from other insurers as from the bookkeepers' lack of time and willingness to handle additional deductions.

To help overcome this obstacle, the insurer considered offering a computerized payroll preparation package for small companies. The development of such software was considered to be well within the capabilities of its IT group, and its sales force was already in contact with many potential customers for the new service. Pricing was designed to provide some profit, but the main intent was to create tighter links to small customers.

Before much work had been done on the new payroll system, the vice president for IT recognized a danger. Although it might well be possible to convince customers to do their payrolls by computer, he could see there was a risk that the business would go not to the insurer but to one of the large, experienced firms that dominate the payroll business. Any of these organizations could, if they chose, offer health and casualty insurance as well through a relationship with another insurer. The link to customers might well be tighter, but it was not clear who would be at the other end! The company postponed the idea of offering payroll service until such time as their customers began to show some interest in doing their payroll by computer. To continue the project would, in the company's opinion, have risked opening its primary line of business to new competitors.

Systems that Bring on Litigation or Regulation. These systems are in the category of things that work too well for their own good. They achieve their initial objectives and then continue to grow in size and effectiveness, eventually giving rise to claims of unfair competition and cries for government regulation. Other possible outcomes are forced divestiture of the system and an agreement to share the system with competitors.

The airline reservations systems used by travel agents are a clear example of this danger. The United and American reservation systems control the offices of nearly 80 percent of U.S. travel agents. Some of the two carriers' competitors have claimed that this level of penetration allows the two big airlines to effectively control the industry's channels of distribution. Examples of such alleged domination include biased display of data, close monitoring and control of travel agents, and inaccurate data on competitors' flights.

After a lengthy investigation of these claims, the Civil Aeronautics Board (CAB) ordered changes in the operation and pricing of computer reservations systems. Nevertheless, United and American were sued by 11 competitors, who demanded that the two carriers spin off their reservations systems into separate subsidiaries. United and American opposed the suit but did agree, along with TWA, to provide unbiased displays. As this book is being produced, the lawsuit is in abeyance because of financial stresses unrelated to the issues in the lawsuit, but its central themes that there is such a thing as an unfair "information monopoly" and that control of electronic channels of distribution may be unacceptable to the public cast a shadow over the 1990s. A similar set of lawsuits and challenges has been engendered around ATMs.

Although they deny unfair practices, United and American have never denied using their reservations systems to gain competitive advantage. Indeed, the two airlines claim that the systems are not economically viable on the basis of usage fee income alone—they were *intended* to generate increased sales. United and American may in fact already have recovered their investments in the reservation systems. The precedent of government intervention suggests, however, that future developers of competitively effective systems may find their returns limited by law or regulation.

Systems that Increase Customers' or Suppliers' Power to the Detriment of the Innovator. Strengthening relationships with customers and suppliers is an area in which information systems have been used most effectively. In some circumstances, however, companies appear to give their customers or suppliers the tools and expertise to get along without them. This change may be inevitable over the long run, but there is no reason to hasten its onset.

An overnight delivery company, for example, instituted very fast delivery of electronically transmitted messages between its offices. The original was picked up from the sender and put through a facsimile machine at a nearby office; the transmitted image was received at an office near the recipient and delivered by hand.

As fax technology grew, the delivery company announced that it would place facsimile machines on its customers' premises and act as a switch among the installed machines. Delivery promised to be even quicker, since there would be no need to take the original copy to the sending office or to deliver the received copy. The value the delivery company was able to add to off-the-shelf facsimile technology was questionable. Little existed to prevent its customers from installing similar equipment directly; indeed, the manufacturer of the facsimile machines advertised its products prominently as the ones supporting the delivery company's system. The firm soon abandoned this line of business.

A somewhat similar risk is created by systems that unintentionally lower switching costs in an attempt to make the customer's life easier. The American Hospital Supply Corporation (now a division of Baxter Travenol) provides an interesting example of steps taken to avoid this danger. American's "ASAP" system, installed in more than 3,000 U.S. hospitals, allows on-line ordering of medical and surgical supplies from American's extensive product line. Substitutes are suggested for out-of-stock items, and the hospital can specify several options for delivery time, depending on how urgently each item is needed. ASAP is generally felt to have contributed heavily to the steady growth that made American the largest company in its field by the mid-1980s.

Some of American's competitors developed similar systems of their own but found it difficult to overcome American's lead. (Hospitals, like travel agents, were generally reluctant to install more than one on-line system.) The extensive use of computerized order-entry systems, however, offered another potential competitive opportunity. Why not develop a "master system" that would take data from hospitals and pass it to suppliers' systems? The hospitals could retain the advantages of a single system and might get lower prices as well, since the master system could "shop" among suppliers for the best price.

As long as American continued to develop and enhance ASAP, this danger was manageable. During its successful life, in fact, the company had taken the system well beyond the order-entry stage. Later versions of ASAP allowed the hospital to order on the basis of its own stock numbers as well as American's, to create and store files of frequently ordered items, and to "personalize" ASAP to its own environment in other ways. After American's acquisition by Baxter Travenol, in a well-meaning effort to control costs, all development expenditures were frozen. Over a two-year period ASAP's competitors caught up.

Baxter finally responded by developing an industry system for all competitors aided by a public accountant to ensure that all players would be treated equitably. Although costly to develop, the new system promises to stabilize the situation. A once formidable technological advantage disappeared, and ASAP now competes primarily through the breadth of its product line and its ability to execute fast delivery.

Bad Timing.   A delicate analysis balances cost and culture in determining the time to make a bold move. Get there too early with an expensive, clumsy technology in an unreceptive customer environment, as Chemical Bank did with its electronic home banking product in the early 1980s, and you can create a real fiasco. (They lost $100 million on the venture.) Get there too late, as the regional airlines and hundreds of drug wholesalers did, and you may lose your life. Behind the technology issues lie very real marketing and business policy issues.

Investments that Turn Out to Be Indefensible and Fail to Produce Lasting Advantages.   There are numerous reasons an investment can turn out to be indefensible. In general, interorganization systems with high potential daily transaction rates with the other party have turned out to be very successful. Where low daily transaction rates exist (one to two per day or less), they have often turned into strategic liabilities with end users getting lost in the procedural details. In another vein, features that have great value to end users but that are easily replicable by the firm's competitors are of much less value than those that, because of size and/or peculiar reinforcing linkage with the firm's products, are hard to replicate. Similarly, systems where the firm can start simple and continue to add new features and services as technology and industry conditions change are much more effective than one-time moves, which then stand as fixed targets for competitors to shoot at.

Systems that Pose an Immediate Threat to Large, Established Competitors.   Several organizations in the hotel industry have recognized that they cannot by themselves develop a link to travel agencies because they would risk being crushed by the airline systems anxious to prevent erosion of their franchise. By putting together a group of hotels as an association, they have combined sufficient market power and purchasing power to make this viable.

Inadequate Understanding of Buying Dynamics across Market Segments.   It is very easy to apply inappropriately a set of concepts that works in one set of market niches to another set. For example, airline reservations systems have been widely cited as an example of effective IT use. Over the past decade, however, two of the most consistently profitable routes in the United States have been Washington National to New York La Guardia and New York La Guardia to Boston Logan. A passenger cannot get a reservation on these routes; rather, each route is served by an every-half-hour shuttle concept. Different market niches may have very different dynamics, and you can get into great trouble by ignoring these differences.

Cultural Lag and Perceived Transfer of Power.   Some systems are beyond the customers' technical comfort level. This was clearly the case with the earlier mentioned electronic home banking failure. It is the great imponderable issue in the early 1990s as one considers the massive joint venture between IBM and Sears that is targeted at bringing hundreds of electronic databases into U.S. homes using a menu-driven architecture. It has worked in the very different environment in France. Whether it will work here is a matter of heated debate. A second related issue is the concern by one party in an interorganization system (IOS) that it may be manipulated by another party and that it may not be able to resist the pressure without losing the business relationship. Not all IOS's are win–win situations.

These are hard but very important questions to address. Quite separate are the areas of technical project management addressed in Chapter 10. Chapter 10 focuses primarily on the real problems of implementation, while this chapter is focused on failures of conceptualization.

Assessing Competitor Risk

Understanding competitive risks is the first step in managing them. Understanding, in turn, is a two-phase process: (1) describing in advance and in detail the industry-level changes that may be brought about by development and implementation of particular information technologies, and (2) determining the potential impact of these changes on the company. Such views of the future, sadly, are very cloudy, and their probabilities are only rough estimates. But together with estimates of project costs and benefits, they must be analyzed before a decision is made on whether to proceed.

Increasing use of information systems is often naively viewed as inevitable. Certainly, situations occur where firms must invest in and adapt to IT in order to remain viable, even if the increase in technological intensity causes a complete reevaluation and reformulation of the firm's strategy. Yet some technological "advances" have remained in an embryonic stage for years. Electronic home banking and home shopping, as noted earlier, are two examples. Sometimes these developments are stalled for reasons of cost, IT capability, or consumer acceptance. Others are held back by lack of support from established industry participants. Rather than uniformly criticizing these firms for technological backwardness, it is more appropriate to entertain the possibility that they understand the technology completely and are prepared to utilize it when it becomes necessary but are unwilling to precipitate a potentially unfavorable change in their competitive environment.

An appropriate place to start in considering the potential impact of a new strategic use of information systems is with the motivation for the new system. As noted earlier, potential justifications include raising entry barriers, increasing switching costs, reducing the power of buyers or suppliers, deterring substitute products, lowering costs, and increasing differentiation. Inevitably, if the initiative is successful, the outcome over time will be a change in the competitive forces affecting the industry. It is tempting but dangerous and shortsighted to consider these forces as impacting only current industry participants— suppliers, buyers, and competitors. As some of the examples indicate, certain IT uses can open up an industry to new and potentially dominant players in a way so threatening to a firm that it is an entirely prudent reason to delay offensive moves.

Equally practical as a firm considers new investments in strategic information systems, it must candidly assess whether it will obtain any sustainable competitive advantage or if a more likely outcome is an extension of the current competitive situation at an increased level of cost. Additional caveats in this area include recognizing that IT software purchased from a nonexclusive source is unlikely to confer lasting advantage. Also, the mobility of skilled IT personnel between firms often results in the rapid proliferation of key ideas, leaving the pioneering firm relatively no better off than before. In the absence of strong, first-mover advantages, some investments in information systems, regardless of their short-term glitz and appeal, may simply not pay off competitively over the long run.

As will be discussed later, the long-term commitment of top management must be obtained before firing the first shot on the IT battlefield. Before starting an IT effort a clear view must exist of the company's long-range strategy and how this move fits into it. Further, the resources and capabilities of competitors, both current and potential, should be considered carefully.

Most crucial is the assessment of the likely long-term consequences of a new system. Initial development cost and benefit may not be an accurate indicator of the potential effects. A positive control is the "impact statement" that lays out the competitive changes expected to result from a new information system. Substantial benefits accruing from an improved competitive situation should alert the organization to consider the risks as well. Consideration of the positive impacts of the new system on competition forces broad-gauge thinking on potential negative impacts as well.

Over time the key to managing these sorts of risks will be the organization's ability to learn from its experience so that it can continue to roll out strategic IT applications as and when appropriate. There must be a common understanding among general managers and senior IT executives about which pieces of software should be considered "directional"—that is, likely to have a major effect on the organization's future competitive position. A thorough review of the potential impacts should be carried out before such systems are developed and again before they are implemented.

THE CHALLENGE

Achieving these advantages while avoiding the pitfalls requires broad IT management–user dialogue plus imagination. The process is complicated by the fact that, while many IT products are strategic, the potential benefits are very subjective and not easily verified. Often a strict return-on-investment (ROI) focus by senior management may turn attention toward narrow, well-defined targets rather than to broader, strategic opportunities that are harder to analyze.

Visualizing their systems in terms of the strategic grid (see Figure 2–4), senior and IT managements in a number of organizations have concluded that their company or business unit is located in either the "support" or the "factory" quadrant and have set up staffing, organization, and planning activities accordingly. Because of the sharp change in IT performance and the evolution of competitive conditions, this categorization may be wrong as one looks to the future. For the new conditions, for example, the competitor of the distributor described in this chapter's opening paragraph was complacent about its position in the support quadrant. The company did not realize what was happening until it was too late. Playing catch-up can be difficult and expensive in the IT area.

A number of companies and industry groups will appropriately remain in the support and factory quadrants. Technical changes, however, have been so sudden in the past several years that the role of a company's IT function needs reexamination to ensure its placement is still appropriate.

A NEW POINT OF VIEW

To address the issues raised here, management will need to change the way it operates.

Planning Issues

The CEO must insist that the end products of IT planning clearly communicate the true competitive impact of the expenditures involved. Figure 3–5 provides a framework for thinking about how to accomplish this by identifying priorities for the allocation of financial and staff resources.

In this connection, managers should realize that an extraordinarily large amount of the systems development effort is often devoted to repairing worn-out systems and to maintaining them in order to meet changed business conditions (over 50 percent in many settings). Also, a vital but often unrecognized need exists for research and development to keep up with the technology and to ensure that the company can know the full range of possibilities. (This idea is developed in depth in Chapter 13.) Distinctly separate are the areas where a company spends money to obtain pure competitive advantage (very exciting) or to regain or maintain competitive parity (not so exciting, because the company is trying to recover from its shortsightedness). Finally, projects where the investment is defined for pure measurable return on investment (ROI) are also separate.

The aim of the ranking process is to allocate resources to areas with the most growth potential. Each company should have an IT plan summary, about three pages long, that vividly communicates to the CEO the data derived from Figure 3–5, explains why IT expenditures are allocated as they are, and enumerates explicitly the types of competitive benefits the company might expect from its IT expenditures. Few companies do this today.

Confidentiality and Competition

Until recently it has been the industry norm for organizations and individuals to share data about information systems technology and plans, on the grounds that no lasting competitive advantage would emerge from IT and that collaboration would allow all firms to reduce administrative headaches. Managers today, however, must take appropriate steps to ensure the confidentiality of strategic IT plans and thinking. Great care should be taken in determining who will attend industry meetings, what they may talk about, and what information they may share with vendors and competitors.

Evaluating Expenditures

Executives should not permit use of simplistic rules to calculate desirable IT expense levels. Judging an IT budget as a percentage of something, such as sales, has always been an easy way to compare the

FIGURE 3–5   Identifying Resource Allocation Priorities by Strategic Business Unit

Goal of IT expenditure	Growing, highly competitive industry	Relatively stable industry, known ground rules	Static or declining industry
Rehabilitate and maintain system	1	1	1
Experiment with new technology	2	3	3
Attain competitive advantage	2	2	3*
Maintain or regain competitive parity	2	3	4
Defined return on investment †	3	3	4

*Assuming the change is not so dramatic as to revolutionize the industry's overall performance.

†In an intensely cost-competitive environment, defined ROI is the same as gaining competitive advantage.

Note: Numbers indicate relative attractiveness or importance of the investment, with 1 denoting the highest priority.

performance of different companies. In today's more volatile competitive arena, such comparisons are very dangerous. We have observed some companies that are spending 6 percent of their total sales in this area and that are clearly underinvesting. We have seen others spending 1 percent of their sales volume that are overspending.

The IT–Management Partnership

To make full use of the opportunities that IT presents, managers need close partnership with technical experts. Bridging the gap between IT specialists and general management for purposes of strategic planning is, however, an enduring problem. Often uncomfortable with technology, many general managers are unaware of new options IT provides and the ways in which it can support strategy. For their part, IT professionals are often not attuned to the complexities and subtleties of strategy formulation. They are generally not part of the strategy development process (discussed further in Chapter 13).

Partnership is necessary. IT experts understand the economies of the technology and know its limits. They can also help move the organization toward the potential of tomorrow's technology. A change that is clumsy and inefficient in today's technology might eliminate the need for architecture redesign in the next generation. For example, very rich, interrelated databases today may be so slow to access as to present serious cost (and possibly response-time) problems. Tomorrow's technology, conversely, may remove the speed and cost problems and highlight the usefulness of the data.

General managers bring insight to overall business priorities. They have detailed knowledge of the various value chains and their potential in the real world and can help identify the paths of least staff resistance in implementation. Synthesis of the two worlds is essential.

Opening Questions

Finally, as a way of starting the process, establishing joint task forces to address the following questions has proved valuable.

1. What business are we really in? To answer that question, the task force may ask: What value do we provide to our customer? Do widespread, cheap, high-volume data communications and computer technology change this? Are we an insurance company, or should we think of ourselves as a provider of diversified financial services? A videotext service, or a mover of electronic bits? A provider of spare parts, or of parts and parts status reporting?

2. *Who are our biggest competitors? What new competitors will this technology make possible in the future? Who else does, or can, provide the same products or services?* If we see ourselves in the future as an insurance company, our competitors will be companies such as Aetna and Travelers. If we see ourselves as a financial services company, our competitors will be firms such as American Express/Shearson Lehman, Merrill Lynch, Sears Financial Services, and Citicorp.

3. *Can we integrate our clients' operations with our own through telecommunications and offer clients faster, easier, or cheaper service? In particular, how can we lock them in? Can we introduce significant switching costs?*

4. *Can we permanently lock competitors out through aggressive use of telecommunications or other electronic services?*

5. *Has our operating environment been changed by deregulation of our industry? Can technology help us compete for marketing, scheduling, control, and coordination in this new setting?*

6. *Has our environment changed due to deregulation of a related industry? Again, can technology help us compete? How can we add new products and services to retain our existing customer base?*

7. *Can we get there first? Should we attempt to make this move?* These two questions may be the most difficult of all. They require anticipating what's going to happen in the marketplace and in relationships with clients, customers, competitors, and regulators. Also, the company must determine which innovations will provide sustainable advantage versus which competitors can readily copy—adding to the costs of all industry participants or shaving all margins.

A Final Thought

At resource allocation time, the difference between an effective strategic initiative and a harebrained scheme is razor-thin. Only after the passage of money and time is the outcome obvious.

Chapter 4

Interorganizational Systems

In a 1966 *Harvard Business Review* article, Felix Kaufman implored general managers to think beyond their own organizational boundaries to the possibilities of extracorporate system.[1] His was a visionary argument about newly introduced computer time-sharing and networking capabilities. Since that article was written, as noted in Chapter 3, developments in information technology (IT) have made feasible many new applications of strategic importance.

Today many of the most dramatic and potentially powerful uses of IT involve networks that transcend company boundaries. These interorganizational systems (IOS's)—defined as automated information systems shared by two or more companies—will significantly contribute to enhanced productivity, flexibility, and competitiveness for many companies. However, current examples illustrate that some IOS's will radically change the balance of power in buyer–supplier relationships, provide entry and exit barriers in industry segments, and in most instances shift the competitive position of intraindustry competitors.

For example, a major automotive manufacturer has established computer-to-computer communication with its primary suppliers to implement just-in-time inventory systems. As an extension, the automotive manufacturer could add instructions to scan the computers of its primary suppliers and place an order with the company whose computer contained the lowest bid or price for the desired product (assuming that other things such as product quality are equal).

Such an expansion of the system would encourage competition among the vendors, and this rivalry could enhance the manufacturer's

---

[1]Felix Kaufman, "Data Systems that Cross Company Boundaries," *Harvard Business Review,* January–February 1966, p. 141.

bargaining power with them. Unfortunately, many companies make decisions about participating in these systems and the terms of participating without an appreciation for the broader strategic implications of the system. In some cases, in fact, such decisions have been made at the production-clerk level. Approximately half the time, under the guise of faster information flow and greater data integrity, the new system suddenly shifts inventory holding costs and business risk to a supplier. Such an imbalance would clearly far outweigh any advantages that the more efficient information system might bring to the supplier.

Some IOS's already have 10- to 15-year histories that clearly illustrate the economic impact and the social and public policy implications of such systems. The most dramatic and best-documented example is the airline industry's reservation systems, a class of IOS shared by intra-industry competitors and organizations that have a buyer–supplier relationship, as noted in Chapter 3 and the Frontier Airlines case. In testimony before the Civil Aeronautics Board (CAB), Frontier Airlines alleged that United Airlines, developer-owner of the widely used APOLLO reservation system, was enjoying unfair competitive advantage by monitoring loading factors of competitors and then using the system to either lower prices or broadcast special messages to travel agents. Since two major carriers, American and United, own reservation systems that provide the primary market access for almost two thirds of the travelers who make reservations through U.S. travel agents, this issue generated a great deal of public interest.

The CAB's airline reservation system inquiry showed the necessity for participants to anticipate the effects of an IOS. Further, it illustrated a need for social, regulatory, and strategic business perspectives in this rapidly evolving area. Given the rapid diffusion of computer and communications technology into most organizations, the potential is great for similar IOS growth and impact in a broad range of industries. In the following discussion we will describe the trends contributing to IOS development, show what an IOS is and how it works, describe frameworks for analyzing the impact of an IOS on business and industry, and suggest a way to consider alternative forms of participation in these systems.

IOS DEVELOPMENT

The growth of interorganizational systems is due to various technological, economic, and organizational changes:

The Need for Fast, Reliable Information Exchange in Response to Rapidly Changing Markets, Products, and Services.   This trend is mainly based on increasing international competition, shrinking geographic separation, and deregulation with more open competition.

The shift in world economics is shown by the change in the world aggregate GNPs. Shortly after World War II the U.S. GNP was about half the world GNP; by 1986 it was about one fourth. This shift has greatly stepped up international competition.

The new international competitors often have different cost structures (for example, the relative labor component of total costs), production processes, and so on. In many industries the injection of these new competitors has changed fundamental characteristics of products (cars, for example), reduced the time span of product life cycles, and added much new productive capacity (which generally limits prices and margins and/or increases costs).

Increased deregulation in industries ranging from trucking to petroleum, to airline and financial services has accompanied the shifts already mentioned. Together these changes foster redefinition of products, of the relationships between buyers and suppliers in a product-service delivery chain, and of ancillary services to the end consumer. Some industry segments that are still heavily regulated, such as the insurance industry, are also affected by this trend.

The Evolution of Guidelines, Standards, and Protocols. As a response to the need for better and faster information exchange, interest has grown in developing standard definitions, protocols, and product encoding. Historically, government regulation was the primary impetus for establishing standards. Now, however, industry associations, industry groups, and the like, also are introducing standards. Two examples are the universal product code (UPC) in the grocery industry and magnetic ink character (MICR) sets and magnetic strips on credit cards and cards for automatic teller machines (ATM). By forcing consistency of message content and product form, such standards make it much easier for firms to establish and participate in interorganizational systems.

Penetration of Information Technology into Internal Business Processes. The combination of decreasing IT costs and increasing capability has resulted in a broader range of internal computer applications. As more and more data are stored in computers, the logical next step is to transmit these data in machine-readable form to wherever they are needed. This avoids redundant encoding of data, makes information readily accessible, and ensures higher quality of data by eliminating multiple keying of the same item. The money and time savings easily justify such data and resource sharing. With more internal company data on computers, developed standards for intercompany exchange of information, and clear economic justification, participation in interorganizational systems is very attractive.

Technical Quality and Capability of Information Technology. As IT has become increasingly reliable, companies are able to use

IOS's in business-sensitive areas, such as in dealing with customers. For example, a customer's perception of his or her bank's service is tested at each use of an ATM. Too frequent problems may cause users to change banks.

Favorable experience with internal computer and communications systems has led companies to explore external applications of these technologies.

Use of IT to Distinguish Product and/or Company.   An example of such use is a large construction company that developed for its own internal use a program for more efficient project management. Eventually the company gave "dumb" terminals (those with no independent processing ability) to its clients so that they could track progress of the project, analyze changes in specifications, and forecast maintenance schedules and costs. In this second step, the company sought to distinguish itself from its competitors, who lacked such computer backup.

Later the company gave "intelligent" terminals to customers to use primarily for special maintenance management programs that originate with the construction company's computer. In competitive bidding, this IT service distinguishes the construction company from its competitors. Further, it links the customer in a manner that encourages a continuing relationship with the company after the project is completed.

IOS VERSUS DDP

In the broadest terms, an IOS consists of a computer and communication infrastructure that permits the sharing of an application, such as programs for making reservations or ordering supplies. The players in a system are either participants or facilitators.[2] An IOS *participant* is an organization that develops, operates, or utilizes an IOS to exchange information that supports a primary business process. Participants can be competitors, organizations in the buyer–supplier chain, or a combination of these. An IOS *facilitator* is an organization that aids in the development, operation, or use of such a network for exchange of information among participants. The supporting products or services are a part of the primary business of the facilitator.

Although some larger companies have well-established IOS's, many executives barely understand the concept of such systems. The most

---

[2]The definitions in this section are partially based on S. Barrett and Benn R. Konsynski, "Inter-Organizational Information Sharing Systems," *MIS Quarterly,* special issue, Fall 1982, p. 93.

frequent response to a general description of an interorganizational system is "What's different about it? Isn't it a special form of distributed data processing (DDP)?"

IOS differs from distributed data processing in four important ways:

1. Whereas DDP is under the control of a single company, an IOS crosses company boundaries. Thus one company's employee can directly allocate resources and initiate business processes in another company. This capability introduces very different challenges for a company's internal control, planning, and resource allocation systems. As a result, most companies must revise these management control systems to permit the requisite coordination across organization boundaries for IOS.

2. With an IOS, in contrast to DDP, the question of government regulation arises as a result of the information exchange across the boundaries of separate organizations and hence of separate legal entities. Among the numerous potential issues are questions of legal liability. For example, when does the electronic message passing over communication lines in an IOS actually become an order? When an IOS involves competitors, as illustrated by airline reservation systems, what constitutes unfair business practice? When an IOS involves participants engaged in interstate commerce, are current regulations sufficient to protect consumer interests?

3. The IOS facilitator is a player that does not exist in DDP. Although intermediaries are not new in most industry segments, their role in interorganizational electronic communication is new. An example of an IOS facilitator is the CIRRUS nationwide network of ATMs. CIRRUS, which is not a bank, permits subscribing banks to give their customers 24-hour, coast-to-coast access to their ATM system. The home banking system network offered by CompuServe is another example of an IOS facilitator.

4. An IOS frequently has a broader and more significant potential competitive impact than the traditional internal uses of IT. For example, a major bank has developed an application it calls the treasury decision support system (TDSS). TDSS is a microcomputer-based system that the bank makes available to its largest corporate customers for use by their company treasurers. The system communicates with the bank's host computer and accepts input from a range of other systems. TDSS permits a treasurer to track, report, analyze, and perform simple manipulation of data concerning the company's funds. Data for TDSS can be transferred from several sources, including the company's computer or computers owned by competitive banks. The company may ask other banks or repositories to transfer data on company funds under their control to TDSS in machine-readable form. Currently, the bank that developed TDSS is the only organization, in addition to the (customer) company, that can examine all the data in the microcomputer. This examination would yield a complete profile of the company's funds management and would (the bank hopes) provide an excellent basis for developing a new (and tailored) product offering for the customer. Implementation of an IOS is not guaranteed to demonstrably improve return on investment, productivity, or operational efficiency. The impact of such systems may be more subtle.

IOS AND GENERIC STRATEGY

As part of strategic planning, IOS's potential impact on the competitive environment and on the implementation of competitive strategy should be considered. Following are examples of how a company can use an IOS to implement competitive strategy.

Overall Cost Leadership

Interorganizational systems can improve efficiency and scale in production and distribution. A number of these systems have reduced costs through electronic purchasing and ordering. The fashionable just-in-time delivery systems are examples of such electronic links among organizations. In one plant, General Motors has experimentally tied its CAD/CAM (computer-aided design and manufacturing) and order-entry systems to its suppliers' production systems. A supplier's computer communicates directly with GM's robot-based assembly line to provide "flexible" manufacturing.

Differentiation

In support of a differentiation strategy, an IOS can be used to add value to products and services. It may be coupled with a special service that distinguishes the product or company. For example, a company that manufactures maintenance chemicals gave its largest customers microcomputers linked to its host computers. Customers could thus use an application that helped them make decisions on product mix, order frequency, and maintenance schedules (as well as the obligatory direct order-entry capability). Over time, the chemical company changed the basis of competition from price alone to a range of services. And once its customers had accepted the microcomputers, they were unwilling to accept similar systems from the chemical company's competitors.

An IOS may serve as a means of differentiation by a radical modification of access and distribution channels. American Airlines' SABRE and United's APOLLO reservation systems, developed from the late

1960s to 1991, illustrate interorganizational links that control market access in their industry. Travel agencies that use automated reservations systems, on average, use one of these two systems for 65 percent of the reservations they make.[3]

Focus

This strategy usually combines low cost and differentiation. In addition, the business entity chooses to address a particular niche of one industry. An example of this strategy is a consortium of small stock-brokerage and investment firms with various specialties. They are sponsoring the development of an application similar to Merrill Lynch's Cash Management Account. Access to the system will be by a home banking network offered by a major West Coast bank. The target customer for this product is the investor with a portfolio of $40,000 or more. The consortium will attempt to offer a flexible range of integrated services at a much lower cost than its competitors.

ORGANIZATIONAL IMPACT

Interorganizational systems can have a range of impacts on the informal organizational structures of the participants. The amount of internal change triggered by an IOS appears to vary depending on whether an organization is reacting to an IOS implemented by another company or whether it is the initiator or implementer of the IOS.

A company's general management frequently does not participate in the decision to join an IOS proposed by another organization, and it may neither explicitly plan nor consider the change implications of the system. These changes will occur in business process (first-order impact), skills and staff requirements (second-order impact), and then organization structure and business strategy (third-order impacts).

Initial changes generally occur in business processes. The particular process (such as order entry and production) must change to conform with the standards of the IOS, as designed by the facilitator, or to take into account various procedures in internal control, report formats, planning systems, and communication patterns. This shift in the underlying business process and communication pattern brings about changes in the skills needed by employees, and in some cases new employee categories.

---

[3]*Report to Congress on Airlines Computer Reservation Systems* and addendum to the report, prepared by the Civil Aeronautics Board in consultation with the Department of Justice, Spring 1983.

Examples of this include independent insurance agencies that now illustrate products through a computer network and do their back-office accounting through links to the home offices of large insurance companies. This has enabled insurance brokers to become "estate planners" and to sell more complex, customized products than were feasible before. Similarly, customer service representatives in large travel agencies have evolved from clerks who simply flipped pages in airline guidebooks to sophisticated computer users who can access numerous databases on hotels and car rental agencies. When an IOS is used for a key business function such as market-access systems (for example, shared ATMs in retail banking), the IOS may force changes not only in business processes, required skills, and organization structure, but even in business strategy.

The order of these impacts differs in organizations that initiate or implement an IOS, due primarily to the heavy planning and financial commitment for the system, which must be done by the facilitator. The IOS is the enabling vehicle for changes in organization structure and strategy. Skill and staff-level changes are next, and changes in the business process occur last.

IOS PARTICIPATION PROFILES

Managers reacting to or contemplating the implementation of an IOS should also understand the range of involvement alternatives and their financial and strategic implications. Technologically, participation in IOS's falls into three levels:

1. Information entry and receipt.
2. Software development and maintenance.
3. Network and processing management.

As the level of involvement increases, there are also increases in responsibility, cost commitment, and organizational and technical complexity.

Information Entry and Receipt

At the first level, the IOS participant performs no application processing and merely acts as an information entry-receipt node. The user generally has access only through restricted protocols. The IOS simply provides standard messages, such as when an independent travel agency uses one of the major airline reservation systems without additional in-house processing capability. Most current IOS participants are operating at this entry level. Employees using these systems include shipping clerks, order clerks, salespersons, and fund and credit managers—all of whom are involved in information retrieval, authorization, and validations activities.

At this first level of participation, higher-level participants determine the standards and procedures and retain control of the application. In the airline reservation system, for example, the travel agent must follow the policies and procedures embedded in the computer programs written and maintained by the major carrier. At this stage, interconnections exist only at the basic data-exchange level, and the switching cost (for example, the cost of moving from one automated reservation or home banking system to another if simple inquiry is the only use) is low.

Compatibility requirements generally exist, but exact protocols are rarely needed initially. In some situations, the higher-level participant will increase the dependence of lower-level participants. (Some home banking systems, for example, permit automatic payment systems after the customer keys in a large amount of data, which dramatically increases the cost of changing to another system.) The first-level participant can become increasingly dependent on the higher-level participant as tasks or processes require more coordination across organizational boundaries. Although first-level participation is not complex, the relationships established with other organizations over time can help restructure the industrial marketplace in which the participant operates. This restructuring is driven by the provider of the IOS.

For example, IOS brokerage networks have permitted savings and loan (S&L) organizations to offer discount brokerage services. This innovation has given the larger S&Ls a new customer segment, and the resulting increased transaction volume has forced improvements in their software and communications systems. This improvement in turn has had the effect of bringing about economies of scale, driving unit costs down, and introducing other products and services (such as insurance). This chain of events illustrates why the distinctions among brokerage houses, insurance agencies, and banks have become blurred from a consumer perspective and how structural change in one element of an industry can cause industry or marketplace changes. Changes are not isolated; a change in one element brings about changes in other elements.

Software Development and Maintenance

Companies participating at the second level develop and maintain software used by other IOS participants. Usually, the developer of the IOS absorbs development and maintenance costs in order to gain exclusive control over decisions on access, price, and design of the application and the network. The expenses and investment associated with the development and operation of such a system can be truly extraordinary; in the airline case, it is hundreds of millions of dollars. In the airline reservation system examples already mentioned, American and United are second-level participants; they are primarily responsible for developing their SABRE and APOLLO systems, respectively. Data Resources, Inc., an economic modeling and information resource firm that permits customers to access its data and applications, is another example.

Administrative overhead is very significant for second-level participants, as they must initiate and manage the coordination across organizational boundaries. For example, planning the system requires detail inputs (such as estimates of transaction volume for capacity planning) from other participant or facilitator organizations, which increases the time required to develop the plan.

Network and Processing Management

The third-level participant serves as a utility and usually owns or manages all the network facilities as well as the computer processing resources. Examples include public information networks such as the Bell operating companies, The Source, and CompuServe. Costs increase dramatically at this level.

In addition to network development and maintenance costs, the third-level participant accepts considerable internal control responsibility for the integrity of the information exchanged. For example, the CIRRUS network that permits ATM transactions nationwide accepts a great deal of responsibility for the reliability, availability, integrity, security, and privacy of its system.

SUMMARY

In considering IOS's as a strategic possibility, managers must weigh internal and industry aspects, participation issues, and social impact and public policy.

The key internal issue is the organization's readiness to deal with changes in business process, personnel, and structure that it may face as a result of IOS participation. It must also have the ability to adapt to the competitive pressures that may arise.

The industry issues involve the strategy and repositioning of the firm in its market. Companies must also determine the appropriate level of investment and the level of control they expect to exert over an IOS. When an organization becomes a participant in a new entity, new problems as well as opportunities are presented.

The social impact and public policy issues, though not always obvious, are critical. How might continued rapid introduction of IOS systems in the buyer–supplier chain affect the large portion of the work force involved in direct sales, for example? At what point will the consumer have to pay such an inappropriate price because of biases built into dominant systems (such as those in the airline industry) that regulatory or legislative relief is necessary?

Chapter 5

Organization and Control

Imaginative companies are not just using the technology to support existing organization structure and control systems; they are creatively applying the speed and flexibility of low-cost computer and communications systems to transform the control function and the organization structure. Managers once stymied by the slow flow of information from the work force or customers can now grab data from the most remote corners of their companies in an instant. This offers the possibility of moving decision making from the field to corporate headquarters, thus bringing more consistency to decisions. Other firms are using the technology to distribute large amounts of data to the desks of decentralized managers, thus facilitating decentralized decision making. The key point of this chapter is that technology encourages neither centralized structures and controls nor decentralized structures and controls but offers new possibilities.

For example, Wal-Mart, the nation's largest retailer, is now using IT to *centralize* control, whereas Frito-Lay, the largest snack food supplier, is using IT to *decentralize* control. In a way not well understood until recently, existing structures and controls have been heavily influenced by "the art of the possible" in information handling. The technology of the 1990s allows us to readdress some long-dormant issues.

CONTROL AND THE CHANGING ENVIRONMENT

The obvious benefit of this fast, flexible, reasonably priced information management technology is that it can revitalize the three traditional purposes that control systems serve. It can help managers use resources more effectively, better align disparate parts of the organization with companywide goals, and improve the collection of data for strategic and operating decisions.

But information technology—PCs, spreadsheets, networks, and database systems—has done more than just enhance existing processes. It has created a whole new set of options for gathering, organizing, and using information. Those who have selected wisely from the new options have seen their control systems and structures transformed. They have found ways to channel the power of information to the muscles of their corporations. As a result, they have boosted their efficiency and overall competitive position.

So far, only the most progressive companies have fully utilized the new technology, perhaps because only they could bridge the gap between the financial systems group and the IT group and effectively engage the enormous change in management issues. We believe the success of these efforts is stimulating many other companies to address these issues. The following examples show the kinds of benefits a business can obtain when it uses information technology to overhaul its control processes. Each of the enterprises described below has capitalized on the technology by organizing information in one of three ways: by consolidating it, by centralizing it, or by decentralizing it.

Consolidating Data to Transform Retail Banking Relationships.
The new technology speed and lower costs permit managers to get information more quickly and to shape data files into new forms as needed. This means that if the rules of the game change, managers can reshuffle material into whatever forms are needed in order to analyze it and meet the challenge. By consolidating reports and raw numbers, companies in essence create new information from old, and new data can stimulate solutions to nagging problems or point to unexploited opportunities.

A prominent bank recently spent millions of dollars to consolidate and reorganize its computer files by customer and by product. The old system of data files meshed with the company's long-standing incentive system, which focused on individual products and product-oriented organizations. Relationship managers had no easy way to identify the full set of relationships each customer had with the bank. Consequently, they were frequently embarrassed when making individual calls and tended to avoid cross-selling opportunities. They lacked a mechanism for reviewing a customer's total holdings regularly and seeking an appropriate mix of products for the customer. Compounding the problem was people's names appearing in several variations on purchase records—sometimes two initials, sometimes the full name, and so on. Even if salespeople had wanted to plow through mountains of product files for customer information, it is doubtful they could have caught all of the listings for every customers.

The new system enables the organization to regularly review a customer's entire product portfolio. They can use this information for suggesting replacement of outdated financial products and additions where appropriate. The company thus helps to forestall customers' switching to other financial institutions and continually generates new business. A new incentive system has been instituted that pays commissions to customer-oriented managers who develop comprehensive long-term relationships with customers, thereby aligning the manager's goals with company goals. Simultaneously, management is also able to measure performance by product line.

Many of the company's competitors are now scrambling to install similar systems but they face two or more years of costly systems programming to reorder their large, inflexible data files. This type of capability is becoming a requirement for retail and wholesale banks that want to stay in business.

Centralizing Data to Improve the Elevator Service Call.   Corporate headquarters can now promptly gather information from branch offices at low cost. This allows close performance tracking and timely corrective action when needed.

A passenger elevator company used information technology to replace its decentralized service system with a centralized one by which customer trouble calls bypass field service offices and come directly to corporate headquarters. Since service contracts are highly profitable in the elevator business and customers' switching costs are low, competition for such contracts is intense. Sustained high service levels are critical for staying in business. For this reason, providing excellent service and dealing with customer problems immediately are primary corporate goals.

Under the old system more than 100 branches fielded customer calls, serviced them, recorded the results, and sent monthly reports to headquarters summarizing their activity. Many important customer complaints and product-line service problems did not reach top management, because the write-ups filtered up through four reporting levels. In fact, company executives suspected that some troubled branches regularly underreported complaints and problems in an attempt to avoid the spotlight. This system was the only possible way of operating until recently.

The new system, in contrast, pumps out weekly service reports from a massive, centralized database and allows management to zero in on trouble spots at once. The database keeps track of *all* service activity on every elevator they have serviced. The system identifies troubled customers, troubled product lines, low-volume service branches, and incompetent mechanics in a way that facilitates appropriate management action. For instance, after several months' data had come in, top management discovered that certain elevators had been breaking down between 18 and 30 times each quarter. The problem had existed for years but had been buried in files at field offices. Focused action on these data initiated a sweeping reorganization that included training in use of systems and adapting the system to the field organization. Elevator service problems have decreased to 50 percent of their previous level.

Whether such old difficulties stem from the inattention of service personnel or product design weaknesses, field managers can now respond with quick action. Further analysis of recurring problems now leads executives to adjust staff levels, retrain service representatives, or send a product back to the engineering department to resolve a design problem. It has also opened the opportunity to remove one level from the organization structure—referred to as "flattening" it.

Additionally, the new system has improved the quality of each service call. The database at headquarters contains the history of every elevator the company has installed. Before headquarters dispatches a service representative by beeper to answer a complaint about an elevator, he or she is briefed on its service history. The service person learns whether the elevator is due for any preventive maintenance, which can save a trip later. The service rep is also given information that permits quicker identification of an emerging pattern of service difficulties on an elevator. Under the old system, the company had to rely on the service rep's memory and often incomplete branch files.

The improved system has increased the company's market share in service while cutting service costs. Needless to say, however, there were enormous implementation challenges as the firm evolved from an independent field system with bottom-up reporting to a totally linked reporting system that challenged 40 years of operating history.

Decentralizing Data to Target Supermarket Inventory.   In other settings the transmission of important data from headquarters to the work force through new control systems gives decentralized staff the information they need for doing their jobs well. It also allows the creation of incentive programs that provide additional motivation for them to do so. Whether funneling new price information to the personal computer in a salesperson's briefcase, providing data to regional market planners, or monitoring customer buying patterns in retail outlets, companies are using IT to leverage effectiveness.

For example, many supermarket chains have applied the speed and flexibility of the new technology to their decentralized inventory monitoring system. The old setup demanded that employees count stock and then translate the numbers into buying and merchandising plans. If sales of an item surged, store managers often learned about it too late. Furthermore, because suppliers had the only up-to-date facts on what was selling where, they acted as consultants and sometimes prodded stores to overstock slow-moving products. This consulting relationship also increased suppliers' bargaining power in price setting.

With the new system, scanners at checkout counters log every item that leaves the store. The scanners post inventory records instantly and far more accurately than earlier methods. As a result, store managers have been able to lower inventory levels, weed out slow-moving items, boost turnover, and match product mixes to their consumers' changing tastes. Managers are better able to offer special promotions or merchandise items in a timely way. Moreover, because they now possess the best information, their bargaining power with suppliers is greater. The system has sharply improved the performance of decentralized managers. In each of these cases the firm's structure and control systems were sharply impacted, albeit in very different ways.

REDESIGN, NOT JUST REPAIR

Traditional control systems often fall short of serving their intended purposes. Failure can usually be blamed on one of three reasons: people do not understand the corporate goals, they understand them but lack the resources to meet them, or they simply are not motivated to fulfill them.

Sometimes people do not know what is expected of them because the corporate plan has changed and dissemination of the new message is lagging. For instance, a cash-flow crisis may cause the vice president of finance to cut budgets. In a huge conglomerate that relies on old technology, management can take weeks to rework budgets and get new spending guidelines out to operating units. In the meantime, large amounts of cash may be drained away. (As noted elsewhere, IT-enabled time compression can be a very significant competitive advantage.)

Even after a message has made the long trip from headquarters to dispersed units, the work force may lack the information to act on it. For example, recall the bank that directed its relationship managers to manage each customer's total relationship. Had the bank not given the managers customer-oriented data files, they would not have had the information they needed in order to meet the company goal. When performance is not measured accurately or promptly it's more difficult to maintain motivation, and bad work habits may evolve. Sales reps whose bonuses are tallied only once a year have no way of knowing where they stand six months into a new year. They may not realize until too late that their techniques are off the mark and need redirection.

Control systems made possible by new technologies arm managers with the tools to solve problems. More importantly, however, they enable managers to step back and rethink what they want a control system to do and to make meaningful adjustments. Some of the new options are discussed here.

Meaningful Budgets

Because budgets identify individual and unit tasks in detail, managers use them to tell people what is expected of them. When individuals help to develop the budgets, however, those individuals tend to become bound to organizational goals. Each blank on a budget form forces a question into a manager's mind. With the old technology, the sheer time required to fill in the blanks prevented managers from trying out several alternative combinations of numbers and looking down the road to see the implications of each.

New spreadsheet technology not only speeds the budgeting process by allowing managers to "plug in" numbers faster; it also improves the quality of those budgets by letting managers try out a variety of "what if" scenarios and compare the outcomes. If a business is trying to project revenues, say, it can run through several iterations based on possible changes in the market in a very short period of time.

A first run-through might assume a regulatory change that bolsters the sales of one product. In another, the absence of the new law might cause sales to remain flat. By using computer models to test various assumptions, managers can think more carefully about plans and expenditures associated with them and then follow these ideas through to their logical conclusions. In this way, the technology drives management to better anticipate and prepare for contingencies. Also, since individual unit budgets can be almost immediately consolidated into overall corporate financial plans, the process helps companies to coordinate diverse activities.

The new technology also lets managers continuously update budgets based on actual performance. Organizations are no longer bound to immediately out-of-date documents. They can quickly change plans in midstream based on performance data. For instance, a telecommunications network can quickly notify manufacturing to step up production as actual sales exceed the forecast. Similarly, the effect of cost overruns on end-of-month profits can be projected as soon as they occur.

In short, information technology permits turning the budget into a meaningful set of instructions that can facilitate optimization of the company's performance under changing conditions. The controller of a large U.S. corporation claims that quickly consolidated on-line spreadsheets for each department and business unit have improved tenfold his company's ability to coordinate action under various alternatives. Moreover, less staff is needed to meet budget preparation deadlines.

Adaptation to Change

More powerful and flexible data architectures help companies adapt to regulatory or other environmental changes. When the 1986 tax law shifted the game rules for insurance companies, one company quickly capitalized on the change. Within weeks of the law's passage, the company launched a campaign to educate its agents and customers about the statute's ramifications and the desirability of repaying loans against insurance policies. While companies whose customer files were policy-oriented scrambled to deliver a coherent message to their clients, this company's computer system produced thousands of individually tailored reports that explained in a few pages how the new rules would affect its policyholders.

The point of the program was to persuade customers to pay back loans against their whole-life policies, since loan interest was no longer tax-deductible and the cash-value buildup on a policy receives favorable tax treatment. (Customers, of course, were in the habit of borrowing against the cash value of their policies at a low rate, deducting the interest on those loans, and pouring the money into high-yield Treasury bills. The net effect was a huge drain on company coffers.) This innovative company succeeded in convincing customers to repay tens of millions of dollars on their loans and at the same time generated massive new sales of single-premium life insurance, which is both liquid and nontaxable under the new law. The ability to respond to environmental change paid a handsome dividend. The flexibility built into the system, of course, was almost impossible to justify at the time the investment was made. Afterward the firm wondered how they could have lived without it.

Solutions for Production

The increased power and versatility of new control systems help managers identify trouble spots in their administrative, field, or factory operations.

One of the widest uses of IT is in production facilities, where monitoring systems track errors per hour, flag equipment downtime, measure machine speeds, and assess worker productivity—allowing managers to remedy production problems before they become disasters. Conventional systems force managers to rely on someone's spotting the variation in a machine's production, or to wait until a piece of equipment breaks completely. Modern systems, however, can detect even the slightest deviation in human or machine performance. Early detection allows early correction, thereby improving the economics of manufacturing.

Examples of this application abound. One cigarette manufacturer has installed an automated system that regularly pulls cigarettes off the line and puts them through 20 tests, noting the smallest inconsistency in quality. Paper companies use sophisticated monitoring devices to detect variations in paper thickness or color that are invisible to the human eye. The precision with which these machines detect slight flaws allows workers to quickly adjust equipment—or their own tasks—as needed. As a refinement of earlier versions of this system, the machine operators and the system designers worked together to develop a set of dynamic graphs on display terminals showing paper thickness versus machine settings. This permits even better control of the paper-making process.

Facts to Make the Sale

Information technology can help management align control and sales-incentive measures with the realities of the market. Failure to use that ability can have embarrassing results. As noted earlier, a prominent retail bank sent salespeople to call on upscale clients with the intention of selling them new financial products. Unfortunately, the bank lacked data on each customer's total holdings. When through ignorance of these holdings, the salespeople pushed products that were wildly inappropriate for the clients, their image as financial counselors was quickly undermined. The bank should have made the investment in its control systems first. The outmoded systems had thwarted efforts to better serve customer needs, and ultimately the bank had to cancel its well-conceived but impossible-to-execute campaign.

Some companies have used IT to spread their sales tentacles ever closer to the customer without relinquishing coordination and control at the top. Banks and travel agencies, for instance, use computer systems to execute transactions at remote sites and instantly post them to centralized files. Automatic teller machines and travel agent terminals have allowed these innovative companies to shift the point of purchase nearer to customers while retaining timely records that top management can easily access.

Opportunities to reshape customer relations take many forms. Consider the case of a trust officer who wants to court the beneficiaries of a trust so that when the trust initiator dies, the money will stay at the bank. In a large bank that handles 10,000 trusts, information about the beneficiaries, many of whom are children, is likely to be buried in computer files or in paper archives. With the right information and an automated "tickler" system, the trust officer can send credit applications to these young beneficiaries as they come of age, thereby founding early relationships with them.

Tracking Inventory and Sales

New inventory tracking systems let companies continuously trace an order, update account balances, monitor inventory, and alert manufacturing and suppliers to upcoming requirements. Companies have applied such systems to control in a variety of ways. An electric sign company installed a sophisticated production control system that pipes orders directly to manufacturing. Under the old arrangement, orders took a week longer to trickle down to the factory floor. The production manager never knew what was in the pipeline, so she could not prepare the materials and staff ahead of time. Production bottlenecks and huge inventories were a way of life. The new system drives down inventory costs by eliminating the need to overstock expensive materials, and it ensures that capacity is better used throughout the 22-step manufacturing process.

Some systems amplify the benefits of low inventory without shortages by linking the order-entry function to suppliers. An automobile manufacturer has electronic ties to its suppliers, which now receive up-to-the-minute information from the company's order-entry system. The supplier can then ensure that necessary materials arrive on time. The system has proved so successful that the manufacturer has reduced its investment in inventory and warehouses—and the savings more than offset the system's cost.

An inventory monitoring system can also help managers get the product to the market where it is selling best. To be most useful, the procedure must be able to capture information and manipulate it quickly. One variety-store chain bought a scanner-based inventory system for its outlets. The old system had used a punch card at the end of each stack of 12 products to signal the need to reorder, but while items were trickling out of stores, corporate management had no idea what was selling in which areas, or how quickly.

Today a wand at the checkout counter reads the bar code off each item sold, and headquarters polls every store across the country every night for inventory data. In this way, management can assess customer trends on a daily basis. An item that turns quickly in 32 upscale locations might stall in inner-city stores, and vice versa. The new system allows managers to tailor product mix to clientele and helps identify emerging market niches that demand new product designs.

Automated order entry and inventory tracking can help companies vary their sales and pricing strategies between regions or customer types and keep their sales force informed of price changes. One national food company with its own truck fleet faced a tough problem: each sales region required its own pricing strategy, and each store its own product mix. What's more, the company wanted to base its strategy for each store on a combination of the items sold and the number of stale items left over from the previous day. Clearly drivers could not sift through customer records every night or new prices from headquarters every morning and still be expected to make their rounds.

The company installed microcomputers in more than 10,000 delivery trucks. Each morning, each driver's PC receives from a headquarters mainframe computer the subregion's prices and recommended stock mix. Every night, the company receives data in electronic form from each driver on what items were delivered and what stale items were removed from the shelves to help it determine the next day's recommendations.

Effective Incentive Systems

Technology can help managers create more effective incentive systems—from corporate profit-sharing plans that eliminate internal rivalries to schemes that automatically pay factory workers bonuses for meeting deadlines. A simple form of automated incentive system in one company continuously tallies sales commissions and allows salespeople to access their records. Salespersons' reviews of how far they are from meeting their quota may motivate them to push harder.

Additionally, incentive-based measurement systems can identify and track the contribution of a working unit that may otherwise go unrecognized. The automotive industry has found this capability attractive. The first dealer a customer visits usually invests a lot of time explaining the various models and demonstrating their features. Nonetheless, the customer may buy the car from a different dealer, who has done far less work but offers a slightly lower price. Knowing this pattern, the first dealer may do a hasty job of educating the customer and try to close the deal quickly. Although automakers may not like this situation, the industry's commission structure, which measures only sales, supports it. One manufacturer is now considering a customer tracking system that would modestly reward a salesperson who makes an initial presentation even though another dealer makes the sale.

Some organizations use innovative systems to influence customers to buy more. With sophisticated on-line analysis, a company can base a customer's discounts on total volume rather than on each other. A contact lens company offers a consignment inventory to opticians who can turn it over 13 times a year. Since opticians can fill 65 percent of their orders from that inventory and get paid on the spot instead of a week later, they are spurred to sell heavily from that manufacturer's line as opposed to some other firm's. Moreover, fast information tells the company and the opticians whether the stores are on schedule to meet their turnover quotas. This system dramatically boosted the lens company's market share over a period of several years.

Different Cost Structures and Asset Investment Levels

Over a period of time, genuinely different cost structures and asset levels may appear. No firm is more illustrative of this than Bergen Brunswig, a $4 billion sales drug wholesaler. In 1970 there were 1,000 firms in the drug wholesale industry, with no firm holding more tha

1.5 percent of the market. Bergen Brunswig's operations costs-to-sales ratio was 16 percent, typical of the industry. In 1989, in a vastly consolidated industry of 200 firms, the top five firms (of which Bergen Brunswig was one) in aggregate held 70 percent of the market. Bergen Brunswig's operations costs-to-sales ratio had shrunk to 2 percent. There was no room left for a 16 percent performance.

Three aspects of this story are important. The first is that these changes evolved over 20 years. The possibilities enabled by information technology can take a long time to play out, both because of the increasing capabilities of the technology and because of the difficulties of change management. When speaking of the competitive uses of technology, we are not talking about a quick checker game but about a chess game that can go on for years. Secondly, in Bergen Brunswig's opinion (1988 company history), the primary driver was information technology, as they slashed operating costs, quintupled the sales revenue handled per marketing representative, and completely transformed the operating structure of the warehouse. Thirdly, on-line ordering to suppliers had shrunk the inventory-to-sales ratio. This type of infrastructure transformation, while not as glamorous as some of the other examples, is absolutely fundamental to survival and competitiveness.

"Flattening" the Organization

The new technologies are allowing very different forms of organizations to emerge. As noted earlier, by facilitating information manipulation, the technology has enabled one or more layers of hierarchy to be eliminated in a number of settings, reducing distance from top to bottom of the organization.

Video conferencing, video cassettes, voice mail, and so on, allow the top of the organization to appear psychologically closer to the middle and the bottom. The CEO and the divisional president now *seem* to be closer and much more real to the managers and staff in the middle of the organization. Some of the techniques used for communicating in the political world have come to the corporate environment. The *form* of communication is changing.

Finally, in this area we come to the networked organization. Voice and electronic mail have radically altered the patterns of communication inside organizations as individuals are able to identify and interact with pockets of expertise they would have been totally unaware of a decade ago. Several years ago one of the authors watched with fascination as a senior sales representative, reacting to a sudden market opportunity, used his firm's electronic mail system to assemble a 200-page proposal in 48 hours with the help of seven sources around the globe whom he had never met within the firm. (The proposal was accepted.) The reach of the network to new sources of expertise and the shrinkage of time make this capability a genuine competitive advantage—albeit one that is extremely hard to justify objectively.

Controlled Complexity—An Example

The ability of some companies to use the technology to execute very complex micromarketing campaigns can put unresponsive organizations at an extraordinary competitive disadvantage. A 1989 interview with the former chairman of People's Express Airlines (chairman until its demise) illustrates this point. He noted that his airline had used a very limited amount of information technology, particularly in its fare structuring. They had only a single weekly fare for any seat on each route; time of day, day of week, and actual loading factors were all irrelevant. He noted that, in his judgment, the key date of their death was January 19, 1985. That was the day when American Airlines introduced their "internal yield management system," which allows them, if desired, to set a different fare for each seat on every flight on a particular route. With that capability, he noted that on every route American flew head-to-head with People Express, depending on anticipated flight loading between 1 and 100, deep/deep/deep discount seats were assigned, with the deep/deep/deep discount seats' fare being $5 below the prevailing People Express fare. American then launched a national advertising campaign.

> Call your travel agent and find out who the *real* low-cost airline is. It is not People Express. It is American Airlines.

Within 20 minutes of the time People Express announced a fare change for a route, American had adjusted its deep/deep/deep discount fare to $5 below the new People Express fare and electronically communicated it to travel agents all over the United States and the world.

Competing against that level of managed complexity is extraordinarily difficult.

SUMMARY

Because changes in organization control systems affect all areas of the corporation, changes in them can be extraordinarily disruptive, with the technical issues and their associated costs being the lesser part of the challenge. For this reason, managers should think long and hard about the changes and their many implications before going forward.

As noted earlier, the technology itself is organizationally neutral. It does not favor centralization over decentralization or one control philosophy over another. It simply offers top managers choices they have not had before. As a by-product, local managers in the elevator company lost some autonomy, and their noses were out of joint for awhile. On the other hand, supermarket automated control systems gave store managers more information, which helped them make better decisions at the store level.

Such choices must be made consciously, giving full attention to the practical details of implementation. For example, reporting relationships may be impaired. Taking away or adding decision-making power may demand that a different type of manager be placed in some posts. The blurring of operational and managerial control may also require restructuring and redefinition of managers' roles.

There is danger, too, in failing to consider all the strategic advantages to be gained from the creative new controls and organization structures. One competitor in the elevator industry copied the other's move to centralize service records. The copycat company, however, went a step further: it identified all of its elevators that chronically failed because of age rather than some defect and then approached the owners of those elevators with proposals to rebuild the units. The innovator has defined a new, very profitable market, at least temporarily.

Expensive data storage, sluggish retrieval, and complex systems that overwhelm their would-be users are all relics of the past. The technology now exists to transform the internal workings of the organization. Consequently, it is appropriate to step back and ponder whether decentralized units are really aligned to company goals, and whether incentive systems are helping or hurting this alignment. Can technology offer new solutions to these issues in your setting?

Chapter 6

Information-Enabled Alliances

Information technology empowers companies to compete, interestingly enough, by allowing them new ways to cooperate. One way is through the information partnership facilitated by the sharing of data between organizations.

THE ALLEGIS EXAMPLE

This competition through cooperation can be illustrated by a notable failure. Allegis Corporation was the brainchild of United Airlines, which acquired Hertz Rent A Car and Westin Hotels in hopes of creating an integrated travel company with real synergies in the eyes of the end customer. The venture was quickly torpedoed by skepticism on Wall Street, where great fear was expressed that the firm was getting involved in businesses whose operations they did not fully understand. Nobody speaks of the Allegis Corporation today without using the word *fiasco,* as the company was forced to divest itself of its pieces at great loss. Yet in retrospect it is hard to imagine a more prescient effort to form a market coalition that exploits the power of information technology.

The Allegis idea seemed to offer something for everyone. From the United Airlines customers' point of view, by renting a Hertz car and staying a Westin hotel, they could earn "frequent flyer" miles on United. The participant divisions could benefit by sharing databases supported by powerful means to transmit, log, and retrieve information. Furthermore, the company could present itself to the customer as a single source of travel services, incentives, and support. Eventually, one could imagine Allegis customizing travel programs for a large number of regular customers.

Implications.   Allegis's hard lesson—and everybody else's excellent one—was that the partnerships engendered by information systems *need not be based on ownership.* Managers of companies in reciprocal industries can plan and coordinate common approaches to customers through relational databases without taking each other over. In retrospect, Wall Street quite rightly reckoned that although United's top managers could develop synergies in servicing customers, they were not likely to enjoy any operational advantages. Indeed the real and legitimate fear was that airline executives would not know how to manage these myriad businesses with specialized operating problems. The insurance industry, with many participants recovering from forays into the "financial supermarket," is learning this same lesson.

The real opportunity, it turns out, is in joining forces *without* merging, the way American Airlines has allied with Citibank. In this arrangement, air mileage credit in the airline's frequent flyer program is awarded to credit card users—one mile for every dollar spent on the card. American has thus increased the loyalty of its customers, and the credit card company has gained access to a new, highly credit-worthy customer base for cross-marketing. This partnership has been expanded to include MCI, a major long distance telephone company, which offers multiple airline frequent flyer miles for each dollar of long-distance billing. Citibank, the largest issuer of Visa and Master-Cards, recently initiated a partnership to steer its 14.6 million Visa card holders to MCI, a response to AT&T's entry into credit cards (the Universal card). American Airlines soon thereafter entered a partnership with Hilton Hotels and Budget Rent-A-Car to build a joint travel service with an investment/contribution from each partner. They have recently added Marriott Hotels and are discussing arrangements with others in the industry. Their next planned move is to provide convention services for cities.

BENEFITS OF INFORMATION PARTNERING

Through an information partnership, diverse companies can offer novel incentives and services or participate in joint marketing programs. They can take advantage of new channels of distribution and introduce operational efficiencies and revenue enhancements. Partnerships enhance opportunities for scale and cross-selling. They can make small companies look, feel, and act big as they reach for customers once beyond their grasp. They can also make big companies look small and close as they target and service custom markets. Information-enabled partnerships, in short, provide a new basis for differentiation. Many more of them will be appearing in the coming decade.

These new forms of market cooperation pass large volumes of electronic data precisely, instantaneously, and relatively cheaply. New computer speeds and cheaper mass storage devices mean that information can be archived, cross-correlated, and retrieved much faster and less expensively than before—and in ways that are customized for recipients. Additionally, the widespread emergence of fiber-optic networks has greatly improved cost-effective delivery of information to remote locations.

Additionally, managers whenever possible are anxious to lessen their financial and technical exposure. Partnerships allow them to share investments in hardware and software as well as the considerable expense of learning how to use both. The cost of developing certain configurations of software is particularly great, posing huge problems for small and mid-size companies that compete against large companies. Software investments may be denominated in hundreds of millions of dollars, which creates impenetrable entry barriers for smaller competitors—unless a number of them consolidate their purchasing power. (The authors have encountered more than one hundred system development projects in the past two years that cost over one hundred million dollars.)

Likewise, as discussed in detail elsewhere, the management cost of organizational learning in this rapidly changing technical environment is mushrooming. While there is no shortcut to learning, information partnerships provide a way to reduce risks in leading-edge technology investments by sharing expenses and exposure. End-customers should provide additional pressure to support this trend. Desktop clutter has led to a demand for simplification. Users want simple, user-friendly interfaces that will enable them to reach out to a variety of services both within and without the firm through a single device and with a minimum of confusing detail. This implies that users want companies to cooperate, at least, on data interface standards where possible and, in fact, they have brought pressure to bear in this regard. Users also continue to demand higher service levels, including faster response time, broader access to data files, and increasingly customized service. Partnerships provide scale and clout for helping companies to satisfy customers in this regard.

KINDS OF INFORMATION-ENABLED ALLIANCES

In response to these opportunities and pressures, four kinds of information partnerships have emerged: joint marketing partnerships, intra-industry partnerships, customer–supplier partnerships, and IT vendor–driven partnerships.

Joint Marketing Partnerships

Information technology offers companies an important new option: co-ordinate with rivals where there is an advantage in doing so, and specialize where it continues to make sense.

The effort by IBM and Sears to market Prodigy is an example of such an effort. At a cost of more than $500 million, these companies have assembled a package of more than 400 electronic data services—home banking, stock market quotations, restaurant reservations, and so on—to be delivered across a standard telephone network to millions of American homes. Individually, these services would be used so infrequently—and cost so much to get hooked into—that few customers would be likely to find any one of them practical. IBM and Sears have perceived that these services have considerable appeal when bundled together. By selling advertising space around the edge of the screen, the partners are able to deliver the product to a home for only $130 per year irrespective of usage.

In another setting, travel companies are making use of electronic linkages to establish combined marketing programs—common customer databases, joint purchasing incentives, and so on—so that airlines, hotels, car rental companies, and bank credit cards are all being combined into a single electronic marketing effort. Spearheading this are such information networks as American Airlines' SABRE, which reaches into thousands of travel agencies and firms. Today all major U.S. airlines are involved in one partnering agreement or another.

In the airline industry, the scale needed to develop and manage a reservation system for travel agencies and individual client firms is beyond the reach of the medium-sized airlines, most of which have become clients of (and hostages to) the reservation information systems of the bigger carriers. In Europe, two major coalitions have been created, the Amadeus Coalition and the Galileo Coalition; software for Amadeus is built around System One, the computer reservation system of Continental Airlines, and Galileo is built around United's software. Of course, there are only a limited number of airlines, and the credit card industry is extremely fragmented. Banks that held back in establishing partnerships with airlines found themselves frozen out once the early movers had made their deals. The painful fact is that the dynamic competitive environment punishes procrastination as much as it does strategic blunders. The first movers may have the capacity to build lasting barriers to entry that punish late entrants. More recently, marketing alliances have been formed among banks, grocery chains, and food companies.

In marketing partnerships, participant companies gain access both to new customers and territories and to economies of scale through cost-sharing. Sharing allows the provider of the data channel to sell excess capacity in the channel, to ensure that the company's image and market position will not be compromised, and to reach customers once thought too expensive to reach. From the customer's perspective, life is simplified when several needed products arrive through a single channel.

The path to these joint marketing programs may be forged with either offensive or defensive objectives in mind. A market leader—as for example, American Airlines—may seize the initiative and establish an imperative for participation, all the while controlling the partnership structure. On the other hand, Johnson & Johnson's development of the COACT system was primarily in response to its concerns that previous initiatives by American Hospital Supply were hurting its sales—clearly a defensive action. Another example of defensive maneuvering is that of Texas Air. A significant motivation for its acquisition of Eastern Airlines was to obtain their reservation system channel as a weapon to partially negate the impact of United and American in the travel agencies, which was seen as unfavorably impacting Texas Air's market share and ability to grow.

Intra-Industry Partnerships

The most important and potentially difficult to manage information partnerships evolve not among companies offering complementary services, but among small or mid-sized competitors who see an opportunity or need to pool resources in order to stay in the game competitively. The ATM banking networks constitute an industry that provides nationwide access to previously *regional* products.

A particularly interesting case is the alliance of 18 mid-sized paper companies that has developed a global electronic information system to link them with hundreds of key customers and international sales offices. Costing $50 million to develop, it was targeted at providing a speed and quality of response that would have been technically and financially unattainable by any of the individual participants acting in their own behalf. With combined sales of nearly $4 billion, these companies made this investment because they could see that to compete effectively in their service-oriented business they must provide online, global data interchange with key customers on order-entry inventory-status product specifications. The alternative was to be driven from key markets by large competitors providing these services. Thus the partnership was driven by the fear of losing. They wanted to provide customers a virtually instantaneous means of placing status inquiries and orders, in contrast with the previous industry norm of 12-day processing cycles. They were all genuinely uneasy about joining the proprietary information networks of their big, global competitors, because they were aware of the harsh penalties and aggressive charging practices in some other industries.

In reaction to the high charges exacted by the airlines' systems, a group of hotels has been actively examining ways to establish their own hotel reservation system. They believe that as a group they might bring enough "critical mass" to the market that they will be able to sharply reduce charges per reservation. This in turn has attracted the interest of a major airline.

Another coalition among competitors is the Insurance Value-Added Network Services (IVANS), which links hundreds of insurance companies' home offices and thousands of independent agents. IVANS permits independent agents across the United States access to distant property and casualty insurance companies for policy issuance, price quotation, and other policy management services. It was initiated and created by the industry trade association ACORD.

These insurance companies were all concerned that several larger companies had invested in electronic channels of their own, giving them the potential to monopolize the business of the independent agents. The IVANS interface presents independent agents with a roster of smaller insurance companies and a level playing field—which benefits the agent, of course, who is concerned about maintaining the competitive environment ensured by multiple providers.

Understandably enough, ACORD's position as a trade organization allows it to be perceived as the fairest, and hence most effective, broker of a collaborative system among businesses. In a similar vein, MEMA/Transnet, which connects hundreds of manufacturers and thousands of retailers in the auto parts industry, resulted from actions by the Motor and Equipment Manufacturers Association (MEMA).

Sometimes, however, suppliers and customers are so fragmented that neither side has the vision or resources to put together any kind of system. In these settings a third party may be positioned to perform this function. The American Gem Market System is an example of this. Put together by a third party independently financed for this purpose, American Gem Market System linked dozens of gem suppliers with hundreds of jewelry stores, in effect replacing what had been a complex interpersonal network. Gems were now traded between partners who had no personal knowledge of each other but who trusted the integrity and reliability of the network provider. Unfortunately, the network provider was unable to attract enough customers and it ultimately failed.

Some intra-industry partnerships are so important to a country or other political body that they are initiated and led by government. An example is the TradeNet system of Singapore, which links the management and operations activities of the world's largest port. The Singapore government has spent an amount approaching $50 million to develop this system for linking trade agents—freight forwarders, shipping companies, banks, and insurance companies—with relevant government agencies—customs officials, immigration officials, and others. Clearing the port used to take a vessel two to four days; now it takes as little as ten minutes. It is hoped that this dramatic reduction in the time ships remain in port will help ensure that Singapore remains a port of choice in Southeast Asia, where the competition among ports is growing.

Customer–Supplier Partnerships

Some information partnerships are built on data networks set up by suppliers to service customers. A good illustration of this noted earlier is the interorganizational system of Baxter Healthcare (formerly American Hospital Supply), a medical equipment and healthcare supplier. Today Baxter Healthcare offers its customers a wide variety of medical supplies manufactured by Baxter and its competitors as well as many other products, including office supplies.

The system has created a platform, a single interface, for buyers to reach their many suppliers and for the participating suppliers to reach new customers at dramatically lower costs. From the viewpoint of Baxter, this system is evolving into a major new revenue stream through its offering of a package of multivendor services. Since its introduction, the system has been one of dynamic reconfiguration and redevelopment—and to some extent, so have the participating companies. Equally important by developing this platform, it allowed Baxter to forestall another company developing their own proprietary platform that could put Baxter at significant disadvantage.

Another example involves a retail grocery chain that has renegotiated its relationship with a supplier of disposable diapers, one of its very profitable, high-turnover items. Under the new partnership agreement, when a shipment of diapers leaves the retailer's warehouse, notice is sent to the manufacturer. No order is transmitted, no delivery schedule is requested. The manufacturer is bound by a performance contract to keep the warehouse sufficiently stocked, and this system provides it the information it needs to ensure this. This partnership is intended to reduce inventories in the retailer's warehouse and to facilitate full-scale coordination and mutual cost reduction, and it appears to be effective. Paperwork has been significantly reduced on both sides (orders, quotes, complicated billing, and so on), production schedules are now more responsive, and each company has trimmed its operations staff.

IT Vendor–Driven Partnerships

On the one hand, these partnerships allow a technology vendor to bring its technology to a new market and, on the other hand, they provide a platform for industry participants to offer novel, technologically sophisticated customer services. General Electric Information Services and Automatic Data Processing are examples of firms that have successfully provided such data interchange platforms. These information companies can become the strategic linchpin for an organization that wishes to pioneer such services.

A good example of this is ESAB, a large European welding-supplies and equipment company that tripled in size between 1973 and 1987 — a period when sales fell off by half in the industry as a whole. A key to the company's growth was an alliance with a large independent network vendor. It used that third party's information services to facilitate acquiring and rationalizing failing companies throughout Europe: closing their plants and moving production of what had been local brands to a central plant in Sweden, while providing the customers an on-line order-entry service. ESAB did not have the IT development resources in-house to build such a Europe-wide telecommunications system.

From the customers' point of view, the old companies' local offices still provided goods and services. In fact, the information system governed the company's production schedule, manufacturing, and shipping so that customers received products, usually overnight, without realizing they were no longer dealing with a local manufacturer. This strategy enabled costs to be slashed dramatically. ESAB has, in effect, replaced inventory and plants with information, using a technology that would have been extremely costly to develop from scratch.

In another type of partnership an information vendor forms a research alliance with a major customer. A common form of this is the joint establishment of a "beta site" — where a manufacturer tests a new technology with selected clients in order to both debug it and learn the extent of its uses. Such coalitions provide advantages to both parties. The vendors gain valuable insight into the practical field problems associated with their technology. Their ability to resolve their customers' problems, especially those of prestige accounts, gives vendors' sales forces highly visible references for further promotion. The customer learns and participates in a new technology that may otherwise be beyond its skill and financial resources and gets a head start in introducing it to appropriate markets.

LAYING THE FOUNDATION FOR A SUCCESSFUL PARTNERSHIP

At its core, partnership is strategy. As a manager starts forward, questions must continually be asked: What lines of business should I provide exclusively, and where should I move to leverage my activities through partnering? What are the appropriate adjunct services that I can use to drive my products to new markets? Where can I profitably offer joint purchasing incentives without confusing or eroding my existing customer base?

Like most activities in the practical world, partnerships are not a sure bet. They can fail because of overly optimistic assessments of the benefits accruing to the several parties or because of inadequate attention to the difficult challenges of administering the relationship. While no single formula will ensure successful partnerships, our research has identified some characteristics of successful partnerships.

Shared Vision at the Top. It may seem a cliché by now, but there are really no substitutes for champions in senior management. If a partnership is to overcome the inevitable divergence of interest among companies, top executives must share both viscerally and intellectually an understanding of the specific benefits of collaboration—cost reductions, new customers, cross-selling. Because of its potential impact, partnering is a strategic matter that needs the stubborn vision of the corporate strategists. For example, the airlines and credit card accord emerged only because their CEOs hammered out details in face-to-face discussions. Neither side was looking for a quick killing; both sought a long-term, mutually profitable relationship.

Reciprocal Skills in Information Technology. Competence in such areas as telecommunications, database design, and programming must be reasonably sophisticated in all partners, and very sophisticated in the partner that is leading the development of the information platform. Minimally, all participant companies must be able to manage telecommunications networks, have high standards of internal quality control (at least with respect to data handling), and be accustomed to working with very large databases. Many companies that have tried to initiate electronic data-interchange agreements have been shocked to find that their potential partners were unable to assimilate even modest data technologies and applications.

Concrete Plans for an Early Success. Partnerships grow from strength to strength. It is important to plan the introduction of the system so that people across participating companies can experience at least limited positive results at the start. Early successes, perhaps at pilot installations in key regions, create a sense of accomplishment and commitment.

Usually, partners must expend considerable effort in testing their hardware and software to ensure that their general direction is technically feasible. Most specifically, they should not settle for the lowest common technical denominator between the organizations. Rather, the more competent side must assist in helping to upgrade the technical or business environment of its partner.

Persistence in the Development of Usable Information.   Mere ownership of a database—say, of a company's current customers—is no guarantee that information is organized in a form that can pass beyond corporate boundaries to partners. In fact, often the most expensive and time-consuming prelude to partnership is organization of data so that it can be usefully and cost-effectively transmitted.

The information must be packaged in ways that make it immediately useful to others without compromising the confidentiality of the company's secrets. In reality, information must be packaged for all partners *by* all partners. This requires the joint design of data definitions, formats, relationships, and search patterns.

Coordination on Business Procedures.   Partnering involves a great deal more than the mere sharing of data. For companies to share data effectively involves a considerable degree of procedural integration across the company lines. A joint team is needed for developing the initial system, and an ongoing task force is needed for guiding its evolution. The partners must involve themselves in such mundane tasks as defining common procedures and common standards of systems development and maintenance. They must develop common codes for products, customers, and data communications as well as articulated procedures for surfacing conflicts, addressing perceived injustices, and rethinking the terms of the partnership when it becomes necessary.

For example, one partnership we have tracked was recently on the verge of collapse because the partner receiving data had not brought its business systems into line with the other partner's systems. For the partnership system to operate, the receiving firm had to first print out all incoming documents and then manually recode and rekey the information to make it compatible with its database architecture.

Appropriate Business Architecture.   Partnering companies must establish structures and guidelines that ensure fairness and profit on both sides. This involves agreeing on rules that will help to assure equal treatment under the system. It also includes addressing possible asymmetries in the partners' underlying interests. That is, the deal should be structured so that partners are not required to contribute more than they can afford and so that they will profit from the system roughly in proportion to what they have contributed.

The sources of potential problems in this area are multitudinous. For example, in the airline industry, the issue of "screen bias"—the listing of competing airlines' flights below those of the lead partner—has been as explosive as exorbitant charging. Additionally, some airlines have contended that American and United have examined their competing partners' booking data to gain insight into competitive market positioning while denying their "partners" access to this data. American and United have denied the charge.

In another setting a small, start-up book distribution company approached a major retailer with the idea of using the retailer's sales data to identify customers' potential interests in books. This would allow the book distributor to promote books about gardening to recent purchasers of gardening tools, for example. As the discussions evolved, however, examination of the retailer's sales data revealed that the two companies would have had to integrate 11 different databases in order to accomplish the joint venture, a task too expensive and risky for the undercapitalized book distributor.

SUMMARY

In the past, the focus of IT thinking and research was on applications for the individual company's management of its information. This led to intense discussion of the chief information officer's role in deployment of IT resources inside the company and the structure and nature of appropriate planning and control systems. More recently, extensive work has been done to develop better understanding of the technical and administrative issues involved in preparing and managing ongoing electronic interorganizational system (IOS) links between a company and its customers and suppliers.

Today, however, the opportunities are broader, and senior managers are discussing the establishment of strategic information partnerships with other companies and in fact implementing them within their industry and without. In tomorrow's business environment, many more companies will find it necessary to analyze and develop these collaborative IT relationships.

Questions for the General Manager

In conclusion, we offer four questions for the general manager:

1. *Is your company vulnerable to new information partnering, and are there ways to forge alliances of your own to preempt them?* In reality, alliances produce many more losers than winners, since in many settings early movers freeze others out of the game or build economies of scale that are hard to replicate. Timing is crucial. If you start too early, you and your partners may get into technical trouble or face a market that does not know it wants your product. (The field is filled with examples of this.) If you start too late, the window of opportunity will close, and real exposure will exist for competitors to damage you.

2.   Does your business strategy realistically assess the implications of the transfer of power and authority to partners in any prospective electronic partnering arrangements? False steps can be extraordinarily expensive and time-consuming to correct.

3.   Are your potential partners financially viable, and do they represent the right collection of players for potential synergy? In selecting these partners, have you analyzed the set of future options that you may be foreclosing? Today's short-term opportunity is often tomorrow's strategic liability.

4.   Is the technical infrastructure you have in place the right one to effect and manage the kinds of strategic alliances you are considering? Are you overreaching your skills or contemplating an approach that does not use your most accessible technical capabilities?

Chapter 7

IT Architectural Alternatives

THE EVOLVING IT ENVIRONMENT

Instability and evolution in the organization structure for delivering IT support have been enduring features of the information technology (IT) environment. In the past decade changes in technology and corporate strategy have repeatedly challenged existing organizational structures for delivering IT support and have led to major reorganizations. Several key reasons lie behind this.

Technological Change

First, both for efficiency and effectiveness reasons, IT in the 1990s incorporates the technologies of office support, image processing, data and voice communications, and data processing. Ideally, all of these technologies are managed in a coordinated, integrated manner. Developing this coordination has not always been easy. In many organizations in the 1960s and 1970s each of these technologies had a different set of implementation issues and was marketed to the company separately. Quite independent internal organizational structures within the firm developed for managing each technology. Very few of these organizations had the necessary staff or the required mix of skills for the new technology or for facilitating its integration with other technologies. The varied managerial histories and decision processes associated with each of these technologies has made their integration exceptionally difficult, and this difficulty continues today. In most firms, the organization of information technology has evolved by experience to its present structure.

Second, ensuring the success of information technologies new to the organization often requires approaches that are quite different from those used with mainframes/minicomputer technologies with which the organization has had more experience. New organization structures have emerged to facilitate handling this problem. The trend is to shift more IT responsibility to the using group.

Third, where the firm's data and computer hardware resources should be located organizationally often requires rethinking. The dramatic hardware performance improvements (in all three technologies) in the past two decades allows very different organizational solutions today than were possible in the early 1970s. These improvements have been facilitated by the technology shifts from the vacuum tube to the very large-scale integrated circuits in computers and from copper wire to optical fiber in telecommunications. In each case vastly improved cost-performance ratios resulted. Equally significant, integrated circuits have permitted development of stand-alone personal computer systems and of office support systems that can be tailored to provide highly specific service for any desired location.

Technological change, then, has brought a dramatic shift in the type of information services being delivered to users and in what constitutes the best organizational structure for delivering them. This new structure involves not only the coordination of data processing, teleprocessing, and office support, but also affords opportunities to change the physical and organizational placements of the firm's technical and staff IT resources. Technical resources include such items as computers, word processors, image processors, private telephone exchanges, and intelligent terminals. Staff resources consist of all the individuals responsible for operating these technologies, developing new applications, or maintaining them.

Productivity improvements will continue as still smaller, more reliable circuits are developed. Table 7–1 shows the cost and performance trends per individual unit and circuit based upon known chip technology. The combination of these reductions in cost, increases in capacity, and the past decade's explosive developments in software have brought linked desktop computers to most office workers' desks.

Environmental Factors

In addition to technology changes, several nontechnological factors have prompted reexamination of effective organization of IT services inside the firm.

Human Resources. The United States has a significant shortage of competent, skilled people who can translate technology into ongoing systems and processes within organizations. These shortages, severe in 1991, are likely to continue in the coming decade as our appetite for complex systems continues to grow. The slow growth problems that

TABLE 7–1　Cost and Performance of Electronics, 1958–the 1990s

Technology	1958 Vacuum Tube	1966 Transistor	1972 IC[a]	1980 LSI[b]	1992 CMOS[c]
Dollars per unit	$ 8.00	$ 0.25	$0.02	$0.001	$ 0
Bits stored per unit	1/32	1	1K	64K	16M
Dollars/logic unit	$160.0	$12.0	$ .200	.008	.0006
Access time	16×10^{-3}	4×10^{-6}	40×10^{-9}	2×10^{-10}	50×10^{-12}

[a]Integrated circuit.
[b]Large-scale integrated circuit.
[c]Complemental metal oxide semiconducter

Source: Georges Anderla and Anthony Dunning, *Computer Strategies 1990–9, Technologies-Costs-Markets,* John Wiley & Sons, p. 18.

have beset the hardware manufacturers have not hit the software and system developers. Partially offsetting this has been the development of user-friendly technologies that allow faster applications to be developed by less-skilled individuals.

Telecommunications Environment.　The highly reliable, inexpensive digital telecommunications systems that have been developed in the United States and the "explosion" of optical fiber provide the potential for dramatically different services in the next decade. The economics and reliability of telecommunications in the rest of the world, however, differ from those in the United States and Canada, and this presents unique environments for the immediate future.

In Western Europe, excessive tariffs (often dramatically higher than in the United States and Canada) and inordinate installation delays have significantly slowed the growth of certain services. During the 1990s, however, better coordination of government-owned systems, increased privatization, and more cost-effective, time-responsive environments are likely to emerge.

In Latin America and other less developed areas, systems and infrastructure reliability problems are combined with the problems encountered in Europe. For example, because of an unacceptable level of communication breakdowns (some more than 24 hours in duration), several South American companies were forced to shut down a sophisticated on-line system supporting multiple branches and to seek solutions that addressed realistically the unreliability of the infrastructure. In another situation, a company was able to achieve acceptable reliability only by gaining permission to construct and maintain its own network of microwave towers. For multinationals this state of affairs poses important problems in developing international networks and common standards and has forced them to be flexible. Recent expansion of satellite links is ameliorating the problem, and paving the way for the inevitable fiber-linked global village. Managing the timing is the key challenge.

Supply–Demand Imbalances. Legitimate user demand for IT support continues to vastly exceed the supply available from an IT organization. Business-justified applications waiting to be implemented and exceeding available IT staff resources by three or more years—the norm rather than the exception—lead to a perception of unsatisfactory support and to dissatisfaction with the central IT organization. This dissatisfaction is intensified when users want types of support that the company cannot afford at the time.

Widespread user frustration provides additional momentum for end-user computing, personal computers, and so on, as alternative ways to meet legitimate needs or to circumvent oppressive financial controls. Personal computer technologies have increasingly permitted users to bypass central IT control, which is helping to relieve some of these frustrations. In addition, users' confidence in their ability to develop and operate a computer system because of their experience on personal computers has grown, and the growth is likely to continue.

Systems Design Philosophy. A fundamental shift has occurred in computer-based systems design philosophy. The prevailing practice in the 1960s and early 1970s involved writing computer programs that intermixed data processing instructions and data elements within the program structure. Today, however, the management of data elements and their architecture are clearly separated from the computer program instructions. Additionally, large amounts of external software are being acquired to be inserted into these systems. Implementing these shifts while coping with legitimate changes in business processing needs is placing enormous pressures on IT organizations. They must balance investing human resources in new systems developments against redesigning old systems to increase their relevance, while ensuring reliable operation of the old systems until the updated ones can be installed. Computer-assisted software engineering is maturing as IBM offers the potential of automated programming in its new depository architecture.

Combined with changing computer hardware economics, these factors have made organization structures designed in the early 1970s seem seriously flawed, and major reappraisals are in order for many firms. Succeeding sections of this chapter deal with the need for and challenges in merging the disparate technologies, various approaches for assimilating IT, and the issues involved in selecting an appropriate centralization/decentralization balance of data and hardware.

MERGING THE "ISLANDS" OF INFORMATION TECHNOLOGY

Problems in the speedy integration of data processing, telecommunications, and office support largely result from these technologies' very different management practices (as shown in Table 7–2). The following paragraphs analyze these differences.

1920. In 1920, an operational style of information services, elements of which persist to this day, was in place in most corporations. The manager and his or her secretary were supported by three forms of information services, each using a different technology. For word processing, the typewriter was the main machine for generating legible words for distribution; a file cabinet served as the main storage device for output, and the various organization units were linked by secretaries moving paper from one unit to another. Data processing, if automated at all, was dependent upon card-sorting machines to develop sums and balances, using as input punched cards that served as memory for this system. The telecommunications system consisted of wires and messages that were manipulated by operator control of electromechanical switches to connect parties. The telecommunications system had no storage capacity.

Also in 1920 (as shown in Table 7–3), the designers of the three "islands" (office support, data processing, and telecommunications) had significantly different roles. For office support, the office manager directed the design, heavily influenced by the whim of his or her manager. Although office system studies were emerging, word processing was the primary means of facilitating secretarial work. The primary means of obtaining new equipment was through purchasing agents and it involved selecting typewriters, dictaphones, and file cabinets from a wide variety of medium-sized companies. Standardization was not critical. Data processing was the domain of the controller-accountant, and its design activity was carried out by either the chief accountant or a card systems manager, whose job it was to design the protocols for processing information. Both data processing and teleprocessing were sufficiently complex and expensive that they required that managers develop an explicit plan of action.

A key difference between data processing and telephones, starting in the 1920s, was that the service of data processing was normally purchased and maintained as a system from one supplier. Thus, from the beginning, a systems relationship existed between buyer and seller. Teleprocessing, however, evolved as a purchased service. As AT&T made available a network of less-expensive inner-city telephones, companies responded by ordering the phones, and the utility developed a monopoly of telephone service. All three islands, therefore, were

TABLE 7–2 Information Technology Equipment, 1920–1990s

Islands of Technology

Functions of the Technology	1920			1965			1990		
	Word Processing	*Data Processing*	*Communication*	*Word Processing*	*Data Processing*	*Communication*	*Word Processing*	*Data Processing*	*Communication*
Human-to-machine translation	Shorthand Dictaphone	Form Keypunch	Telephone	Shorthand Dictaphone	Form Keypunch	Telephone	Dictaphone Terminal Audio input	Terminal	Telephone Terminal
Manipulation of data	Typewriter	Card sort	Switch	Typewriter	Computer	Computer	Computer	Computer	Computer
Memory	File cabinet	Cards	None	File cabinet	Computer	None	Computer	Computer	Computer
Linkage	Secretary	Operator	Operator	Secretary	Computer	Computer	Computer	Computer	Computer

TABLE 7–3 Information Technology Human Roles, 1920–1990s

Islands of Technology

Roles	1920			1965			1986		
	Word Processing	*Data Processing*	*Communication*	*Word Processing*	*Data Processing*	*Communication*	*Word Processing*	*Data Processing*	*Communication*
Designer	Office manager	Card designer	AT&T	Office system analyst	System analyst	AT&T	System analyst	System analyst	System analyst
Operator	Secretary	Machine operator	AT&T	Secretary	Operator	AT&T	Manager Secretary Editor	Manager Secretary Operator	Manager Secretary Multiple suppliers
Maintainer	Many companies	Single supplier	AT&T	Many companies	Single supplier	AT&T	Many companies or single supplier	Multiple suppliers	Multiple suppliers Other
User	Manager	Accountant	Manager	Manager	Manager Accountant	Everybody	Everybody	Everybody	Everybody

served in a different manner in 1920: one by many companies, one by a single systems supplier, and one by a public utility.

1965.   In 1965 the servicing and management of all three islands were still institutionalized in the 1920s pattern. Office support had a design content, but it was still very much influenced by the individual manager and centered around the secretary. Services, such as typewriters and reproducing systems, were purchased as independent units from a range of competitors offering similar technology. There was little long-term planning, and designs and systems evolved in response to available new technical units. Data processing, however, had become an increasingly complex management process, requiring serious evaluation of major capital investments in computers and software and multiyear project management of the design and development of systems support. In addition, all users needed extensive training sessions so that they could take full advantage of the productivity offered by the new system. At times even the corporate organization was changed to accommodate the problems and the new potential created by computer technology. AT&T completely dominated the provision of communications service in 1965; from a user's perspective, management of communications was a passive purchase problem. In some organizations, managing communications implied placing three-minute egg timers beside telephones as an aid in reducing the length of calls.

Today.   Today the management concerns for office support and telecommunications are integrated with those of data processing for three important reasons. First, all three areas now require large capital investments, involve large protracted projects with complex implementations, and may need extensive user training. Further, significant portions of all three services are increasingly being purchased from single suppliers. The corporate managers of these activities, however, are still learning how to handle these very different situations. A special challenge for office support has been the move from multiple vendors with small, individual dollar purchases to a single vendor that provides integrated support. The size of the purchase decisions and the complexity of the applications are several orders of magnitude larger and more complex than those of the 1970s, as networks of thousands of intelligent terminals are being created. For telecommunications the problem is that of breaking the habit of relying on a service purchased from a public utility and, instead, considering multiple sources in making large-capital-investment decisions that may include creating significant in-house networks. Both cases involve a sharp departure from past practices and require a type of management skill that was added to the data processing function in the 1970s.

The second reason for the integration of management concerns is that, to an increasing extent, key sectors of all three islands are physically linked in a network. For example, in a typical mid-sized manufacturing company the same WATS line may be used over a 24-hour period to support on-line data communications, normal voice communication, and an electronic mail message-switching system. A problem of one island, therefore, can no longer be addressed independently of the needs of the other two.

Third, complicating the situation today, dominant suppliers for each island market their products as the natural technological base for coordinated automation of the other islands. Some examples:

- IBM has attempted to extend its data processing base into office support and communications products.
- AT&T is attempting to extend its communications base into products targeted at data processing and office support; it has augmented its line of computers with its acquisition of NCR.
- Xerox is attempting to expand its office support effort into communications and data processing.

Failure to address these management issues appropriately places an organization at great risk. In the past decade most U.S. organizations have consolidated at least policy control and, in the majority of cases, management of the islands in a single IT unit at either corporate or divisional level. The main reasons for this include:

1. Decisions in each island now involve large amounts of money and complex technical/cost evaluations. Similar staff backgrounds are needed in each case to do the appropriate analysis.
2. Great similarity exists in the type of project management skills and staff needed to implement applications of these three technologies.
3. Most applications now require integrated technological networks to handle computing, telecommunications, and office support.

MANAGING THE ASSIMILATION OF EMERGING INFORMATION TECHNOLOGY

Chapters 3, 4 and 5 focused on how developments in information technology have facilitated many new strategic applications. Indeed, as noted, many companies depend heavily on this technology to operationalize and implement their competitive business strategy. For them, relevant new technology (for example, expert systems) must be identified and exploited as quickly as possible. Sustaining a high rate of product innovation, assimilating new vendors, and carefully evaluating new technology options each pose significant organizational challenges as these firms balance the need to run day-to-day operations smoothly while appropriately investigating and assimilating new technologies.

Two key steps must be taken to address this problem. First, corporate management needs to take a *contingency* approach to administrative systems for managing technology assimilation. Each technology requires different management approaches at various points of its life cycle. Introducing technologies to a firm requires an organizational learning perspective as opposed to considering only cost and efficiency. (These concepts are well grounded in organizational theory research. For example, the work of Chris Argyris and Donald Schon[1] describing how organizations successfully exploit new technologies has been particularly helpful.)

The second step is careful consideration of the establishment of a new unit in the IT structure called *emerging technologies (ET)*. This unit, which has been installed successfully in a number of settings, manages the identification and introduction of new technology with high payoff potential.

The Four Phases of IT Assimilation

The notion of information technology being assimilated in stages has been discussed since the mid-1970s. The pivotal work was introduced by Cyrus Gibson and Richard Nolan.[2] Focusing on large-scale computer technology and the development of centralized data processing departments during the late 1960s and early 1970s, they described four stages of assimilating data processing (essentially batch-oriented) technology.

As pointed out in Chapter 2, we have refined this idea when we speak of a company's "portfolio" of information technologies. Each technology application in an individual firm progresses through a set of phases that relate to Nolan and Gibson's original stages and that is also consistent with the organizational change concepts developed by Edgar Schein.[3] These phases are characterized in Figure 7–1 as investment/project initiation, technology learning and adaptation, rationalization/management control, and maturity/widespread technology transfer.

Phase 1.   The first phase is initiated by a decision to invest in a new (to the organization) information-processing technology. It involves

---

[1]C. Argyris and D. A. Schon, *Organizational Learning: A Theory of Action Perspective* (Reading, Mass.: Addison-Wesley Publishing, 1978).

[2]R. L. Nolan and C. F. Gibson, "Managing the Four Stages of EDP Growth," *Harvard Business Review,* January–February 1974, pp. 76–88.

[3]Edgar Schein, "Management Development as a Process of Influence," *Industrial Management Review* 2 (1961), pp. 59–77.

FIGURE 7–1 Phases of IT Assimilation

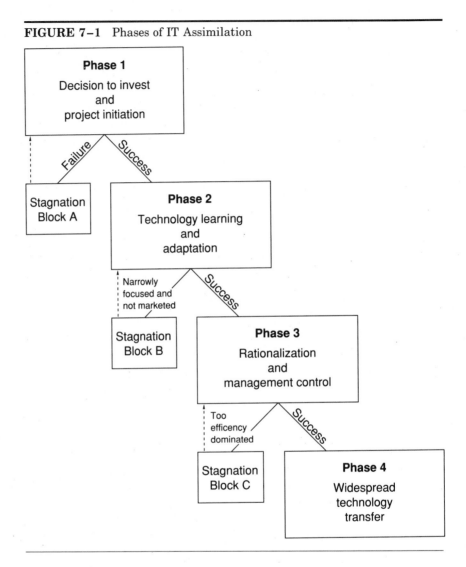

one or more complementary project development efforts and initial individual training. These projects are characterized by a lack of precision in both their costs and ultimate stream of benefits and, where possible, are confined to test markets and/or plants. The resulting systems, in retrospect, often seem quite clumsy. Each step of the project life cycle is characterized by much uncertainty, and considerable learning takes place. The second phase follows unless there is a disaster in Phase 1 —such as vendor failure, discovery that the technology is inappropriate to the firm, or poor user involvement—that results in "Stagnation Block A."

Stagnation Block A typically generates a two-year lag before new investments in this technology are attempted again, usually accompanied by a complete change of personnel. The decision to disinvest is normally a result of there being increased work and little benefit from the system. Sources of these problems may be vendor failure, lack of genuine management attention to the effort, incompetent project management, poor fit of technology to organizations, or merely bad choice. Rarely are the causes recognized immediately. The complexity and time requirements of implementing new information technology normally hide perception of the developing failure for 18 to 36 months. The project typically is not a clear technological disaster, but rather, an ambiguous situation that is perceived as adding more work to the organization with little perceived benefit. Rejection of the system follows. All aborted projects of this type that were studied had significant cost overruns. Each failure created anxieties and prevented development of coordinated momentum. Typically, organizations frozen in this state end up purchasing more services of a familiar technology. They become relatively adept at adapting this familiar technology to their use but become vulnerable to obsolescence.

At the CEO's urging, an insurance company launched a major desktop Executive Information System (EIS) project to put a device on every senior executive's desk. Eight months into the process, the CEO had to retire suddenly for health reasons. Without its key sponsor, the project died over the next six months. Only today, three years later, is the problem far enough in the past that the company is willing to start over, and it is significantly behind the state of the art.

Phase 2. The second phase involves learning how to adapt the new technology to particular tasks beyond those identified in the initial proposal. As learning occurs, the actual benefits coming from the projects in this phase are often quite different from those anticipated. Again, retrospectively, the resulting systems look clumsy. Although the project life cycles in this phase are not characterized by great technical problems, they tend to be hard to plan. A study of 37 office support sites showed that in none of them was the first utilization of technology implemented as originally planned.[4] In each case, significant learning took place during implementation. Indeed, many of the competitive successes discussed in Chapters 3, 4 and 5 evolved over a decade or more as the systems were successively refined through new technologies and experience. If the second phase is managed in an adaptive manner that permits managers to capture, develop, and refine new understanding of

---

[4]Kathleen Curley, *Word Processing—First Step to the Office of the Future* (New York: Praeger Publishers, 1983).

how this technology could be more helpful, the organization moves to Phase 3. Failure to learn from the first applications and to effectively disseminate this learning leads to "Stagnation Block B."

A typical Stagnation Block B situation occurred in a large manufacturing company and involved automation of clerical word processing activities that were under the control of a very cost-conscious accounting function. Highly conservative in its approach to data processing technology, the firm had developed automated accounting systems centrally controlled in a relatively outmoded computer operating system, and it had no plans to enter into database systems. Focusing on only word processing for its mass mailing activities in order to save costs, it forfeited additional benefits. After three years of use, mass mailing was the only activity on its word processing system. Only with new management did the company solicit a proposal that led to the understanding of how this architecture could be the base for an executive information system and many other applications. The organization, however, had been frozen in underutilization for an unconscionably long period.

Phase 3. This phase typically involves a significant change in the organization's approach to the technology, continued evolution of the uses of technology to ones not originally considered, and most important, development of precise controls for guiding the design and implementation of systems that use these technologies (to ensure that later applications can be implemented more cost-efficiently than the earlier ones). In this phase the various aspects of the project life cycle are analyzed, with the roles of IT staff and user becoming clearer and the results more predictable.

If, in Phase 3, control for efficiency does not excessively dominate and room is left for broader objectives of effectiveness, then the organization moves into Phase 4, which involves broad-based communication and implementation of the technology to other groups in the organization. "Stagnation Block C" is reached if excessive controls are developed that are so onerous as to inhibit legitimate, profitable expansion in the use of technology. An example of Stagnation Block C with respect to data processing is the case of a manufacturing company that built a large-scale, centralized distribution center and redesigned all its systems to support this structure. To justify the expense of this new center, it focused on gaining all possible cost economies of a very standardized, highly efficient distribution center. In its single-minded effort to gain this efficiency, the organization became so focused on standard procedures and cost squeezing that it lost its ability and enthusiasm for innovation and change utilizing this technology. This served to discourage users who had useful new ideas. Further, the rigorous protocols of the standard programs in the branches irritated users and helped set the stage for surreptitious branch-office support experimentation (Phase 1 in a different technology). Too rigorous an emphasis on control prevented logical growth.

Phase 4. This final phase can be characterized as a program of technological diffusion. Here firms take the experience they have gained in one operating division and expand its use throughout the corporation.

Quite naturally, as time passes, new technologies will emerge that offer the firm the opportunity either to move into new applications areas or to restructure old ones. A firm is thus confronted over time with a series of waves of new technologies and at any one time is adapting to managing and assimilating several technologies, each in a different phase (see Figure 7–1). For example, a financial organization studied in 1990 was in Phase 4 in terms of its ability to conceptualize and utilize enhancements to its demand-deposit accounting (check processing) systems over a multiyear period. At the same time, it was in Phase 3 in terms of organizing protocols to roll out a new type of branch platform work station that had been successfully piloted in its branches and was now ready for systemwide use. It had recently made an investment in image processing in two departments, and although the firm was highly optimistic about the long-term results, it was clearly in Phase 1 with respect to this technology. Finally, it had just been decided that executive information systems was an important technology, and the firm was at the beginning of Phase 1 in terms of planning what to acquire and how to place it on the desks of key senior managers.

For organizational structure planning, the four phases can be grouped into two broader categories. Phases 1 and 2 comprise a category called *innovation phases,* and Phases 3 and 4 can be grouped as *control phases.* The differences between them can be described as forecasting, assessing, learning, creating, and testing (innovation) versus general usage, acceptance, and support (control).

Work in this area suggests that different parts of the organization will (or should) be responsible for these two functions. Keeping innovation-phase activities separate from control-phase activities helps ensure that the efficiency goals of one do not blunt the effectiveness goals of the other. This idea initially emerged from the organizational behavior literature. For example, James March and Herbert Simon, in their classic book on organizations,[5] referred to the innovation versus control phases as *unprogrammed* versus *programmed* activity. To enable and encourage unprogrammed or innovative activity, they recommended that organizations make special and separate provisions for it. This would frequently involve creating special units for the innovative purpose.

---

[5]J. S. March and H. A. Simon, *Organizations* (New York: John Wiley & Sons, 1958).

Managing the Emerging Technology (ET) Group

Increasingly, a new, explicitly separate organization unit to address innovation-phase technology exploitation and management appears to be a promising approach. Called the *emerging technology (ET) group,* it often resides initially in the IT organization on a level equal with applications development and operations departments. A historical analysis of 12 firms found that the key difference between leading and lagging financial institutions, airlines, and manufacturers was the early formation of an ET group. In some large, strategic IT organizations, the ET unit has been placed outside the IT department to help ensure that it is not swamped by the IT control philosophy.

Three issues must be dealt with by general management in structuring the ET group: organization, management control, and leadership (Table 7–4). The following paragraphs address these three issues in relation to the innovation and control phases. Because the innovation phase is more troublesome for most organizations, it is discussed in more detail.

Innovation Phase.   The atmosphere within the ET group should be exploratory and experimental. Examples of current technologies that such a group might be exploring are interorganization image processing and small-scale expert systems. The organizational structures and management controls are loose and informal. Cost accounting and reporting are flexible (though accuracy is essential), and little or no requirement exists for pro forma project cost-benefit analysis. The leadership style resembles what Hersey et al. refer to as "participating"; that is, the distinctions between leaders and subordinates are somewhat clouded, and the lines of communication are shortened. The level of attention to relationships is high compared to that of task orientation. As noted earlier, this informality is key to innovation and organizational learning.

TABLE 7–4   Characteristics of Effective Management of Emerging Technology (ET) Groups by Phase

	Characteristic	
Management Issue	*Innovation-Phase Effectiveness*	*Control-Phase Efficiency*
Organization	Organic (ET)	Mechanistic (traditional IT)
Management control	Loose, informal	Tight
Leadership	Participating	Directive (telling, delegating)

A study of the tobacco industry[6] referred to such informality as *organizational slack* and stated that "the creation or utilization of slack normally requires the temporary relaxation of performance standards." In the effective companies standards of efficiency were greatly reduced during the early testing phases of a new IT innovation. Organizations strategically dependent on IT should view innovation-phase activities as an integral part of their ongoing response to pressures to adapt to changing environments and should fund them appropriately.

Illustrative of the pressure and responses that lead to establishment of a separate department is the dramatic growth of "information centers" in response to end-user computing. These facilities are generally staffed with nontraditional data processing professionals and have very different accounting, justification, and cost-benefit systems. Firms that are strategically dependent on IT cannot afford to establish such centers reactively. They must proactively forecast, assess, and test appropriate technology to introduce it at an early stage. These activities are unlikely to occur without specific responsibility being assigned to a person or an organizational unit. The role of this unit may be seen as being similar to that of a corporate R&D department.

Two key features contained in a position analysis for ET are noteworthy because of their deviation from the general corporate R&D model. The first is that the manager of ET and the department staff serve primarily as facilitators as opposed to gurus. This implies the use of professionals outside the ET organization to forecast, track, and assess specific technology evolution. For example, a person in the database administrator's organization might be partially funded by ET to forecast, track, and test new database management system products. The second feature is that ET is responsible for what we call *intraorganizational technology transfer.* This refers to the role of designing and managing the Phase-2 introduction and diffusion of the targeted technology in the company. This is the key role of an ET group when contributing to the broad-based learning in a company. ET must first facilitate the development of user-oriented, creative pilot applications of the new technology. They then participate in discussions about how the new applications can best be developed and implemented, the education and training needs of users and IT professionals for using the new technology, and the changes in strategy or structure that may result from implementing the new technology and associated applications.

After the personnel directly involved with the new technology (the ET group) develop the ability to support it, general management then decides whether to provide additional resources to continue the diffu-

[6]R. Miles, *Coffin Nails and Corporate Strategies* (Englewood Cliffs, N. J.: Prentice-Hall, 1982).

sion of the technology throughout the organization (Phase 2). With requisite support of senior management, the ET group begins to teach others throughout the organization how to utilize it and encourages experimentation. A chief concern of the ET manager at this point becomes how to market it effectively to the rest of the organization. (In some organizations the job of selling the new technology is easy because the organizational culture encourages innovation and experimentation.) In the words of March and Simon, innovation in such companies is "institutionalized."[7]

Again the cultural differences between laboratory and operations are important. Part of the task of successfully selling this technology to other parts of the organization is finding a way to translate the unique language associated with the technology to a language compatible with the larger organizational culture. It was noted in a study of the electronics industry that these cultural differences exist more in the minds of the organizational participants than in any objective reality. The "artifacts" identified in the study resulted from the natural tendency of people "when faced with problems in human organizations of an intractable nature, to find relief in attributing the difficulties to the wrong-headedness, stupidity, or delinquency of the others with whom they had to deal."[8]

The issue is not whether the cultural differences exist only in the minds of the participants but, rather, given that they do exist somewhere, what can be done about them. The study identified two useful solutions employed by the sample companies. One solution was assigning members of the design department to supervise production activity and production personnel to supervise the design activity. For IT this means assigning responsibility for user implementation work to ET staff, as well as putting the user in charge of ET group projects. To be effective, this solution must be implemented with consideration for the wide gaps in technical expertise between subordinates and their managers. (Usually the subordinates know more about the technology or business process than the manager does.) However, this has proven to be a viable approach when the key individuals are chosen carefully.

A second solution was effective in other settings. It is the creation of special intermediaries to serve as liaison between the design department and production shops in the organizations. IT steering committees and user department analysts are examples of these intermediaries which have worked effectively in the IT environment. This strategy unfortunately increases the bureaucracy of the organization structure,

---

[7]March and Simon, *Organizations* (see footnote 4).

[8]Burns and Stalker, *Management of Innovation* (London: Tavistock Publishing, 1979), p. 53.

but for many organizations has proven to be a very effective solution to improved communication.

ET managers must analyze existing or potential resistance by organization members to the change brought about by the new technology. Resistance to change often stems from the reluctance of organization members to disturb delicately balanced power and status structures. ET managers need to adopt a "selling" leadership style, which is characterized by high task orientation and high levels of interpersonal interaction. Major organizational changes threaten long-established power positions and open up opportunities for new ones to develop. The advocate of a new technology who is insensitive to the political ramifications of the new system will face unpleasant, unanticipated consequences.

Once the range of potential uses of the new technology has been generated and appropriate users are acquainted with the new technology, management must make a decision about putting the technology permanently into place. At this juncture the assimilation project moves from the innovative phases to the control phases.

Control Phase.   The focus of the control phase is to develop and install controls for the new technology. Whereas the main concern during the innovation phase was the *effectiveness* of the technology, control-phase management is concerned with *efficiency*. In installing the necessary controls over the technology, management's task is to define the goals and criteria for technology utilization. The most effective leadership style here is one of "informing," with lower interpersonal involvement relative to task orientation. During this phase the organizational users (non-IT staff) are better able to judge the appropriateness and feasibility of the new technology to their tasks than they were during the innovation phase. The traditional IT organization and associated administrative systems are generally appropriate for this task.

For technologies in the later aspects of the control phase, IT managers typically exhibit a "delegating" leadership style. Interpersonal involvement and task orientation are low. With operation procedures now well understood and awareness high, the effective managers let subordinates "run the show."

PATTERNS OF HARDWARE/DATA DISTRIBUTION

As technology capabilities evolve (apart from issues in handling emerging technology), another key organizational issue concerns the physical location of the data and hardware elements. (Issues associated with the location of the development staff are dealt with in the next chapter.) At one extreme is the organization that has a large centralized hub connected by telecommunications links to remote input/output devices. At the other extreme is the organization with a small or nonexistent hub, most or all of its data and hardware being distributed to users. Between these two extremes lies a rich variety of intermediate alternatives.

The early solutions to this organizational problem were heavily influenced by technology. The high cost of hardware and the significant economies of scale associated with it in the early 1960s made consolidation of processing power into large data centers very cost effective. In contrast, the cost characteristics of the technology of the 1990s permit but do not demand cost-effective organizational alternatives. (In the 1990s technological efficiency of hardware per se is not a prime reason for having a large central data center.)

Pressures toward a Large Central Hub of a Distributed Network

In order to retain market share as the difference in efficiency between large and small computers has eroded, the vendors of large computers are suggesting that many members of an organization have a critical need to access the same large data files. Hence one ideal structure of an information service is a large central processing unit with massive data files connected by a telecommunications network to a wide array of intelligent devices (often at great distance). The alternative is a network of powerful intelligent terminals containing most of the organization's data files linked to each other. This dichotomy poses a set of complex architectural decisions.

Resolution of the IT organizational-structure problem depends on the key factors of management control, technology, data, professional services, and organizational fit. The impact of each of these factors is discussed here, with Table 7–5 presenting a summary.

Management Control. The ability to attract, develop, maintain, and manage staffs and controls in order to assure high-quality, cost-effective operation of existing systems is a key reason for a strong central processing unit (CPU). The argument is that a more professional, less-expensive, higher-quality operation (from the user's perspective) can be put together in a single large unit than through the operation of a series of smaller units. A dominant trend of the early 1990s is the notion of data-center consolidation for reducing costs by eliminating duplicate software charges, technical support staff, operations, and so on. It was the primary force behind one large decentralized company's decision not to eliminate its corporate data center and move to regional centers. In the final analysis, the firm's management was unconvinced that eight small data centers could be run as efficiently in aggregate and that even if they could, the cost and trauma of making the transition would be justifiable. The company felt that

TABLE 7–5   Pressures on Balancing the Hardware/Data Distribution

Pressure	Toward Increasing the Hub	Toward Increasing Distribution
Management control	More professional operation. Flexible backup. Efficient use of personnel.	User control. User responsiveness. Simpler control. Improvement in local reliability.
Technology	Access to large-scale capacity. Efficient use of capacity.	Efficiency of small scale. Reduction of telecommunications costs.
Data	Multiple access to common data. Assurance of data standards. Security control.	Easier access. Fit with field needs. Data relevant to only one branch.
Professional services	Availablity of specialized staff. Reduced turnover disruption. Richer professional career paths.	Stability of work force. User career paths.
Organizational fit	Corporate style: centralized. Corporate style: functional. IT centralized from the beginning.	Corporate style: decentralized. Business need: transnationals.

through its critical mass, the corporate data center permitted retention of skills for corporatewide use that could not be attracted or retained in a series of smaller data centers. They decided to keep the operation and maintenance of all three technologies central, and to emphasize user input to projects in the design and construction phases through development departments in the several divisions.

In 1990 a large aerospace company consolidated eleven data centers to two. This produced savings of nearly $50 million by eliminating 350 jobs and duplicate software rentals, and management believed it also provided a higher degree of control.

Further, provision of better backup occurs through the ability to have multiple CPUs in a single site. When hardware failure occurs in one CPU, the network can be switched from one machine to another by simply pushing a button. Obviously this does not address the concern that a major environmental disaster could strike the center.

Technology.   Another justification for a large hub is its ability to provide very large-scale processing capacity for users who need it but whose need is insufficient to justify their own independent processing system. In a day of rapid explosion in inexpensive, powerful computing, it is easy for users to do significant amounts of their computing on desktop computers or stand-alone minicomputers. At the same time, however, some users have huge "number crunching" problems—such as large linear programming models, petroleum geological reservoir mapping programs, and weather forecasting models—that require the largest available computing capacity. The larger the computer capacity available, the more value-added detail they can profitably build into the infrastructure of their computer programs.

Many firms see consolidation as an opportunity to better manage aggregate computing capacity in the company, thus reducing total hardware expenditures. When many machines are present in an organization and each is loaded to 70 percent, the perception may be that the "waste" of a vast number of CPU cycles could be eliminated if the processing was consolidated. Although such thinking was an important issue in the technology economics of the 1960s, its significance as a decision element has largely disappeared. The ability to eliminate duplicate software rentals and reduce operating staff remain important reasons for consolidation.

Data. Another pressure for the large central hub is the ability to provide instantaneous, controlled, multiple-user access to common corporate data files on a need-to-know basis. An absolutely essential need since the early days for organizations such as airlines and railroads, this access has become economically desirable in many other settings. Management of data at the hub is also very effective for controlling access and thus security. The issue has become extraordinarily complex, however. Where there is high local need for file access and only occasional need outside the area, locally sited files linked by telecommunications has proven to be a highly satisfactory and less expensive alternative. The geographic dispersal of data files is a very important and complex issue to study.

Professional Services. In itself, the sizable staff required for a large IT data center enhances the organization's ability to attract and retain a specialized technical staff. The ability to work on complex problems and share expertise with other professionals provides a desirable air of excitement, which helps to attract competent IT specialists to the firms and to keep them involved and excited about their work. Availability of these skills in the organization permits individual units to undertake complex tasks as needed without incurring undue risks. Furthermore, when staff and/or skills are limited, consolidation in a single unit permits better deployment of them. Additionally, having the large staff resources at a hub permits more comfortable adaptation to inevitable turnover problems. Resignation of one person in a distributed three-person group is normally more disruptive than five resignations in a group of 100.

For the ambitious individual who wants to remain in the IT field, the large unit provides more opportunity for stimulation and personal development. Perceived opportunity for technical and professional growth has proven to be a key element in reducing turnover. The opportunity for professional growth is a critical weapon in battling the so-called burnout problem.

Organizational Fit. In a centralized organization, the above-mentioned factors take on particular weight, since they lead to congruency between IT structure and overall corporate structure and help to eliminate friction. This point is particularly important for organizations where IT hardware was introduced in a centralized fashion and the company adapted its management practices to IT's location in this way. Reversal of such a structure can be tumultuous.

Pressures toward a Distributed Network

Other pressures push toward the placement of significant processing capacity and data in the hands of the users and only limited or non-existent processing power at the hub of the network.

Management Control. Most important among these pressures is that the distributed network structure better satisfies the user's expectation of control. The ability to handle most transactions locally is consistent with users' desires to maintain a firm grip on their operation. The concept of locally managed data files suggests that the user will be the first person to hear about deviations from planned performance of the unit and hence have an opportunity to analyze and communicate on a planned basis his or her understanding of what has transpired. Further, there now exist a greater number of user-managers with long experience in IT activities who have an understanding of systems and their management needs. These individuals are justifiably confident in their ability to manage IT hardware and data.

The user is offered better guarantees of stability in response time by being removed from the fluctuations in demand on the corporate network. The ability to implement a guaranteed response time on certain applications has been found to be very important to the user.

A distributed network also permits the user to predict in advance more accurately what the costs of computer use are likely to be. Not infrequently the distributed network appears to offer the possibility of lower costs (a careful cost analysis, however, sometimes reverses this conclusion).

Distribution of processing power to the user offers the potential to reduce corporate vulnerability to a massive failure in the corporate data center. A network of local work stations can keep key aspects of an operation going during a service interruption at the main location. A large forest products company decentralized to local fabricators all raw-material and product decisions through installation of a network of work stations with substantial local file storage capacity and processing capability. This reduced the volatility of on-line demand at the corporate computer center and increased the productivity of both corporate and distributed users. Reuters news service scatters key pieces of its database around the globe, and each module has multiple communications paths into it. If a large-scale disaster should occur in any location, the network will not collapse but will only slightly degrade. This system will work for information services, but it would be unviable for an airline reservation system, for example, where an informed opinion (as to whether a seat on a particular flight is or is not sold) must exist in a single setting.

From the user's perspective the distributed network offers a simpler environment, in terms of feeding work into the system and constructing the operating system. The red tape and delay of routing work to a data entry department are eliminated, and the necessary processing procedures can be built right into the ongoing operation of the user department. (Surprisingly, in some cases regaining this control has been viewed with trepidation by the user, although after the fact it is a "non-issue.") Similarly, the new desktop software has dramatically simplified the task of user/technology communication. (In the jargon of the trade, they are "user friendly.") Today's graphic/user interfaces, executive information systems, and electronic mail systems have revolutionized the use of the technology and have propelled such firms as Apple, Microsoft, and COMSHARE to the forefront.

Technology.   In the early days the efficiency of large central processing units was superior to that of smaller units. Today, however, several important changes have occurred:

1. The economics of CPUs and memories in relation to their size have altered. The rule that the power of computers rises as the square of the price (commonly called *Grosch's law*) no longer applies.
2. The economics of Grosch's law never did apply to peripheral units and other elements of the network. The CPU and internal memory costs are a much smaller percentage of the total hardware expenditures today than they were in 1970, with network and peripheral unit costs being the dominant hardware items.
3. The percentage of hardware costs as a part of the total IT budget has dropped dramatically over the past decade as personnel, telecommunications, and other operating and development costs have risen. (In several industries teleprocessing investment and ex-

penses constitute more than half of the computer configuration expenditures.) Efficiency of hardware utilization is consequently not the burning issue it was a decade ago, except for a limited number of super computer applications. Considering these factors, as well as the much slower reduction in telecommunications costs (11 percent per year) and the explosion of user needs for on-line access to data files that can be generated and stored locally, the economic case for a large hub has been totally reversed in many cases.

4. As more systems are purchased rather than made, users are becoming better informed in the procedures of selecting and managing a local system.

Data.   Universal access by users to all data files is not a uniformly desired goal. Due to telecommunications costs and most users' infrequent need to access data files at other sites, it is often uneconomical or undesirable to provide central access to all data. Further, building in the inability to interrelate data from different segments of the firm may in fact be part of corporate strategy.

As a case in point, consider a large decentralized financial services company with a central corporate computing center that serves its four divisions. (All development staff reside in the division.) Almost no common application or data file exists between even two of the divisions in the company except for personnel. Even if its survival depended on it, the company could not identify in less than 24 hours its total relationship with any individual customer. In senior management's judgment, this lack of data relationships between divisions appropriately reinforces the company's highly decentralized structure; indeed there could be significant negative implications in terms of units poaching on each other's customers. No pressure exists anywhere in the organization for change. The corporate computing center, an organizational anomaly, was conceived as a cost-efficient way of permitting each division to develop its network of individual systems. In place for several years, no need has yet emerged for managers to develop common systems or to share data.

Technicians can readily suggest interesting approaches for providing information that has no practical use. Indeed those ostensibly sound suggestions if implemented would destabilize soundly conceived organizational structures.

Professional Services.   Moving technical support functions away from an urban area offers the opportunity to reduce employee turnover, the bane of metropolitan-area IT departments. Recruiting and training can be more difficult in such settings, but once the employees are there, and if they are sensitively managed, the relative scarcity of "headhunters" and nearby attractive employers reduces turnover pressures.

When the IT staff is closely linked to the user organization, it becomes easier to plan employee promotions that may move technical personnel from the IT organization into user departments. This is critical for the department with low employee turnover, as the former change agents begin to develop "middle-age spread" and burnout symptoms. Two-way staff transfers between user departments and IT are a growing trend for expanding the experience base and facilitating closer user–IT relations. This is discussed further in the next chapter.

Organizational Fit.   In many settings the controls implicit in the distributed approach better fit the corporation's organization structure and general leadership style. This is particularly true for highly decentralized structures (or organizations that wish to evolve in that direction) and for organizations that are geographically very diverse.

Finally, widely distributed facilities fit the needs of many multinational organizations. Although airline reservation data, shipping container operations, and certain kinds of banking transactions must flow through a central location, the overwhelming amount of work in many settings is more effectively managed in the local country, with communication to corporate headquarters either by fax, mail or delivery service, telecommunications link, or some other means, depending on the organization's management style, size of unit, and so on.

Assessing the appropriateness of a particular hardware–data configuration for an organization is very challenging. In all but the most decentralized of organizations, there is a strong need for central control over standards and operating procedures. The changes in technology, however, both permit and make desirable in many settings the distribution of significant amounts of the hardware operations and data handling. What in a previous technology was an either/or situation, today is a wide portfolio of difficult options, as we move to ever more networked organizations.

SUMMARY

The trend to merge technologies and the ability to distribute data and hardware must be carefully managed in combination, because they are interdependent. Since firms vary in their use of IT, history, culture, and business strategy, they may appropriately develop radically different structures. When new needs arise for central integrated files in industries in which IT is *strategic* (such as banking and insurance), there is a strong tendency to accelerate the merging of all services into single-site support systems, often at the cost of great organization disruption. (Industries in which IT is *supportive* can move more slowly.)

On the other hand, even some banks have maintained distributed stand-alone systems providing similar support. Key reasons for these structures lie in the bank's internal culture, geography, and other factors relating to its business practices.

Periodic reexamination of the organization's deployment of hardware and software resources for the IT function should have high priority. Changing technology economics, merging of formerly disparate technologies whose managerial traditions differ, and the problems of managing technology innovation have made obsolete many organizational structures that were appropriate as late as the mid-1980s. To ensure that these issues are being properly addressed, six steps must be taken:

1. Establish, as part of the objectives of a permanent corporate policy group, the development of a program to periodically review IT architecture. Foremost, this involves balancing the desires for a strong hub against the advantage of a strongly distributed approach and ensuring that different technologies are being guided appropriately. A structure that is appropriate for the technology and competitive environment of 1993 may not be appropriate in 1997.

2. Ensure that uniformity in management practice is not pushed too far and that appropriate diversity is accommodated. It may be appropriate for the different parts of the organization to evolve different patterns of support for hardware and data. (Just because four units are supported out of a central hardware facility does not automatically imply that it is appropriate for the fifth). Differing phases of development of specific technologies and geographical distance from potential central service support, for example, are valid reasons for different approaches.

3. Show particular sensitivity to the needs of international activities. What works in the United States may not work at all in Thailand. Neither companies that operate primarily in a single country nor transnationals that operate in many countries can assume that enforcing the same approaches in all countries is appropriate. Each country has different cost and quality structures of telecommunications, different levels of IT achievement, different reservoirs of technical skills, different cultures, and so on. These differences are likely to endure for some time. A common hardware/data architecture standard will have to be flexible.

4. Address these issues in a broad strategic fashion. The arguments and reasoning leading to a set of solutions are more complex than simply the current economics of hardware or deciding which persons should have access to particular data files. Corporate organization structure, corporate strategy and direction, availability of human resources, and current operating administrative processes are other critical inputs. In both practice and writing, the technicians and information theorists have tended to oversimplify a very complex set of problems and options.

5. Ensure adequate innovation-phase investment; that is, investments in experimental studies, pilot studies of new technologies, and development of prototypes. Attention must be paid to ensure that proven expertise is being distributed appropriately within the firm, even to places where the technology's availability or potential may not be obvious. Establishing an ET group is a highly effective approach, particularly for firms that have high strategic dependence on information technology. Firms that have strong commitments to R&D in non-IT areas have found it easier to deal with these issues than firms that lack a strong research tradition.

6. Ensure an appropriate balance between long-term and short-term needs. A distributed structure optimally designed for the current technology and economics may fit rather poorly five years from now. It may make sense to postpone feature development or to design an approach that is clumsy in today's technology but which will be quite efficient in the anticipated technologies five years in the future.

Chapter 8

IT Organizational Issues

In the preceding chapter we noted that the management structures needed for guiding new technologies into the organization are quite different from those for the older, established technologies. The corporation must encourage *innovation* by information technology (IT) staff and users with the newer technologies while focusing on *control* and *efficiency* in the more mature technologies. In this chapter we will discuss two aspects of IT management that are rapidly changing: first, the range of organizational alternatives that have emerged for effectively assigning responsibility for IT development, and second, the coordination and location of IT policy formulation between users, IT, and general management.

ORGANIZATION ISSUES IN IT DEVELOPMENT

Policies for guiding the deployment of information technology development staff and activity in the future must deal with two sets of tensions. The first, as noted in the previous chapters, is the balance between *innovation* and *control*. The relative emphasis a firm should place on the aggressive innovation phase varies widely from firm to firm, depending on a broad assessment of the potential strategic impact of information technology on the firm, general corporate willingness to take risk, and so on. If IT is perceived to be of great impact in helping the firm reach its strategic objectives, significantly greater investment in innovation is called for than if it is seen to be merely helpful.

The second set is the tension between *IT dominance* and *user dominance* in the retention of development skills and in the active selection of priorities. The user tends toward short-term need fulfillment (at the expense of long-term IT hygiene and orderly development). IT, on the other hand, can become preoccupied with the mastery of technology and an orderly development plan at the risk of slow response to legitimate user needs. Balancing the roles of these two groups is a complex task that must be dealt with in the context of the corporate culture and the potential strategic IT role.

Table 8–1 illustrates some consequences of excessive domination by IT and by users. It shows clearly that very different application portfolios and operating problems emerge in the two settings. This chapter emphasizes the need for experimentation because of the difficulty of anticipating the implications of introducing a new technology. The following four cases illustrate this problem.

Some Examples

Case 1: A Short-Term User-Need Situation, Strategically Important.
The number-one priority in a large machine-tool manufacturer's engineering department was computer-aided design (CAD). Early success

TABLE 8–1   Possible Implications of Excess IT and User Dominance

IT Dominance	*User Dominance*
Too much emphasis on database hygiene.	Too much emphasis on problem focus.
No recent new supplier or new distinct services (too busy with maintenance).	IT says out of control.
All new systems must fit data structure of existing system.	Explosive growth in number of new systems and supporting staff.
All requests for service require system study with benefit identification.	Multiple suppliers delivering services. Frequent change in supplier of specific service.
Standardization dominates; few exceptions.	Lack of standardization and control over data hygiene and system.
IT designs/constructs everything.	Hard evidence of benefits nonexistent.
Benefits of user control over development discussed but never implemented.	Soft evidence of benefits not organized.
Study always shows construction costs less than outside purchase.	Few measurements/objectives for new systems.
Head count of distributed minis and development staff growing surreptitiously.	Technical advice of IT not sought; if received, considered irrelevant.
IT specializing in technical frontiers, not user-oriented markets.	User buying design/construction/maintenance services and even operations from outside.
IT spending 80% on maintenance, 20% on development.	User building networks to own unique needs, not to corporate need.
IT thinks they are in control of all.	Some users are growing rapidly in experience and use, while others feel nothing is relevant because they do not understand.
Users express unhappiness.	No coordinated effort for technology transfer or learning from experience between users.
Portfolio of development opportunities firmly under IT control.	Growth in duplication of technical staffs.
No strong user group exists.	Dramatically rising communications costs because of redundancy.
General management not involved but concerned.	

had led to a major expansion of the effort. Department personnel modified the digital information design output to enable them to control computer-driven machine tools directly. This work was deliberately kept independent of their bill of materials/cost system, which was in a database format and was maintained by the IT unit.

Short of staff to integrate the new system in their database structure, the user department decided to go ahead despite the major system integration problems that would result. The work was done over the objection of IT management, but the engineering department received full support from senior management because of the project's potential major, immediate impact on shortening the product development life cycle.

The engineers enthusiastically worked on the CAD project to make it work, while the IT unit was decidedly lukewarm. The project slashed development time by half for new designs. The IT database integration issue remains, but realistically, the firm is no worse off in this regard than it was before.

Case 2: User Control to Achieve Automation. A substantial investment in office automation was undertaken by a division of a large consumer products manufacturer with modest up-front cost-benefit justification. Managers and administrative support personnel were encouraged by IT to "use" the systems with only cursory direction and some introductory training on the Wang word processor that was made available to them. After four months, three product managers had developed independent networks to support sales force activities; two had automated portions of their word processing, with substantial savings; two others did little but were encouraging their administrative support staff to "try it out." The users were gaining confidence and pursuing new programs with enthusiasm.

The challenge to the IT management now, after only six months, was to develop and evolve an efficient program with these seven "experienced" users. The IT manager estimated it would take roughly two years to achieve this efficient integration. However, both he and divisional management felt, retrospectively, that it would have been impossible to implement office support with a standard IT-dominated systems study and that the expense of the after-the-fact rationalization was an acceptable price for these benefits. The control over this word processing program contrasted sharply with the strong central control IT was exerting over its mature data processing technologies.

Case 3: Step-by-Step Innovation of a New Technology. A large grocery chain acquired a system of point-of-sales terminals. These terminals were initially purchased by the retail division (with the support of the IT manager) to assist store managers in controlling inventory. They were to be used exclusively within individual stores to accumulate daily sales totals of individual items. These totals would permit individual stores to trigger reorders in case lots at given times.

Once installed, however, these isolated systems were evolved quickly into links to central headquarters at the initiative of corporate management. These links were established to feed data from the stores to new corporate computer programs that provided a measurement of advertising effectiveness and the ability to manage warehouse stock levels chainwide.

Implementation of this nonplanned linkage involved significant extra expense, because the communication protocols in the selected terminals were incompatible with those in the computer at headquarters. Nonetheless, the possibilities and benefits of the resulting system would have been difficult to define in advance, because this eventual use was not considered important when the initial point-of-sale terminals were being installed. Further, in management's opinion, even if the organization had considered it, the ultimate costs of the resulting system would have been seen as prohibitive in relation to benefits (in retrospect, *incorrectly* prohibitive). Success of the first system laid the baseline for the next ones. In an uncertain world, there are limitations to planning.

Case 4: User Innovation as a Source of Productivity.   A large bank introduced an electronic mail system and a word processor system to facilitate its preparation of loan paperwork. The two systems soon evolved to link the bank's loan officers (initially not planned to be clients of either system) to a series of analytical programs—an evolution that developed out of conversations between a loan officer and a consultant. They discovered that the word-processor loan system had bundled with it a powerful analytical tool that could be used by the officers to analyze loan performance. Because of the bank's electronic mail system, this analytical tool could be easily accessed by loan officers (at headquarters and in branches).

After three months of use, the bank faced a series of internal tensions as the costs of both the electronic mail system and the word processing system unexpectedly rose due to this added use. This was compounded by the lack of a formal means to review "experiments" or evaluate unanticipated uses of the systems by participants not initially involved. Eventually a senior management review committee supported the new use of the two systems, and it was permitted to continue. Substantial enhancements were added to the word processing software to make it even more useful to the loan officers.

Implications

These examples are typical of emerging new services that support professionals and managers in doing work. They form the underpinning of our conviction that it is impossible to foresee in advance the full range of consequences of introducing information technology systems. Excessive control and focus on quick results in the early stages can deflect important learning that may result in even more useful applications. Neither IT professionals nor users have outstanding records in anticipating the consequences of new technologies' impacts on organizations. Consequently, a necessary general management role is to help facilitate this assimilation.

This chapter is divided into three sections. The first discusses the pressures on users to gain control, not only over a system's development activities, but when possible, to have the resulting product run on a stand-alone mini or micro system located in their department. The second section identifies the advantages of strong IT development coordination and the potential pitfalls of uncontrolled proliferation of user-developed systems. The third section identifies the core policies that must be implemented by IT management, user management, and general management, respectively, in order to ensure a good result. In our judgment, the general manager's role is particularly critical in creating an environment that facilitates technological change and organizational adaptation.

PRESSURES TOWARD USER DOMINANCE

A number of intense pressures encourage users to exercise stronger control over their systems development resources and acquisition of independent IT resources. These pressures can be clustered into five categories: pent-up user demand, the needs for staffing flexibility, competitive and service growth in the IT market, user desire to control their destiny, and fit with the organization.

Pent-Up User Demand

The backlog of development work facing an IT systems development department is frequently very large in relation to its staff resources; three- to five-year backlogs tend to be the norm. The reasons for these staffing "crunches" are many, and the problems are not easily solved. One reason is that existing systems require sustained maintenance in order to deal with changing regulatory and other business requirements. As more systems have been automated, the maintenance needs have continued to rise, forcing either increases in development staff or the postponement of new work. This problem has been intensified by the shift in systems design philosophy in the early 1970s from one that incorporates data into programs to one that clearly separates database management from processing procedures.

Effecting this one-time conversion has been very expensive in terms of staff resources.

Further, the most challenging, high-status, high-paying jobs tend to be with computer vendors and software houses, which puts great pressure on an organization's IT department. Its most talented staff is tempted to move on to more challenging, perhaps more financially remunerative jobs. Frequently it is easier for the IT systems development unit to get the budget allocations than to find the staff resources to use them. The delays caused by these factors have led to enormous user frustration and a strong desire to take matters into their own hands.

Staff Flexibility and Growth. The central IT department appears to be unresponsive to users' demands, and user-developed systems and stand-alone minis or micros become attractive to users as a nonconfrontational way of getting work done. Using either their own staffs or outside software houses, users see that they are significantly speeding up the process of obtaining "needed" service.

Staff Professional Growth. An IT staff decentralized by both their physical and organizational presence in the end-user department helps educate users to the legitimate potential of IT. It also reduces communications problems between IT professionals and end users. Particularly important, it makes it easier to plan employee promotions that rotate IT staff to other (non-IT) jobs within the department, thus enhancing user–IT coordination. This also facilitates the movement of end users to IT positions.

Finally, from the viewpoint of a local department, the protocols of interfacing with the corporate network and of meeting corporate control standards can be very time-consuming and complex. A stand-alone system purchased by a user that is independent of this corporate network may simplify the job of the end user and permit less-skilled staff resources to be utilized. It may require no major changes, particularly if it is a system familiar to one or more employees due to prior experience.

Competitive and Service Growth in the IT Market

Thousands of stand-alone computer systems are available for specific applications. They range from simple accounts-payable systems to complete office automation products. Their existence makes them beguilingly easy solutions to short-term problems. Marketed by hardware and software vendors to end-user managers, the systems' functional features are emphasized, and any technical and software problems are soft-pedaled. For example, most standard word processing systems are marketed without mention of their computer foundation.

A stand-alone local hardware platform may seem particularly attractive to the user, because its on-line response times are faster and more consistent than those of devices that depend on a central unit. The stand-alone unit also provides easy access to on-line systems when needed. With it, the user avoids the problems associated with sharing a many-user system, which can result in a highly variable volume of transactions and lead to variation in response times. Also, the system is seen as operationally simple, needing only an operator to run it when developed. Air conditioning, physical maintenance, and power availability, all of them issues in big IT shops, are less critical in these settings.

Frequently the local solution "appears" to be more cost-effective than work done or purchased by a central IT development group. Not only is there no cumbersome project proposal to be written and defended in front of IT technicians who have their own special agendas, but often a simple up-front price is quoted. Developed under user control, the project is perceived to be both simple and relatively free of red tape.

User Control

The idea of regaining control over a part of their operations, particularly if information technology is a critical part of their units' operations, is very important to users. In many cases this reverses a trend that began 20 years ago in a very different technology. Control in this context has at least three dimensions.

Development.   Users can exercise direct control over systems development priorities. By using either their own staffs or self-selected software houses, which may offer highly specialized skills not present in the firm, users often hope they can get a system functioning in less time than it would take to navigate the priority-setting process in the corporate IT department—and to get staff assigned to the project. A user systems staff is also seen as closer and more responsive to user needs. Development mistakes made by a local group are more easily accepted than those made by a remote group and they are rarely discussed; successes are often topics of conversation.

Maintenance.   Users gain control over systems maintenance priorities. This is because the work will be done either by themselves or by software houses that are dependent upon them for income. The importance of this point is often overlooked initially by the user. Quite often the assumption is that maintenance will be no problem or that it can be performed by a clerk following a manual. A rare occurrence! Needs and desires relentlessly change.

Operations.   Users gain control over day-to-day operations. Insulated from the vicissitudes of corporate computer scheduling, users believe they will be able to exert firmer control over the pace of their departments' operations. This is particularly important to small, marginal users of heavily utilized data centers with volatile loads. Today these points are intensified in many users' minds because of previous experiences with service degradation at month-end in large computer systems or with important jobs (to them) not being run because of corporate priorities. Further, as a result of their hands-on experience with home computers, managers are much more confident in their ability to manage a computer operation successfully. Additionally, computer vendors' clever marketing has helped to increase their confidence. In general, however, this experience is of insufficient depth, and the user has more confidence than is warranted.

Fit with the Organization

As the company becomes more decentralized in structure and more geographically diverse, a distributed development function becomes a much better fit and avoids heavy marketing and coordination expenses. Among conglomerates, for example, only a few have tried to centralize development; most leave it with the original units. Heavily decentralized companies such as Capital Holding have closed down their central IT coordinating unit and placed all IT staff in key divisions. Another advantage of distributed development is that if the decision is made to divest the corporation of a unit, the divestiture will be easier to implement if its IT activities are not integrated with the rest of the company.

User Learning

As suggested in the previous chapter, predicting the full ramifications of introducing a new technology is very difficult. On one hand, enthusiastic experimentation by the user can stimulate creativity and produce new approaches to troublesome problems. Systems developed by a central IT unit, on the other hand, must overcome greater user resistance in adoption. This IT challenge simply reflects research in the fields of organization development and control, which has identified organization learning as a principal benefit of organizing in multiple profit centers, rather than by function. As noted earlier, this is increasingly evident in office support and new professional support such as CAD.

Summary

In aggregate, these five pressures represent a powerful argument for a strong user role in systems development and suggest when that role might be the dominant one. The pressures driving users toward purchase, development, *and/or* use of stand-alone, mini-based, and local systems and software can be summarized as *short-term user control*. Stand-alone personal computers and local development have been found to offer users more immediate solutions to the problems under their control and to do so in a climate they perceive as enjoyable. While particular benefits associated with Phase-1 and -2 learning can be achieved by this approach, they may be gained with little regard for information hygiene and less regard for control, as discussed next.

PRESSURES TOWARD IT CONTROL

Countering the arguments of the previous section, pressures exist in many settings to consolidate a firm's IT development resource into a single unit or to at least keep it in two or more large clusters.

Staff Professionalism

As pointed out earlier, a large central IT development staff enhances the organization's ability to recruit and retain (attract and keep challenged) specialized technical personnel. Such a central unit also provides useful support for a small division or unit that does not have its own IT staff and needs occasional access to information technology skills.

Additionally, as the average age of many IT development staffs continues to rise, more and more of the employees are becoming comfortable and set in their ways ("the graying of IT"). The central unit is a useful fulcrum to insert a limited number of high-energy new talent to aid in re-energizing and redirecting older staff. The importance of this is intensified by the fact that salary levels, individual interests, and perceived interpersonal relationships of existing staff often make lateral movement out of the central IT system department undesirable. Many of these people must either be retrained or they will have to be let go. The inability of some firms to manage this is a key reason for the current popularity of outsourcing development to external vendors. It is easier to modernize a centralized unit than one in which the development staff is scattered throughout the firm.

Developing and enforcing better standards of IT management practice is also easier in a large group. Documentation procedures, project management skills, and disciplined maintenance approaches are examples of critical infrastructure items in IT systems development departments. In 1981 a large financial service organization faced with a deteriorating relationship between its central development department and key users was forced to split the development department into a number of smaller units distributed around the company, thereby changing both reporting responsibility and office location. Although the change was initially successful in stimulating new ideas and better relationships with users (many development people came to identify better with users than with technical development issues), by 1987 the quality of IT staff professionalism had dropped so low through neglect that several major project fiascoes occurred that required assistance from an outside service organization. Significant parts of the development function had to be recentralized, and much tighter controls had to be installed over management practices in the remaining distributed development groups. This periodic swing of the centralize/decentralize pendulum has occurred in numerous settings as the benefits of a change over time give way to problems that require redirection.

Central staff expertise is particularly important for supporting user-designed and user-selected computer-based systems. Lacking practical systems design experience and purchased software standards, the user often ignores normal data control procedures, documentation standards, and conventional costing practices. Consequently, purchasing from several suppliers or incrementally from one often results in a clumsy system design that is hard to maintain.

For example, a large financial organization discovered that all of the people who were involved in the design and purchase of software for three of the stand-alone computer systems used to process data on a daily basis had left the company. Further, no formal documentation or operating instructions had been prepared, and all source programs had been lost. All that remained were disk files with object programs on them. The system ran, but why it ran no one knew; and even if the company's survival depended on it, changes would at best have been very difficult and time-consuming to execute.

A recent study of a firm that had invested heavily ($8 million) in personal computers in the past five years showed it had also invested $15 million in systems development for those machines. Locally developed and largely unmanaged, more development money was being spent on the distributed systems than in the central development unit, which had extensive documentation and other controls. The situation was rectified before serious damage occurred.

Feasibility Study Concerns

A user-driven feasibility study may contain major technical mistakes that result in the computer system's being inadequate to handle growing processing requirements or in its having large amounts of excess capacity. Repeatedly, because of inexperienced staff, the feasibility study may underestimate both the complexity of the software needed and the growth in the number of transactions to be handled by the system. (The risk increases if competent technical staff inputs to the feasibility study were limited and if the real business needs were not well understood.)

Additionally, users often focus a feasibility study on a specific service without recognizing that successful first applications tend to generate unanticipated second applications, then third applications, and so forth. Each application appears to require only a modest incremental purchase price and, therefore, does not receive a comprehensive full-cost review. The result may be that in a very short period of time the hardware configuration or software approach selected cannot handle the necessary work. Unless great care was taken in the initial hardware selection and system design process to allow for growth, expansion can result in major business disruptions and very expensive software modifications.

User-driven feasibility studies are more susceptible to recommendations to acquire products from unstable vendors because of some unusually attractive product features. Stability of vendors is an important consideration in this rapidly growing industry sector; significant numbers of software vendors have failed, and a number of hardware manufacturers are in trouble as well. The same trends that hit the pocket calculator and digital watch industries in the late 1970s began to hit this industry sector as it reached a point of maturity in recent years. Stability of the vendors is critical, because many of these systems insinuate themselves into the heart of a department's operations. With software-intensive investments, failure of a hardware vendor can mean both expensive disruption in service provided by the department and intensive, crisis spending efforts to convert the software to another machine unless appropriate standards have been selected. These concerns apply equally to hardware suppliers and to the packages and services provided by software suppliers. A single experience with a product from a failed software vendor provides painful learning.

Some care must be taken on local development, since user groups tend to buy or develop systems tailored to very specific situations, which may lead to long-term maintenance problems. In many environments characterized by local development, there is also poor technology transfer between similar users and thus consequent lack of corporate leverage, an issue of low importance to the local unit.

A large forest products company, organized geographically, combined a system-minded regional manager with an aggressive growth-oriented IT manager who was promoted to responsibility for all administrative support in the region. Within three years their budget for IT was double that of a comparable region. Although their applications were extraordinarily effective, only one was exported to another region. Subsequent review of this unit's work indicated that nearly half of the systems they developed were focused on problems of potentially general interest and consequently could have been exported to other parts of the company.

Corporate Database System

Development of corporate database strategy involves both the collection of data files at a central location for reference by multiple users and the development of networks and procedures that will allow users to access data files easily regardless of their physical location in the firm. A central staff provides a focal point for both conceptualizing and developing the architecture of these systems to serve multiple users across the firm. The need for this corporate database varies widely with the nature of the corporation's activities. A conglomerate usually has much less need for this data across the firm than does a functionally organized, one-product company. Even here, however, electronic mail, videoconferencing, and shared financial performance information have become legitimate needs. If such needs exist, a central department is better able to develop and distribute such systems to users or to coordinate a development process in which key parts of the systems development are farmed out to local development units.

Inevitably the first concern raised when discussing distributed development and hardware in the several business units is that the company will lose the ability to manage and control its data flows—that data of significance to many people beyond those in the originating unit will be locked up in a nonstandardized format in inaccessible locations. Without denying the validity of this concern (there is substantial truth in it in many settings), several mitigating factors demand that such objections be carefully examined in any specific situation.

Timing.   One factor is the issue of timing. In many cases the argument raised against a stand-alone system is the erosion of data as a corporate resource. Allegedly, in order to preserve flexibility for future database design, this stand-alone computer should not be acquired. However, it frequently turns out that this flexibility is not needed as adaptive communication systems can provide control as well as access to distant users. In this context a well-designed stand-alone system may be an equally good (if not better) starting point for these long-term systems as jumping directly from the present set of manual procedures would be. This possibility must be pragmatically assessed.

Abstraction of Data. Another mitigating factor, often overlooked, is the capability for abstracting data, if necessary, from a locally managed system at planned frequent intervals and sending it directly to a central computer. Ordinarily not all information in a stand-alone file is relevant to or needed by other users. Indeed, often only a small percentage is.

On the other hand, locally designed data-handling systems can prove expensive to maintain and to link with each other. The firm must identify in operational terms the data requirements of the central files and provide guidelines for what data can be stored locally and how accessible it should be to others. This problem is exemplified by the branch-office office support systems that generate voluminous records in electronic format. Unless well-designed, these files can be bulky, lock up key data from potential users, and pose potential security problems. For example, a mail-order house recently discovered that each customer representative was using more than 200 disks per day and storing them in boxes by date of order receipt, making aggregate customer information impossible to obtain in a timely manner. A new procedure reduced the number of disks to five.

Organizing and accessing electronic files may require central storage to ensure appropriate security. Managing effective security—a topic of intense interest in a world of "hackers"—is usually easier when all files are in a single location rather than dispersed. Realistically, however, some data is so sensitive that it is best kept off the network, the only way to ensure real security.

Fit with the Corporate Structure and Strategy

Centralized IT development's role is clearest in organizations where there is centrally directed planning and operational control. A large farm-equipment manufacturer with a tradition of central functional control from corporate headquarters successfully implemented a program by which all software for factories and distribution units worldwide was developed by the corporate systems group. As the company grows in size, however, the company's structure is becoming more decentralized. Consequently, the cost of effective central systems development is escalating, and the firm is having to implement a marketing function to educate users on the virtues of central services *and* to decentralize some development functions. It is becoming increasingly common for centralized development groups to have an explicitly defined and staffed internal marketing activity.

Cost Analysis

Because of its practical experience in other systems efforts, a centralized IT development group has the ability to produce a realistic software development estimate (subject to the problems discussed in Chapter 10) that takes into account the interests of the company as a whole. Software development estimates are problematic in user feasibility studies for two key reasons. The first is that most new systems are more software intensive than hardware intensive. Typically software costs are 75 percent to 85 percent of the total cost for a customized system. Few users have had experience in estimating software development costs, and an order-of-magnitude mistake in a feasibility study—particularly if it is an individually developed system and not a "turn-key" (i.e., general purpose) package—is not unknown.

Users also lack understanding of the true costs of an existing service. A major contributor to this is complicated corporate IT charge-out systems, many of which present calculations in terms of utilization of computer resource units that are completely unfathomable to the user. The result is that each month or quarter an unintelligible bill arrives, the amount of which is unpredictable. (In management control environments where the user is held closely responsible for variance from budget, this legitimately causes intense frustration.) A locally developed system, particularly if it is for a stand-alone personal computer, is seen as producing both understandable and predictable costs for the user. Further, since many corporate charge-out systems are designed on a full-cost basis, their charges to the end user seem high and thus offer great inducements to purchase locally. Since much of corporate IT is fixed cost in the short run, many of these savings are false.

Because there are significant fixed-cost elements to a corporate information systems center, particularly in the short run, what appears to the individual user to be an opportunity to reduce costs may be a cost increase for the company—more hardware/software acquired locally and no possible savings at the corporate IT facility. Policies for ensuring that appropriate cost analyses are prepared must be established.

Summary

The pressures toward centralized IT control can be summarized as *long-term information hygiene.* Inexorably over the long run, most (but not all) stand-alone units will become part of a network and need to both receive and share data with other users and systems. In many respects these pressures are not immediately evident when the system is installed but tend to grow in importance with the passage of time.

Policies for managing the trade-offs between the obvious short-term benefits and long-term risks are delicate to administer but necessary.

COORDINATION AND LOCATION OF IT POLICY

Effective management of the tension between IT and users can be managed by establishing clear policies that specify the user domain, the IT domain, and senior management's role. Senior management must play a significant role in ensuring that these policies are developed and that they evolve appropriately over time. Both IT and users must understand the implications of these roles and the possible conflicts.

IT Responsibilities

The following tasks constitute the central core of IT responsibilities—the minimum for managing the long-term information hygiene needs of an organization:

1. Develop procedures to ensure that, for potential IT projects of any size, a comparison is made of internal development versus purchase. If projects are implemented outside the firm or by the user, establish the appropriate professional standards for project control and documentation. These standards must be flexible, since user-developed systems for personal computers pose demands quite different from systems to be run on large mainframe computers. Further, define a process for forcing adherence to the selected standards.
2. Maintain an inventory of installed or planned-to-be-installed information services.
3. Develop and maintain a set of standards that establishes:

   a. Mandatory telecommunication standards.
   b. Standard languages for classes of acquired equipment.
   c. Documentation procedures for different types of systems.
   d. Corporate data dictionary with clear definitions as to which elements must be included. Identification of file maintenance standards and procedures.
   e. Examination procedures for systems developed in local units to ensure that they do not conflict with corporate needs and that any necessary interfaces are constructed.

4. Identify and provide appropriate IT development staff career paths throughout the organization. These include lateral transfers within

and between IT units, upward movement within IT, and appropriate outward movement from IT to other functional units. (Although this is more difficult in distributed units, it is still possible.)

5. Establish appropriate internal marketing efforts for IT support. These should exert catch-up pressure and coaching for units that are lagging and slow down units that are pushing too fast into leading edge technologies that they do not understand.

6. Prepare a detailed checklist of questions to be answered in any hardware/software acquisition to ensure that relevant technical and managerial issues are raised. These questions should ask:

   a. Does the proposed system meet corporate communication standards?
   b. For office support systems, has upward growth potential been addressed, and are adequate communication capabilities in place so that local files can be reached from other locations if appropriate?
   c. Are languages being used that are appropriate and that can be maintained over the long term?

7. Identify and maintain relationships with preferred systems suppliers. Before a relationship is established with a vendor, the conditions for entertaining exceptions to the established standards must be agreed upon. For example, size, number of systems in place, and financial structure requirements should be clearly spelled out.

8. Establish education programs for potential users that communicate both the potential and the pitfalls of a new technology and that define the users' roles in ensuring its successful introduction in their departments.

9. Establish an ongoing review of systems for determining which ones have become obsolete and should be redesigned.

These questions apply with particular force to the design of systems that embed themselves in the company's daily operations. Decision support systems do not pose quite the same problems, although the need to obtain data from the rest of the organization is rapidly putting them in the same situation.

These core responsibilities, of course, can be significantly expanded to impose much tighter and more formal controls if the situation warrants it.

User Responsibilities

To assist in the orderly implementation of new IT services and grow in an understanding of their use, cost, and impact on the organization, the following responsibilities should be fulfilled by the user of IT service:

1. Clearly understand the scope of all IT activities supporting the user. Increasingly in the more experienced organizations a user-understandable IT charge-out system has been installed to facilitate this.
2. Realistically appraise the amount of user personnel investment that will be required for each new project, both to develop and to operate the system, in order to ensure a satisfactory service. These costs are often much higher than planned and are frequently ignored.
3. Ensure that comprehensive user input takes place for all IT projects that will support vital aspects of the unit's operations. This might include, for example, nature of service, process of introduction, and level of user training for both staff and managers.
4. Realistically ensure that the IT–user interface is consistent with IT's strategic relevance to the business unit. If it is very important, the interface must be very close. If it is less important, more distance between the parties and more friction can be tolerated.
5. Periodically audit the adequacy of system reliability standards, performance of communications services, and adequacy of security procedures.
6. Participate in the development and maintenance of an IT plan that sets new technology priorities, schedules the transfer of IT among groups, and evaluates a portfolio of projects in light of the company strategy.

These represent the very minimum policies that the users should develop and manage. Depending on the firm's geography, corporate management style, stage of IT development, and mix of technology development phases, expanded levels of user involvement may be appropriate, including full-time assignment of their own staff. As these facets evolve over time, the appropriateness of certain policies will also evolve.

General Management Support and Policy Overview

Distinct from the issues involved in the distribution of IT services is a cluster of broad policy and direction activities that require *senior management perspective*. In the past these activities were built into the structure of a central IT organization. Now, because of the need to link IT to business, IT operations are frequently separated from IT planning. A chemical company reorganized in 1990 to establish a 500-person systems and operations department reporting directly to the head of administrative services, which works on corporate applications. (An additional 400 analysts and programmers are employed in the major divisional staffs.) This department does the implementation and operational IT work of the company on a month-to-month, year-to-year basis. At the same time, a 25- to 30-person IT policy group reports directly to the head of research. This policy group works on overall IT policy and long-range IT strategy formulation for the firm. In a similar vein, a major conglomerate whose development staff and hardware are distributed to key users has a three- to four-person group at headquarters level.

Key responsibilities of a corporate IT policy group should include these:

1. Ensure that an appropriate balance exists between IT and user inputs across the different technologies and that one side is not dominating the other inappropriately. Initiate appropriate personnel and organizational transfers if the situation is out of balance. Establishment of an executive steering committee, for example, is a common response to inadequate user input.
2. Ensure that a comprehensive corporate IT strategy is developed. Particularly in organizations where the resources are widely distributed it is critical that there be a comprehensive overview of technology trends, current corporate use of information technology, and linkage between IT initiatives and overall corporate goals. The resources to be devoted to this effort appropriately varies widely from organization to organization as IT's perceived contribution to corporate strategy, among other things, changes. (This is discussed in more depth in Chapter 13.)
3. Manage the inventory of hardware and software resources and assure that the corporate view extends to the purchasing relationships and contracts. In most settings the corporate group is the appropriate place to identify and manage standard policies for relationships with vendors.
4. Facilitate the development and evolution of appropriate standards for development and operations activities, and ensure that the standards are applied appropriately. In this regard, the corporate policy group plays the combined role of consultant on the one hand and auditor (particularly if there is a weak or nonexistent IT auditing function) on the other hand. This role requires staff that is both technically competent and interpersonally sensitive.
5. Facilitate the transfer of technology from one unit to another. This occurs through recognizing the unit's common systems needs as well as the stimulation of joint projects. Actual transfer requires regular visits to the different operating units, organization of periodic corporate MIS conferences, development of a corporate information systems newsletter, and other means.
6. Actively encourage technical experimentation. A limited program of research is a very appropriate part of the IT function; an important role of the corporate policy group is to ensure that it does not get swept away in the press of urgent operational issues. Further,

the corporate policy group is in a position to encourage patterns of experimentation that smaller units might feel pose undue risk if they are the sole beneficiary.

7. Assume responsibility for developing an appropriate planning and control system to link IT firmly to the company's goals. Planning, system appraisal, charge out, and project management processes should be monitored and (if necessary) encouraged to develop by the policy group. In this context, the group should work closely with the corporate steering committee.

As these responsibilities imply, the corporate IT policy group needs to be staffed with individuals who, in aggregate, have broad technical backgrounds and extensive practical IT administrative experience. Except in very limited numbers, it is not an appropriate department for entry-level staff members.

SUMMARY

Chapters 7 and 8 have focused on the key issues surrounding the organization of information technology for the next decade. A significant revolution has occurred in what is regarded as good managerial practice in this field. Important contributors to this change have been the development of new hardware and software technologies and managerial experience with IT. These technologies not only permit quite different types of services to be delivered, but also offer the potential for quite different ways of delivering these services. Consequently, what constitutes best practice has changed considerably, and the evolution seems likely to continue; many IT organization structures that were effectively put together in the 1970s are being found inappropriate for the 1990s.

The subject of determining the appropriate pattern of distribution of IT resources within the organization is complex and multifaceted. The general manager should develop a program that will encourage appropriate innovation on the one hand while maintaining overall control on the other. The final resolution of these organization and planning issues is inextricably tied to non-IT-oriented aspects of the corporate environment. The leadership style of the person at the top of the organization and that person's view of the future provide one important thrust for redirection. A vision of tight central control presents a different context for these decisions than a vision that emphasizes the autonomy of operating units. Closely associated and linked to this is the corporate organizational structure and culture and the trends occurring within it. Also, the realities of geographical spread of the business units heavily impact on IT organizational and planning possibilities; for example, the corporate headquarters of a large insurance company poses different constraints than the multiple international plants and markets of an automobile manufacturer.

On a less global scale are the present realities of quality and location of existing IT resources (organizationally and physically), which provide the base from which change must be made. Equally important is how responsive and competent current users perceive these resources to be. The unit that is seen (no matter how unfairly or inaccurately) as unresponsive has different organizational challenges than the well-regarded unit. Similarly, the existing and the perceived-appropriate strategic roles of IT on the dimensions of the firm's applications portfolio and operations have important organizational implications. If the firm is in the "support" quadrant, for example, the IT policy unit must realistically be placed lower in the organization structure in order to deal with its perceived lack of burning relevance to corporate strategy.

In dealing with these forces, one is seeking an appropriate balance between innovation and control and between the inputs of the IT specialist and the user. Not only do appropriate answers to these questions vary among companies; different answers and structures are often appropriate for individual units within an organization. In short, there is a series of right questions to ask and there is an identifiable but very complex series of forces that, appropriately analyzed, determine for each organizational unit the direction in which the correct answer lies—for now.

Chapter 9

IT Management Control

The IT management control system is a critical network and set of activities that integrates IT activities with the rest of the firm's operations and ensures that IT is being managed in a cost-efficient, reliable fashion. Whereas the project management system *guides* the life cycle of individual projects (many of which last more than a year) and the firm's planning process takes a multiyear view in assimilating technologies and systems to match the company's evolving needs and strategies, the IT *management control system* focuses primarily on guiding the entirety of the information technology department on a year-to-year basis. The management control system builds on the output of the planning process to develop a portfolio of projects, hardware/software enhancements and additions, facilities plans, and staffing levels for the year. It then monitors their progress, raising red flags for action when appropriate. The broad objectives of an effective IT management control system include these:

1. Facilitate appropriate communication between the user and provider of IT services and provide motivational incentives for them to work together on a day-to-day, month-to-month basis. The management control system must encourage users and IT to act in the best interests of the organization as a whole. It must motivate users to use IT resources appropriately and help them to balance investments in this area against those in other areas.

2. Encourage the effective utilization of the IT department's resources and ensure that users are educated in the potential of existing and evolving technologies. In so doing, it must guide the transfer of technology consistent with strategic needs.

3. Provide the means for efficient management of IT resources and give necessary information for investment decisions. This requires developing the standards for measuring performance and the

means for evaluating performance against the standards to ensure that productivity is being achieved. This should help to facilitate "make" or "buy" decisions and it should ensure that existing services are delivered in a reliable, timely, error-free fashion.

Early IT management control systems tended to be very cost focused, relying heavily, for example, upon return-on-investment (ROI) evaluations of capital investments. These systems proved workable in situations where the technology was installed on a cost-displacement justification basis. However, in firms where the computer was a competitive wedge (such as CAD/CAM or industrial robotics today) or where the technology was pervasively influencing the industry's structure of operations (such as in banking and financial services), cost analysis and displacement alone did not provide appropriate measurements of performance. Development of additional management control techniques has been necessary. For example, several years ago a large metropolitan bank instituted an expensive, complex charge-out system for improving user awareness of costs. Poorly thought out in broad context, the system generated a surge in demand for "cheap" minicomputers and inadequate investment in integrating network services, triggered an overall decline in quality of central IT support in comparison with leading-edge banks, and ultimately created market image and sales difficulties for the bank as a whole. Ultimately the system had to be completely restructured to correct these problems.

Four special inputs now appear to be critical to an appropriate IT management control system structure for an organization:

1. The control system must be adapted to very different software and operations technology in the 1990s than was present in the 1970s. An important part of this adaptation is the development of appropriate sensitivity to the mix of phases of information technologies in the company. The more mature technologies must be managed and controlled in a tighter, more efficient way than those in early phases, which need protective treatment appropriate to a research development activity.
2. Specific factors of the corporate environment determine the appropriate IT management control system. Key issues here are the IT sophistication of users, geographic dispersion of the organization, stability of the management team, the firm's overall size and structure, nature of the relationship between line and staff departments, and so on. These factors influence what is workable.
3. The architecture of the organization's overall management control system and the philosophy underlying it influence IT control systems.
4. The system is affected by the perceived strategic significance of IT, in both the thrust of its applications portfolio and the ever more important dependence on existing automated systems in many settings.

IT EVOLUTION AND MANAGEMENT CONTROL

Software Issues

The management control problem posed by software development has become more complex. An increasing percentage of central data processing software support is for maintenance, while most office support (OS) software is bought. Thus the operational changes necessary for keeping the business running have become intermixed with a stream of small, long-term, service-improving capital investments. Since these two streams are not easily separated in many organizations, controls designed to influence operating expense maintenance are often inappropriately applied to stimulate or choke off systems enhancements that are really capital investments.

A second software issue arises with outside software sourcing. As the percentage of development money devoted to outside software acquisition grows, management control systems designed for an environment where all sourcing was internal are often inappropriate for environments dominated by software make/buy alternatives.

Operations Issues

For IT operations, management control is complex because of the difficulty in measuring and allocating costs in a way that will encourage appropriate behavior. In the short term overall operations costs are relatively fixed and there is considerable volatility in the mix of applications running on a day-to-day basis. The operations cost control problem is further complicated by the cost behavior of IT over time. Technical change has created a world where a replacement computer generally has 4 to 10 times the capacity and costs less. This has created an interesting control issue: Should the cost per unit of IT processing be lower in the early years (to reflect the lower load factor) so that it can be held flat over the life of the unit while permitting full (but not excessive) recovery of costs? Conversely, as utilization grows over the years, should the user's cost per unit of IT processing decline?

An example of coping with this problem is provided by a large insurance company that replaced an IBM 3084 several years ago with an Amdahl V7A, gaining four times the computing capacity at 15 percent less cost. After conversion, the machine was loaded to barely 30 percent capacity. The managers were faced with the choice of either spreading the present costs among their current users or forecasting future costs (assuming future volume activity) and setting a three-year average that would recover costs at the period's end. The first approach would have covered expenses from the start but, through its higher prices, would inhibit the initiation of useful work that was economically justified in the long term. They therefore chose the three-year-average cost as the price basis in order to encourage use and pass on the immediate productivity improvement to their current users. The unabsorbed costs became part of corporate overhead.

The selection of a particular method of cost allocation varies with the firm's experience with technology. In many organizations the current control system gives complete management of office support (OS) to the user and complete management of communications to IT. As we have noted, however, OS and telecommunications are so interrelated that such a separation of management is highly suspect. A critical contemporary problem is to ensure that IT control systems evolve along with changes in the organization's technical environment. For example, a large industrial organization gave free OS technology to stimulate users while simultaneously charging for its traditional database time-sharing decision-support system. Very quickly users started creating their own databases on the OS equipment, which both limited their OS experimentation and underutilized the time-sharing, thereby undercutting the firm's objectives. Our discussion of control structure, while recognizing these issues, does not attempt to resolve them definitively.

Corporate Culture Forces

Growth in User Influence.   A major stimulant to growth in IT usage has been the emergence of a group of users who are familiar with problem solving using information technology. After 20 years it is clear that effective user applications generate ideas for additional applications. This is desirable and healthy, provided a control system exists to encourage appropriate appraisal of the new use's potential costs and benefits (broadly defined) to the organization. The absence of such controls can result in explosive growth (often unprofitable and poorly managed), requiring additional processing capacity every one or two years, or alternatively, in little growth with frustrated users obtaining necessary services surreptitiously (and more expensively). Both situations erode confidence in the IT department and its management control system. Also, for many of the new generation of user demands, articulating their benefits is more difficult than determining their costs. In repeated situations the control system has given the hard cost of an applications implementation undue weight against the soft, but often very strategic, management benefits.

This presents a paradox in the control of information services: while the area is technologically complex, most factors critical to its effective, efficient use are human factors. This poses very familiar management control challenges. A complicating factor is that since both technology and user sophistication are continually changing, the types of applications are also changing. Many individuals are sufficiently set in their ways (reinforced by a control approach) that they find change difficult to implement and thus resist it. As a by-product, these users' perceptions of the change agent (IT department) are often unnecessarily poor. For example, these users attribute all sorts of spurious effects to the introduction of new computer systems, word processors, and so on.

External and Internal Factors.   Forces of change also exist in external items such as new tax laws and in numerous internal strategic items. Internal changes include the addition of new customers and products, moving to new offices, and modifications in the organization. A well-designed management control system recognizes these changes and handles them appropriately.

Geographic and Organizational Structure.   Other important control aspects relate to the organization's geographic dispersion and size. As the number of business sites grows and staff levels increase, substantial changes may be needed in organizational structure, corporate management control, and IT management control. Informal personnel supervision and control that fit the more limited setting can fall apart in the larger, more dispersed setting. Similarly, the nature of relationships between line and staff departments within the company influences expectations about the evolving IT-user relationship and thus the appropriate IT management control.

The organizational structure of the firm plays an important role in the IT management control architecture. A firm with a strong functional organization that maintains the central services function as an unallocated cost center may find it appropriate to keep IT as an unallocated cost center. On the other hand, a firm that is heavily decentralized into profit or investment centers or that has a tradition of charging out for corporate services is propelled down the path of charging for corporate IT activities—and may go as far as setting it up as a profit or investment center. Over time it becomes increasingly difficult to manage with good results an IT organization whose control architecture is sharply different from that of the rest of the firm.

Corporate Planning and Control Process

In concept, the IT planning and management control system should be similar to that of the corporation. Ideally in both cases there is a multi-year plan linked appropriately to the overall business strategy, which in turn is linked to a budget process that allows the responsible managers to negotiate their operating budgets. As such, IT planning/budgeting should be compatible with the overall business planning/budgeting. If business planning primarily consists of an annual budget with periodic follow-up of performance during the year, however, a very difficult environment exists for IT management control. Implementation of any sizable IT change can easily take two or more years—including as much as a year to formulate, select, and refine the appropriate design approach. Thus an IT organization often must maintain at least a three-year view of its activities to ensure that resources are available to meet these demands. In many cases, this extends the IT planning horizon beyond the organization's planning horizon.

To be useful, IT project plans must systematically and precisely identify alternative steps for providing necessary service. For example, to upgrade reservation service in a large hotel chain, the IT department, in concert with key hotel managers, had to project the type of service the hotels would need four years out. This was necessary in order to select the proper terminals and provide an orderly transition to the new system over a 30-month period. A key bottleneck in this massive, one-time, 600-terminal installation was a corporate planning and control approach that extended only one year into the future.

This combination of short corporate time horizons, long IT time horizons, and technical innovation can generate intense corporate management control conflict. These conflicts, which can only be resolved by repeated judgments over time, involve two major clusters of managerial issues.

1. How congruent/similar should the IT management control architecture and process be with that of other parts of the organization? Where differences exist, how can the dissonance best be managed? Should it be allowed to exist long term?
2. How can the tension between sound control and timely innovation best be balanced?

Control typically depends on measuring costs against budgets—actual achievements versus predictions—and returns against investments. Innovation calls for risk taking, gaining trial experience with emerging technologies, relying on faith, and at times moving forward despite a lack of clear objectives. A portfolio excessively balanced in either direction poses grave risks. (As will be discussed in Chapter 10, different companies will appropriately balance their portfolios quite differently.)

Strategic Impact of IT on the Corporation

An important consideration in determining how closely the IT control system should match the business's planning/control process is the strategic importance of IT systems developments for the next three years. If they are very strategic to the firm's achievement of its goals, then close linkage between corporate planning and control and IT planning and control is important, and any differences between the two will cause great difficulty. Additionally, IT investment decisions and key product development innovations must be subject to periodic top-management review.

The control system for these strategic environments must encourage value-based innovations even if only one out of three will pay off. Often in this situation the key challenge is to encourage the generation, evaluation, and management of suggestions for new services from multiple unplanned sources while maintaining adequate control. Several now-defunct brokerage houses and soon-to-be-merged banks were unable to do this.

If IT is not strategic to the business but is more a "factory" or "support" effort, congruency of links to the rest of the business planning and control activities is not as critical. IT can more appropriately develop an independent planning and control process to deal with its need to manage changing user demand and the evolving technology. A "factory" environment, for example, must emphasize efficiency controls, while a "turnaround" should focus upon effective utilization of new technology.

A useful way of looking at management control was developed by Ken Merchant, and we will use it to frame the issues in this chapter. Merchant suggested that controls can be grouped into three categories: results controls, personnel controls, and action controls. The specific mix of these controls that is appropriate to a setting depends on its context.

- *Results* controls are those that focus on the measurement of concrete results; they include such measurements as amount of profit, percentage of variance from the budget, number of items procured/hour versus the budget, and the like.
- *Personnel* controls focus on hiring practices, types of training and testing in place, evaluation procedures, and so on.
- *Action* controls involve the establishment and monitoring of certain protocols and procedures; examples include segregation of duties, establishment of certain task sequences, control of access to certain areas, and so on.

All of these are important in the IT context and will be discussed. Because of the special managerial problems historically associated with results control issues, however, the rest of this chapter pays particular attention to them.

Looking Ahead: Other Aspects of Control

To achieve appropriate results the specific approach to IT management control is tailored to an organization, based on one or more of the dimensions discussed. Further, as circumstances change it will evolve over time. The remainder of the chapter describes additional key factors that influence selection of control architecture (financial), control process (financial and nonfinancial), and the audit function. Briefly defined here, each aspect of control is discussed in depth later in the chapter.

Control Architecture. *Should the IT function be set up as an unallocated cost center, an allocated cost center, a profit center, or an investment or residual income center? Further, if costs are allocated from the IT function to the users, should the transfer price be market-based, cost-based, cost-plus, split-level, or negotiated?* Each of these alternatives generates quite different behavior and motivation, and each decision is a fundamental decision; once made, it is not lightly changed. Finally, *what nonfinancial measurements should be designed to facilitate effective use of IT?*

Control Process, Financial and Nonfinancial. *What form of action plan is most appropriate?* Typically this is represented by the annual budget and drives both operations and project development. *What forms of periodic reporting instruments and exception* (against budget targets) *reporting tools are appropriate during the year?* These forms change much more frequently than architectural forms.

Audit Function. Issues here include ensuring that an IT audit function exists, that it is focused on appropriate problems, and that it is staffed appropriately.

RESULTS CONTROL ARCHITECTURE

Unallocated Cost Center

Establishment of the IT department as an unallocated cost center is a widely used approach that offers many advantages. Its being essentially free to the users stimulates user requests and creates a climate conducive to user experimentation. This is particularly good for technologies in Phase 1 or 2 of their assimilation into the firm. The lack of red tape makes it easier for the IT department to sell its services. All the controversy and acrimony over the IT charge-out process is avoided, since no charge-out system exists. Further, very low expenditures are required for developing and operating IT accounting procedures.

In aggregate, these factors make this a good alternative for situations in which the IT budget is small. Innovation is facilitated in settings where financial resource allocation is not a high-tension activity. A large bank, operating as an unallocated cost center, introduced electronic mail and word processing over a two-year period. It had been decided at the most senior levels that this infrastructure was critical to its long-term operational viability. The lack of an end-user charge-out system was seen as an important facilitator to its introduction.

On the other hand, significant problems can exist when IT is treated as an unallocated cost center. With no financial pressure, the user can quickly perceive IT as a free resource where each user should be sure to get a piece of the action. This can rapidly generate a series of irresponsible user requests for service that may be difficult to turn down. Further, in a situation where staff or financial resources are short, the absence of a charge-out framework increases the possibility of excessive politicization of IT resource-allocation decisions. The unallocated cost center also insulates the IT department from competitive pressures and external measures of performance, permitting the hiding of operational inefficiencies. Further, this approach fits the management control structure of some firms poorly (that is, firms that have a strong tradition of charging out corporate staff services to users). Finally, an unallocated cost center poses particular problems for organizations where IT charges are perceived to be both large and strategic by blurring important revenue/cost trade-offs. In combination, these pressures explain why many firms that start with an unallocated cost center approach evolve forward to another approach, at least for their more mature technologies and users.

One approach widely followed is to keep IT as an unallocated cost center but to inform users through memos what their development and operations charges would be if a charge-out system were in place. Without raising the frictions (described next) associated with charge-out procedures, this shows users that they are not using a free resource of the corporation and gives them an idea of the magnitude of their charges. The approach is often adopted as a transitional measure when a firm is moving IT from an unallocated cost center to some other organizational form. Unfortunately, however, a memo about a charge does not have the same bite as the actual assignment of the charge.

Allocated Cost Center and Charge-Out

From a corporate perspective, establishing the IT department as an allocated cost center has the immediate virtue of helping to stimulate honesty in user requests. This approach fits rather well the later phases of technology assimilation, where the usefulness of the technology has been widely communicated within the firm. While it may open up heated debate about costs, it avoids controversy about whether an internal IT department should be perceived as a profit-making entity. An allocated approach particularly fits environments that have a strong tradition of corporate services charges.

Allocation Problems. The allocated cost center introduces a series of complexities and frictions, since such a system necessarily has arbitrary elements in it. The following paragraphs suggest some of the practical problems that come from allocating IT department costs to users (whether in a cost center or using some other approach).

The first problem is that the IT charges will be compared to IT charges prepared both by other companies in the same industry and by outside service organizations, raising the possibility of misleading and invidious conclusions. The words *misleading* and *invidious* are related, because the prices prepared by other organizations often have one or more of the following characteristics:

1. The service being priced out is being treated as a by-product rather than as a joint costing problem, and thus the numbers may be *very* misleading.
2. IT is being treated under a management control system different from that of the company making the evaluation (that is, a profit center in one organization and a cost center in the other). Thus the cost comparison is highly misleading, because the charges have been developed under very different bases.
3. An independent IT services firm or an in-house operation selling services to outside customers may deliberately produce an artificially low price as a way of buying short-term market share. Thus their prices may be perceived as fair market when in fact they are nothing of the sort over the long term.

Since the prices produced by other companies are not the result of an efficient market, comparing them to in-house prices may easily produce misleading data for management decisions.

Another issue of concern is innovation. Unless carefully managed, the charge-out system tends to discourage Phase-1 and Phase-2 research projects. These activities must be segregated and managed differently from projects utilizing the more mature technologies. In our view, nothing particularly useful is accomplished by charging 100 percent of all IT costs to the users. Segregating as much as 15 to 25 percent as a separately managed, emerging-technology function and including it in corporate overhead (after careful analysis) is a sound strategy.

On a more technical note, in the majority of companies that are charging out IT costs today, two major concepts underlie the charge-out process:

1. The charge-out system for IT operations costs uses a very complex formula (based on use of computer technology by an application) that spreads the costs in a supposedly equitable fashion to the ultimate users. Featuring terms such as *XCP*, the concept is that users should bear computer costs in relation to their pro rata use of the underlying resource.

2. The charge-out system ensures that all costs of the activity are passed to consumers of the service. Not infrequently this involves reimbursement by users of all IT operations costs incurred by the firm each month and certainly by year-end.

Rigorous application of these concepts has led to a number of unsatisfactory consequences from the user's perspective. Most important, in many cases the charges are absolutely *unintelligible* and *unpredictable* to the end user, as they are clothed in technical jargon and highly affected by whether it has been a heavy or light month in the IT department. There is no way for the user to predict or control them short of disengaging from the IT activity. This is one reason for the explosion of stand-alone minis and personal computers in the early and mid-1980s.

Not infrequently the charges are highly *unstable*. The same application processing the same amount of data, run at the same time of the week will cost very different amounts from week to week depending on what else happens to be running in the IT department during the week. In addition, if all unallocated costs are charged out to the users at the end of the year, they are often hit with an entirely unwelcome and unanticipated surprise, which generates considerable hostility.

The charges tend to be *artificially high* in relation to incremental costs. As mentioned earlier, this can cause considerable IT–user friction and encourage the user to examine alternatives that may optimize short-term cost behavior at the expense of the long-term strategic interests of the firm.

In addition, in both operations and development this approach makes no attempt to hold IT uniquely responsible for variances in IT efficiency. Rather, all efficiency variances are directly assigned to the ultimate users, which creates additional friction and allegations of IT irresponsibility and mismanagement. Finally, administration of a charge-out system of this type frequently turns out to be very expensive.

These factors in combination have generated a number of charge-out systems that do not satisfactorily meet the needs of many organizations. We believe this is a direct result of the technical and accounting foundations of the system. For most situations, technology and accounting are the wrong disciplines to bring to the problem. The task can be better approached as a problem in applied social psychology: What type of behaviors do you want to trigger in the IT organization and the users? What incentives can be provided to them to help assure that as they move to meet their individual goals, they are moving in a more or less congruent fashion with the overall goals of the corporation?

The design of such a system is a very complex task, requiring trade-offs along many dimensions. As the corporation's needs change, the structures of the charge-out system will also need to change. Critical issues to be dealt with include:

1. Should the system be designed to encourage use of IT services (or components thereof), or should it set high barriers for potential investments?
2. Should the system encourage IT to focus on efficiency or on effectiveness? The answer to this question may well evolve over time.
3. Should the system favor the use of IT department resources or outside resources?
4. What steps must be taken to ensure that the system is congruent with the general control architecture of the organization, or if it is not congruent, to ensure that the deviation is acceptable inside the firm?

Desirable Characteristics.   While the answers to these questions will dictate different solutions in different settings, some generalizations that fit most settings and represent the next step in the evolution of a charge-out system are possible. First, for an IT charge-out system to be effective in this environment, it is critical that the users understand it. This means that the system needs to be simple. Again and again, evidence suggests that an IT operations charge-out system that is a gross distortion of the underlying electronics but that the user can understand is vastly preferable to a technically accurate system that no one can comprehend. User understanding that encourages even partial motivation and goal congruence is better than no motivation or goal congruence. In this context, systems that are based on an agreed upon *standard cost* per unit of output are better than those that allocate all costs to whomever happened to use the system. Even better (and a clear trend today) is designing these standards not in IT resource units, but in transactions that users understand (for example, so much per paycheck, so much per order line, so much per inquiry), where the prices of these transactions are established at the beginning of the budget year.

A second desirable characteristic is that the IT operations charge-out system should be *perceived* as fair and reasonable on all sides. In an absolute technical sense it does not have to *be* fair; it is enough that all involved believe that it is a fair and reasonable system. In this vein the IT operations charge-out system should produce replicable results; processing a certain level of transactions at 10 A.M. every Tuesday should cost the same amount week after week. If it does not, an air of skepticism sets in that undermines the system's credibility.

A third desirable characteristic of an IT operations charge-out system is that it should distinguish IT efficiency issues from user utilization of the system. IT operators should be held responsible for its inefficiencies. Charging month-end or year-end cost efficiency variances to the user usually accomplishes no useful purpose. (It only raises the emotional temperature.) After appropriate analysis of the causes for the variances, they normally should be closed directly to corporate overhead.

IT Maintenance and Development Charges.   The issues involved in charging for IT maintenance and systems development are fundamentally different from those of IT operations and must be dealt with separately. In advance of development and maintenance expenditures of any size, a professional contract must be prepared between IT and the users (as though it were a relationship with an outside software company). Elements of a good contract include:

1. The provisions that estimates of job costs are to be prepared by IT and that IT is to be held responsible for all costs in excess of this.
2. Procedures for reestimating and, if necessary, canceling the job if changes in job scope occur.
3. The provision that if a job is bid on a time and materials basis (very frequent in the software industry), a clear understanding must be reached with the user in advance as to what represents such significant change in scope that the contract should be reviewed.

For many systems, such as database systems, the most challenging (sometimes impossible) task is to identify the definable user (or group thereof) with which to write the contract. Further, an answer is needed for this question: If the contract is written with one group of users and others subsequently join, are the new users charged at incremental cost, full cost, or full cost plus (because they have undertaken none of the development risks and are buying into a sure thing)? Neither easy nor general-purpose solutions to these issues are possible.

An Example.   One company approached these issues in an effective way in our judgment. It provided computer services to 14 user groups, many of which had very similar needs, spreading *operations expenses* in these ways:

1. Every time a piece of data was inputted or extracted on a computer screen, a standard charge was levied on the user, irrespective of the type of processing system involved. This charge was understandable to the user.
2. Since all costs from the modems out (terminal, line) could be directly associated with a user in a completely understandable fashion, these charges were passed directly to the end user.
3. All report and other paper costs were charged to the user on a standard cost per ton basis, irrespective of the complexity of the system that generated them.
4. All over- or underrecovered variances were analyzed for indications of IT efficiency and then closed directly to a corporate overhead account, bypassing the users.

With respect to *maintenance and development cost,* the following procedures were used:

1. Items budgeted for less than 40 hours were charged directly to the users at a standard rate per hour.
2. Projects budgeted to take more than 40 hours were estimated by the IT organization. If the estimate was acceptable to the user, work would be done. Any variances in relation to the estimate were debited or credited to the IT organization, with the user being billed only the estimated amount.
3. A job-reestimating process was created to handle potential changes in job specification, with the users having the option of accepting the new costs, using the old specifications, or aborting the job.
4. Research and development projects were budgeted separately by the IT organization. IT was accountable to corporate for the costs of these jobs, and the users were not charged for them.

Over a several-year period these procedures did a remarkable job of defusing the tensions in user–IT relationships, enabling them to work together more easily.

Profit Center

A third frequently discussed and used method of management control is the establishment of the IT department as a profit center. Advocates of this approach note that this puts the inside service on the same footing as an outside one and brings the pressures of the marketplace to bear on it. It consequently encourages the IT function to hold costs down through efficiency and to market itself more aggressively inside the company. This structure hastens the emergence of the IT marketing function, which if well managed will improve relationships with users. Further, excess IT capacity tends to be dealt with promptly by IT management, and they are willing to run more risks on the user service side.

Excess capacity also encourages sales of services by the IT department to outside firms, which can turn out to be a mixed blessing. Often priced as incremental sales (rather than on a full-cost basis), not only are these sales unprofitable, but many IT departments—excited by the volatile *hard outside* dollars as opposed to the captive *soft* inside ones—begin to give preferential treatment to outside customers, with a resulting erosion of service to inside users.

Establishing IT as a profit center has other problems. First, significant concern is often raised inside the firm as to whether it is appropriate for an inside *service department* to establish itself as a profit center, particularly when it does not sell any products outside the company. "Profits should come from outside sales, not service department practices" is the dominant complaint. The problem is further complicated when, because of geography, shared data files, and privacy and security reasons, users do not have the legitimate alternative of going outside (unless the entire IT department is out sourced). Therefore, the argument that the profit center is subject to normal market forces is widely perceived by users as spurious.

At least in the short run, setting up the IT activity as a profit center leads to higher user costs, because a profit figure is added to the user costs. Not only can this create user hostility, but in many settings it prevents the user from having legitimate full-cost data from the corporation for external pricing decisions.

In summary, all of these issues must be addressed before an organization adopts a profit center approach. A deceptively intriguing approach on the surface, it has many pitfalls.

Transfer Pricing

When an IT activity is set up as a profit center, establishment of the IT transfer price becomes a critical issue. There are at least four different conceptual approaches, each with specific strengths and weaknesses. (The issues involved are very similar to those of transfer pricing arrangements in general.)

For the purpose of this discussion we will assume that IT operations are being priced in end-user transaction terms (such as so much per paycheck, so much per invoice line, etc.), whereas a fixed-price contract is being written for IT development and maintenance. As described in our earlier discussion on charge-out issues, many other ways exist to approach these items. However, these assumptions are useful for introducing the issues involved.

Cost-Based Price. Assuming a full-cost method is used, the cost-based price method has the advantage of producing the lowest cost from the user's perspective and is thus likely to generate few user complaints. In this setting, whether IT is a profit center or a cost center is irrelevant, since profits can be earned on internal business only by the internal sales generating positive efficiency variances (obviously sales outside the company can be priced to generate a profit). This approach does not avoid the previously mentioned issue of what constitutes cost and how it should be determined (joint versus by-product, etc.).

A variation of this approach is the **cost-plus** basis. On the positive side, this makes IT generate profits and at the same time provides an understandable number for users to deal with. On the negative side, the users raise both the narrow issue of capriciousness in selection of the "plus" and the broader issue of the general inappropriateness of an internal service department earning profits.

Market-Based Price.   A key alternative, the market-based price method is used in some companies, particularly as the availability of outside services has grown. Its implementation, however, poses major problems. The first is the near impossibility in many settings of finding comparable products and services for establishing the market price. Unique databases or process control systems are examples of items for which such data are impossible to find. Even so-called standardized services such as payroll and accounting have so many special ramifications and alternative designs that market prices are very elusive. Also, suppliers of IT services treat some IT products as by-products of other activities and price them accordingly. Still other organizations calculate prices for in-house use; since they make no attempt at rigor, they achieve only "ballpark" figures. Using these figures as market-price surrogates produces spurious results.

Dual Transfer Price.[1]   The dual transfer price approach is designed to satisfy the motivational needs of the IT department and the key users simultaneously. As long as a single transfer price is used, it is impossible to come up with a price that will both allow IT to feel that it is earning a fair profit and allow the users to be given prices that will permit them to manage aggregate costs in line with the company's overall interests. The "pain" can be spread around, but in the end it is reallocation of a finite amount of pain as opposed to its elimination. Dual transfer pricing in IT works as follows:

1. The users are charged items at either direct or full cost, depending on the company's overall management control philosophy.
2. The IT department is allocated revenue based on a standard cost of services delivered plus a standard fixed markup (or at a market price if a sound one can be established). Revenue in excess of the planned amount can be derived either from selling more services than planned or from gaining unanticipated cost efficiencies.
3. The difference between the revenue of the IT department and the cost figure charged to the user is posted to an overhead expense account, which is closed to corporate overhead on a monthly basis.

This method, at least in theory, allows both the IT department and users to be simultaneously motivated to behave in the best overall corporate interest. Users are given appropriate economic trade-offs to

---

[1]Robert G. Eccles, Jr., "Control with Fairness in Transfer Pricing," *Harvard Business Review,* November–December 1983, pp. 149–161.

consider, while IT is provided incentives to operate efficiently and to sell extra services.

Dual pricing has worked satisfactorily in a number of settings and has dramatically changed the tenor and quality of relationships by permitting the IT group and the users to work together instead of against each other. Its Achilles' heel is that careful attention must be paid to the establishment of the cost target to ensure that the IT group is being asked to stretch enough and is not building excess slack into its budget. Also, its implementation involves some additional accounting work, although not enough to make the idea disabling.

Negotiated Price. The negotiated-price method is quite difficult to execute in the IT–user arena because the two parties often bring quite different strengths to the negotiating table. For example, systems that interface directly with other systems or that share proprietary databases must be run by the central IT department. Hence the negotiating positions of the two parties cannot be considered equal, since the user realistically has no other options.

Summary. Many potential IT financial control results architectures are possible. None represents a perfect general-purpose solution. The challenge is to pick the one that best fits the company's general management control culture, present user–IT relationships, and current state of IT sophistication. The typical firm has approached these issues in an evolutionary fashion, rather than having selected the right one the first time.

Financial Reporting Process

Budget Objectives. A key foundation of the IT results control process is the budgeting system. Put together under a very complex set of trade-offs and interlocked with the corporate budgeting process, its first objective is to provide a mechanism for appropriately allocating financial resources. While the planning effort sets the broad framework for the IT activity, the budgeting process ensures fine-tuning in relation to staffing, hardware, and resource levels. A second objective of budgeting is to set a dialogue in motion to ensure that organizational consensus is reached on the specific goals and possible short-term achievements of the IT activity. This is particularly important in organizations where the planning process is not well formed. Finally, the budget establishes a framework around which an early warning system for negative deviations can be built. Without a budget it is difficult to spot deviations in a deteriorating cost situation in time to take appropriate corrective action.

Budget Process. The budget system must involve senior management, IT management, and user groups. Its key outputs include establishing the planned service levels and costs of central operations, the amount of internal development and maintenance support to be implemented, and the amount and form of external services to be acquired. The planned central IT department service levels and their associated costs must flow from review of existing services and the approved application development portfolio as well as user desire for new services. In addition, these planned service levels must take into account long-term systems maintenance needs. The budget must also ensure that there are appropriate controls on purchased IT services for the firm as a whole (software and hardware, such as personal computers). The dialogue between users and the IT department regarding their anticipated needs and usage for the budget year helps generate an understanding of the IT department's goals and constraints that iteratively leads to a better IT plan as well as to clarification of the user's plans.

Example. To ensure that this dialogue occurs, a leading chemical company asks both the users and the IT department to develop two budgets, one for the same amount of dollars and head count as the preceding year and one for 10 percent more dollars and 2 percent more head count. Typically the IT department's proposals involve an expansion of distributed services. To help ensure communication, the main descriptions of key items are stated in user terms—such as the number of personnel records and types of pension planning support—with all the jargon relating to technical support issues being confined to appendixes. Both groups are asked to rank services of critical importance as well as to identify those that are of lower priority or that are likely to be superseded. A senior management group then spends a day reviewing a joint presentation that examines the budget in terms of probable levels of expenditure and develops a tentative ranking of the priority items. This meeting allows senior management to provide overall direction to the final budget negotiations between the two groups. The priorities established in these discussions are then consolidated by the IT manager for final approval. This modified, zero-based budgeting approach is judged to have provided good results in this setting.

Budget Targets. The IT budget must establish benchmark dates for project progress, clarify type and timing of technical changeovers, and identify needed levels and mixes of personnel as well as set spending levels. A further mission is to identify key milestones and completion dates and tie them to the budget. This helps to ensure that periodic review will allow for early detection of variance from the plan. Budgeting the key staff head count and levels is a particularly important management decision. In many situations a major cause of project overruns and delays is lack of talent available to support multiple projects in a timely manner. Shortage of personnel must be dealt with realistically in fitting projects together. (This should be done periodically through the year as well.)

An important benefit of involving users and suppliers in the budget process is the education that results. On the one hand, it helps the IT department to understand the particular needs of each user department and to assess their needs for IT support relative to other departments. On the other hand, the users develop an awareness of what is possible with available technology and better define their potential needs. In one financial institution the budget process is used heavily as a stimulus for innovation. During budget preparation both users and IT staff take many trips to other installations and receive information from their hardware/software suppliers to generate thinking on potential new banking services. Over a several-year period this has significantly improved the relationship between the two groups.

Periodic Reporting. Effective monitoring of the department's financial performance requires a variety of tools, most of which are common to other settings. These normally include monthly reports that highlight actual performance versus the plan and exception reports as needed. Design and operation of these systems are rather routine. Obvious issues include: (1) Are budget targets readjusted during the year through a forecasting mechanism? (2) If so, is the key performance target actual versus budget or actual versus forecast? (3) Are budgets modified for seasonal factors, or are they prepared on a basis of one-twelfth of the annual expense each month?

The IT financial reporting task is a bit different in that an IT organization requires a matrix cost reporting system as it grows in size. One side of the matrix represents the IT department structure and tracks costs and variances by IT organizational unit. The other side of the matrix tracks costs and variances by programs or projects.

An issue that is beyond the scope of this book is whether budget numbers and actual results should be reported in nominal dollars or in inflation-adjusted dollars. This is an issue of major importance for corporate management control systems today, particularly for multinational firms.

Nonfinancial Reporting Process

At least in an operational sense, the nonfinancial controls are of more importance than the financial ones in assuring management that the day-to-day and month-to-month activities of the IT function remain on target. Critical items here include preparation of regular six-month surveys of user attitudes toward the IT support they are receiving. Such surveys identify problems and provide a benchmark against which progress can be measured over time. Their distribution to the users for completion also clearly communicates that IT is concerned about user perception of service. Problems surfacing in such a survey need to be acted on promptly if the survey is to be an effective control.

Another category of controls are those relating to staff. Reports that monitor personnel turnover trends can provide critical early insight into the problems of this notoriously unstable group. These data allow timely action to be taken on such items as sensitivity of leadership, adequacy of salary levels, and workplace climate. In the same vein, formal training plans and periodic measurement of progress are important management tools for ensuring a professionally relevant group and maintaining morale.

Reports and other procedures that generate absolute measures of operational service levels are very important in IT operations. These include data on such items as trends in network uptime, ability to meet schedules on batch jobs, average transaction response time by type of system, and number of missends and other operational errors *and* a customer complaint log. Critical to the effectiveness of these systems is that they be maintained and adhered to; when quality-control errors are allowed to creep in better performance is shown than is actually present. These issues are discussed further in Chapter 11, with the emphasis that all dimensions of service cannot be optimized simultaneously.

In relation to systems development, reports on development projects in terms of elapsed time and work-months expended (vis-à-vis budget) provide a critical early warning system for assessing overall performance. The type of data needed and appropriately available varies widely by company. The company's maturity in dealing with information technology, the relative strategic role of IT development and operations, and the corporation's general approach to managerial control also influence both the form of these issues and the detail with which they are approached.

IT AUDIT FUNCTION

Located as a part of the office of the general auditor, the IT auditor function provides a vital check and balance on IT activity. The basic elements of its mission are threefold. The first is to ensure that appropriate standards for IT development and operations have been developed and installed consistent with the control architecture. With changes in both technology and the organization's familiarity with it, development of these standards is not a one-time job but requires continuous effort.

The second element is to ensure that these standards are being adhered to by the various operating units. This includes both regular progress reviews and the conduct of surprise audits. Such audits should reduce fraud and loss. Ensuring adherence to these standards should help reduce operations errors and omissions and increase user confidence and satisfaction. Audits also act as a prod toward improving operating efficiency.

The third element is active involvement in the systems' design and maintenance functions to ensure that systems are designed to be easily auditable and that maintenance changes do not create problems. This clearly compromises the supposedly independent mission of the auditor but is a necessary accommodation to the real world. Such involvement helps ensure the smooth running of the final system. Successful execution of all three mission elements helps to reduce the amount of outside assistance needed by the firm.

These seemingly straightforward tasks are very difficult to implement in the real world. The three main causes of this IT auditing difficulty are discussed here.

1. The most important barrier is the difficulty in maintaining necessary auditing staff skills. Operating at the intersection of two disciplines (IT and auditing), good practice demands thorough mastery of both. In fact, because IT auditing is frequently a "dead end" career path, staff members who can be retained are often sufficiently deficient in both disciplines to be ineligible as practitioners in either. Higher salaries and visibly attractive career paths are essential preconditions to reversing this situation.
2. The "art" of IT auditing continually lags behind the challenges posed by new technologies. For example, understanding methodologies for controlling batch systems for computers is not very relevant today for a world dominated by complex operating systems, networks, and on-line technologies. Managing catch-up for such lags poses a key IT auditing challenge for the future.
3. There has been an unevenness of senior management support for IT auditing, due in part to the lack of formally defined requirements from an outside authority. Support for a strong IT auditing function tends to be very episodic, with periods of strong interest following conspicuous internal or external failure. This interest, however, tends to erode rapidly once the calamity is corrected.

The role of the IT auditing function is poorly defined in most organizations at this time. Typically part of the internal auditing organization, and often not reporting to senior management, this is a function that deserves serious consideration at that management level.

SUMMARY

As noted earlier many of the IT management control issues are clearly similar to the general issues of management control that face an organization. Several aspects, however, make them different. The first is posed by the rapid changes in the underlying technology and the long time span required for users to adapt to new technologies. Phase-1 and Phase-2 technologies require a commitment to R&D and user learning that is in direct conflict with the charge-out techniques appropriate for Phase-3 and Phase-4 technologies. It is very easy for an organization to become too uniform in its control system and to try to standardize in order to use systems "efficiently," stamping out appropriate innovation as a by-product. In most organizations today, different divisions (at varying stages of learning, and using varying mixes of technologies) require quite different control approaches. Further, as organizational learning occurs, other control approaches become appropriate. Thus, quite apart from any breakthroughs in the general area of IT control methods, their practice in an organization undergoes continual evolution.

As IT becomes more firmly established in an organization's operation, the penalties of uneven performance of technology may impose very severe consequences for the organization as a whole, and action controls become vital. As a company, department, or system evolves from "turnaround" to "factory" to "support," very different control philosophies become appropriate.

Adding these issues to those discussed at the beginning of the chapter concerning the changing corporate environment and evolving corporate planning and control processes (in a world shifting from "make" to "buy" in software), the full complexity of the IT management control problem is apparent. Different organizations must adopt quite different control approaches, which then must evolve over time to deal with a changing corporate environment, changing strategic role of IT, and changing technologies.

Chapter 10

A Portfolio Approach to IT Development

A large insurance company deactivates its old systems for a major affiliate on June 30 and implements a new one on July 1 on a new technology. Seven weeks pass before the firm can issue a policy, write a commission check, or send out a premium notice. Nearly 70 percent of the sales force resign in disgust during this period.

A large consumer products company budgets $100 million for a new computer-based order-entry and marketing information system to be ready in two years. Two years later $50 million has been spent, an estimated additional $100 million will be spent to complete the job, and the project completion time has been extended to five years. Both the project manager and the chief information officer have been replaced.

A mid-sized bank has spent $2 million on a new consumer loan system. Developed in complete isolation from the end users, its functions are judged so limited that its conversion is delayed eighteen months, and the system must be completely rewritten.

Nine months after it had installed a state-of-the-art office automation system at a cost of $900,000, a Midwest mail-order house found that 50 percent of the terminals were unused in spite of 90 percent of the work being simple word processing. Further, the communications system was incompatible with the main data processing, and system support was unobtainable. The firm returned the system to the vendor.

Stories from the Stage-1 and Stage-2 days of the late 1960s and early 1970s? Unfortunately not! These examples are from the late 1980s and early 1990s. Although it is embarrassing to admit, the day of the big disaster on a major information technology (IT) project has not passed. Given business's more than 30 years of IT experience, the question is, Why? An analysis of these cases (all of them domestic companies; we could have selected equally dramatic examples from overseas) and firsthand acquaintance with a number of IT projects in the past 10 years suggest three serious deficiencies in practice that involve both general management and IT management: (1) failure to assess the individual project implementation risk at the time a project is funded; (2) failure to consider the aggregate implementation risk of the portfolio of projects; (3) lack of recognition that different projects require different managerial approaches.

These aspects of the IT project management and development process are so important that we address them in this separate chapter. Chapter 11 will discuss the influences of corporate culture and the technology's perceived strategic relevance on the balance of control between IT and the user over the various stages of the project management life cycle. Since many projects have multiyear life cycles, these project management issues must be dealt with separately from those of the management control system with its calendar-year focus, as discussed in Chapter 9.

PROJECT RISK

Elements of Project Implementation Risk

In discussing risk, we are assuming that the manager has brought appropriate methods and approaches to bear on the project— mismanagement is obviously another element of risk. Implementation risk, by definition here, is what remains after application of proper tools. Also, we are not implying that *risk* is *bad.* These words denote entirely different concepts, and the link between the two normally is simply that higher-risk projects must have potential for greater benefits.

The typical project feasibility study covers exhaustively such topics as financial benefits, qualitative benefits, implementation costs, target milestone and completion dates, and necessary staffing levels. In precise, crisp terms the developers of these estimates provide voluminous supporting documentation. Only rarely, however, do they deal frankly with the risks of slippage in time, cost overrun, technical shortfall, or outright failure. Rather, they deny the existence of such possibilities by ignoring them. They assume the appropriate human skills, controls, and so on, are in place to ensure success.

Consequences of Risk.   By risk we are suggesting exposure to such consequences as:

1. Failure to obtain all, or any, of the anticipated benefits because of implementation difficulties.
2. Implementation costs that are much higher than expected.
3. Implementation time that is much longer than expected.
4. Technical performance of resulting systems that is significantly below the estimate.
5. Incompatibility of the system with the selected hardware and software.

In practical situations, of course, these risks are not independent of each other; rather, they are closely related.

Project Dimensions that Influence Inherent Risk. At least three important project dimensions influence the inherent implementation risk:

Project Size. The larger the project in terms of dollar expense, staffing levels, elapsed time, and number of departments affected by the project, the greater is the risk. Multimillion-dollar projects obviously carry more risk than $50,000 projects and, usually, also affect the company more if the risk is realized. A related concern is the size of the project relative to the normal size of an IT development group's projects. A $1 million project in a department whose average undertaking costs $2 million to $3 million usually has lower implicit risk than a $250,000 project in a department that has never ventured a project costing more than $50,000.

Experience with the Technology. Because of the greater likelihood of unexpected technical problems, project risk increases as the project team's and organization's familiarity with the hardware, operating systems, database handler, and project application language decreases. Phase-1 and Phase-2 technology projects are intrinsically more risky for a company than Phase-3 and Phase-4 technology projects. A project that would pose a slight risk for a leading-edge, large-systems development group may be highly risky for a smaller, less technically advanced group. (The latter group can reduce its risk by purchasing outside skills for an undertaking involving technology that is in general commercial use. This rapidly growing market for outside skills is served by the major systems integrators such as Arthur Andersen, Computer Science Corporation, Electronic Data Services, and IBM.)

Project Structure. In some projects the nature of the task defines the outputs completely from the moment of conceptualization. Such schemes are classified as "highly structured." They carry much less risk than those whose outputs are more subject to the user-manager's judgment and hence are vulnerable to change. The outputs of a highly structured project are fixed and not subject to change during the life of the project.

An insurance company's automating the preparation of its agents' rate book is an example of a highly structured project. At the project's beginning, planners reached agreement on the product lines to be included, the layout of each page, and the process of generating each number. Throughout the life of the project there was no need to alter these decisions. Consequently the team organized to reach a stable, fixed output rather than to cope with a potentially mobile target.

Quite the opposite was true in the "low structure" order entry–marketing information project described at the beginning of the chapter. In that situation the users could not reach a consensus on what the outputs should be, and these decisions shifted almost weekly, crippling progress.

Project Categories and Degree of Risk

Figure 10–1 combines in a matrix the various dimensions influencing risk. It identifies eight distinct project categories with varying degrees of implementation risk. (Figure 10–2 gives examples of projects that fit this categorization.) Even at this grossly intuitive level, such a classification is useful to separate projects for different types of management review. IT organizations have used it successfully for understanding relative implementation risk and for communicating it to users and senior executives. The matrix helps to address the legitimate concern that all people viewing a project will have the same understanding of its risks.

Assessing Risk of Individual Projects

Figure 10–3 shows excerpts from a questionnaire developed by a company for assessing project implementation risk: a list of 42 questions that the project manager* answers about a project prior to senior management's approval of the proposal and then several times during project implementation.The company developed the questions after analyzing its experience with successful and unsuccessful projects. No analytic framework underlies the questions, and they may not be appropriate for all companies. Nonetheless, they provide a good starting point—and a number of other companies have used them as such in developing their own instruments for measuring implementation risk.

These questions not only highlight the implementation risks but also suggest alternative ways of conceiving of the project and managing it. If

---

*Actually, both the project leader and the key user answer these questions, and then they reconcile differences in their answers; of course, the questionnaire data are no better than the quality of thinking that goes into the answers.

FIGURE 10–1   Effect of Degree of Structure, Company-Relative
Technology, and Project Size on Project Implementation Risk

		Low Structure	High Structure
Low Company-Relative Technology	Large Project	Low risk (very susceptible to mismanagement)	Low risk
	Small Project	Very low risk (very susceptible to mismanagement)	Very low risk
High Company-Relative Technology	Large Project	Very high risk	Medium risk
	Small Project	High risk	Medium-low risk

FIGURE 10–2   Comparison of Project Implementation Risk by Degree of
Structured and Company-Relative Technology—Examples

	Low Structure	High Structure
Low Company-Relative Technology	Spreadsheet support for budgeting	Inventory control of oil tank farms
High Company-Relative Technology	On-line graphic support for advertising copy	AI-driven bond trading

FIGURE 10–3   Project Implementation Risk Assessment Questionnaire (sample from a total of 42 questions)

Size Risk Assessment

Risk Factor			Weight
1. Total development work-hours for system[a]			5
100 to 3,000	Low	1	
3,000 to 15,000	Medium	2	
15,000 to 30,000	Medium	3	
More than 30,000	High	4	
2. Estimated project implementation time			4
12 months or less	Low	1	
13 months to 24 months	Medium	2	
More than 24 months	High	3	
3. Number of departments (other than IT) involved with system			4
One	Low	1	
Two	Medium	2	
Three or more	High	3	

Structure Risk Assessment

Risk Factor			Weight
1. If replacement system is proposed, what percentage of existing functions are replaced on a one-to-one basis?			5
0% to 25%	High	3	
25% to 50%	Medium	2	
50% to 100%	Low	1	
2. What is severity of user-department procedural changes caused by proposed system?			5
Low		1	
Medium		2	
High		3	
3. What is degree of needed user-organization structural change to meet requirements of new system?			5
None		0	
Minimal	Low	1	
Somewhat	Medium	2	
Major	High	3	
4. What is general attitude of user?			5
Poor; against IT solution	High	3	
Fair; sometimes reluctant	Medium	2	
Good; understands value of IT solution		0	
5. How committed is upper-level user management to system?			5
Somewhat reluctant, or unknown	High	3	
Adequate	Medium	2	
Extremely enthusiastic	Low	1	
6. Has a joint IT–user team been established?			5
No	High	3	
Part-time user representative appointed	Low	1	
Full-time user representative appointed		0	

FIGURE 10–3   *(continued)*

Technology Risk Assessment

Risk Factor			Weight
1. Which of the hardware is new to the company?[b]			5
None		0	
CPU	High	3	
Peripheral and/or additional storage	High	3	
Terminals	High	3	
Mini or micro	High	3	
2. Is the system software (nonoperating system) new to IT project team?[b]			5
No		0	
Programming language	High	3	
Database	High	3	
Data communications	High	3	
Other (Please specify)	High	3	
3. How knowledgeable is user in area of IT?			5
First exposure	High	3	
Previous exposure but limited knowledge	Medium	2	
High degree of capability	Low	1	
4. How knowledgeable is user representative in proposed application area?			5
Limited	High	3	
Understands concept but has no experience	Medium	2	
Has been involved in prior implementation efforts	Low	1	
5. How knowledgeable is IT team in proposed application area?			5
Limited	High	3	
Understands concept but has no experience	Medium	2	
Has been involved in prior implementation efforts	Low	1	

Source: This questionnaire is adapted from the "Dallas Tire" case, No. 180-006 (Boston, Mass.: Harvard Business School Case Services, 1980).

Note: Since the questions vary in importance, the company assigned weights to them subjectively. The numerical answer to the questions is multiplied by the question weight to calculate the question's contribution to the project's risk. The numbers are then added to produce a risk score for the project. Projects with risk scores within 10 points of each other are indistinguishable in their relative risk but those separated by 100 points or more are very different in their implementation risk to even the casual observer.

[a]Time to develop includes systems design, programming, testing, and installation.

[b]This question is scored by multiplying the sum of the numbers attached to the positive responses by the weight.

the initial aggregate risk score seems high, analysis of the answers may suggest ways of lessening the risk through reduced scope, lower-level technology, multiple phases, and so on. Thus managers should not consider risk as a static descriptor; rather, its presence should encourage better approaches to project management. Questions 5 and 6 in the "Structured Risk Assessment" section are particularly good examples of questions that could trigger changes.

The higher the assessment score, the greater is the need for corporate approval. Only the executive committee in this company approves very risky projects. Such an approach ensures that top managers are aware of significant hazards and are making appropriate trade-offs between risk and strategic benefits. Managers should ask questions such as these:

1. Are the benefits great enough to offset the risks?
2. Can the affected parts of the organization survive if the project fails?
3. Have the planners considered appropriate alternatives?

Periodically during the undertaking, the questionnaire is used again to reveal any major changes. If these assessments are positive, the risk continuously declines during implementation as the number and size of remaining tasks dwindle and familiarity with the technology grows.

The questionnaire data facilitate a common understanding among senior, IT, and user managers as to a project's relative implementation risk. The "fiascoes" commonly occur when senior managers believe a project has low implementation risk and IT managers know it has high implementation risk. In such cases IT managers may not admit their assessment because they fear that the senior executives will not tolerate this kind of uncertainty in information systems projects and will cancel a project of potential benefit to the organization.

PORTFOLIO RISK

In addition to determining relative risk for single projects, a company should develop a profile of aggregate implementation risk for its portfolio of systems and programming projects. While there is no such thing as a universally appropriate implementation risk profile for all firms, different types of companies and strategies suggest different risk profiles as being appropriate.

For example, in an industry where IT is strategic (such as banking and insurance), managers should be concerned if there are no high-risk projects. Such a cautious stance may be leaving a product or service gap for competition to step into. On the other hand, a portfolio loaded with high-risk projects would suggest that the company may be vulnerable to operational disruptions if projects are not completed as planned. In "support" companies, heavy investment in high-risk projects may not be appropriate. It is the wrong area for them to take strategic gambles. Often, however, even those companies should have some technologically exciting ventures in order to ensure familiarity with leading-edge technology and maintain staff morale and interest.

These examples suggest that the aggregate implementation risk profiles of the portfolios of two companies could legitimately differ. Table 10–1 lists the issues that influence toward or away from high-

TABLE 10–1   Factors that Influence Implementation Risk Profile of Project Portfolio

	Portfolio Risk Focus	
Factor	Low	High
Stability of IT development group.	High	Low
Perceived quality of IT development group by insiders.	High	Low
IT critical to delivery of current corporate services.	No	Yes
IT important decision support aid.	No	Yes
Experienced IT systems development group.	Yes	No
Major IT fiascoes in last two years.	No	Yes
New IT management team.	No	Yes
IT perceived critical to delivery of future corporate services.	No	Yes
IT perceived critical to future decision support aids.	No	Yes
Company perceived as backward in use of IT.	No	Yes

risk efforts. (The risk profile should include projects executed by outside software houses as well as those of the internal systems development group.) As the table shows, the aggregate impact of IT on corporate strategy is an important determinant of the appropriate amount of implementation risk to undertake.

Summary

In summary, it is both possible and useful to assess a project's implementation risk at the feasibility study stage. Discussion of risk is helpful to those working on the project and to the department as a whole. Not only can this systematic analysis reduce the number of failures, but equally important, its power as a communication link helps IT managers and senior executives reach agreement on the risks to be taken in relation to corporate goals.

PROJECT MANAGEMENT: A CONTINGENCY APPROACH

Much of the literature and conventional wisdom suggest that there is a single right approach to project management. A similar bias holds that managers should apply an appropriate cluster of tools, project management methods, and organizational linkages uniformly to all such ventures.

While there may indeed be a set of general-purpose tools, the contribution each device can make to planning and controlling the project varies widely according to the project's characteristics. Further, the means of involving the user—through steering committees, representation on the team, or as leader—should also vary by project type. In short there is no universally correct way to run all projects.

Management Tools

The general methods (tools) for managing projects are of four principal types:

- **External integration tools** include organizational and other communication devices that link the project team's work to users at both the managerial and the lower levels.
- **Internal integration devices** ensure that the team operates as an integrated unit. These include a variety of personnel controls.
- **Formal planning tools** help to structure the sequence of tasks in advance and to estimate the time, money, and technical resources the team will need for executing them.
- **Formal results-control mechanisms** help managers to evaluate progress and to spot potential discrepancies so that corrective action can be taken.

Results controls have been particularly effective in the following settings:[1]

1. Where clear knowledge of the desired results exists.
2. Where the desired result can be controlled (at least to some extent by the individuals whose actions are being influenced).
3. Where the controllable result areas can be measured effectively.

Highly structured projects that involve a low degree of technology satisfy these conditions very well. Formal results-control mechanisms are very effective in those settings. For low-structured projects which involve a high degree of technology, none of the above conditions apply; consequently results control can make only a limited contribution. In those settings major contributions are derived from internal integration devices (personnel controls).

Table 10-2 gives examples of the types of integration and control tools that are commonly used by companies. The next paragraphs sug-

---

[1]Kenneth A. Merchant, *Control in Business Organizations* (Marshfield, Mass.: Pitman Publishing, 1985).

TABLE 10–2   Tools of Project Management

Integration Tools, External	Integration Tools, Internal
Selection of user as project manager.	Selection of experienced IT professional to lead team.
Creation of user steering committee.	Frequent team meetings.
Frequent in-depth meetings of user steering committee.	Regular preparation and distribution of minutes within team on key design evolution decisions.
User-managed change control process.	Regular technical status reviews.
Frequent and detailed distribution of project team minutes to key users.	Managed low turnover of team members.
Selection of users as team members.	Selection of high percentage of team members with significant previous work relationships.
Formal user specification approval process.	Participation of team members in goal setting and deadline establishment.
Progress reports prepared for corporate steering committee.	Outside technical assistance.
User responsibility for education and installation of system.	
User management decision on key action dates.	

Formal Planning Tools	Formal Control Tools
PERT, "critical path," etc.; networking.	Periodic formal status reports versus plan.
Milestone phases selection.	Change control disciplines.
Systems specification standards.	Regular milestone presentation meetings.
Feasibility study specifications.	Deviations from plan, reports.
Project approval processes.	
Project postaudit procedures.	

gest how the degree of structure and the company-relative technology influence the selection of tools.

Influences on Tool Selection

High Structure–Low Technology Projects. Projects that are highly structured and that present familiar technical problems are not only the lower-risk projects but also the easiest to manage (see Figure 10–1). They are also the least common. High structure implies that the outputs are very well defined by the nature of the task and that the possibility that the users will change their minds about the desired outputs is essentially nonexistent. The project leaders, therefore, do not have to develop extensive administrative processes in order to get a diverse group of users to agree to a design structure and then to stick to their decision. Such external integration devices as inclusion of analysts in user departments, heavy representation of users on the design team, formal approval of the design team by users, and formal approval of design specifications by users are cumbersome and unnecessary for this type of project. Other integrating devices, such as training users how to operate the system, remain important.

The system's concept and design stages, however, are stable. At the same time, since the technology involved is familiar to the company, the project can proceed with a high percentage of persons having only average technical backgrounds and experience. The leader does not need extraordinary IT skills. This type of project readily provides opportunities to the department's junior managers; it can give them experience that they can apply to more ambitious tasks in the future.

With their focus on defining tasks and budgeting resources against them, project life-cycle planning concepts—such as PERT (Program Evaluation and Review Technique) and "critical path"—force the team to develop a thorough and detailed plan (exposing areas of soft thinking in the process). Such projects are likely to meet the resulting milestone dates and keep within the target budget. Moreover, the usual results-control techniques for measuring progress against dates and budgets provide very reliable data for spotting discrepancies and building a desirable tension within the design team to work harder to avoid slippage.

An example of this type of highly structured project is the insurance agents' rate-book project mentioned earlier. A portfolio in which 90 percent of the projects are of this type should produce little unplanned excitement for senior and user managers. It also requires a much more limited set of skills for the IT organization than would be needed for portfolios with a different mixture of project types.

High Structure–High Technology Projects.   Vastly more complex than the high structure–low technology projects, these projects involve some significant modifications of practices outlined in project management handbooks. A good example of this type of project is the conversion of one computer manufacturer's systems to those of another where all the code must be rewritten with no enhancements. Another example is the conversion of a set of manual procedures onto a minicomputer with the only objective being performance of the same functions more quickly.

The normal mechanisms for liaison with users are not crucial here; the outputs are so well defined by the nature of the undertaking that both the development of specifications with user inputs and the need to deal with systems changes from users are unimportant aspects of the project. Liaison with users is nevertheless important in two respects:

(1) to ensure coordination on any changes in input/output or any other manual procedure changes necessary for project success, and (2) to deal with any systems restructuring that must follow from unexpected shortcomings in the project's technology.

In this kind of project it is common to discover during implementation that the technology is inadequate, which forces a long postponement while new technology is chosen or vital features modified to make the task fit the available technology. In one such situation an industrial products company had to convert some computerized order-entry procedures to a manual basis so that the rest of an integrated materials management system could be shifted to new hardware that had already been purchased.

Such technological shortcomings were the main difficulty faced by the insurance company described at the beginning of the chapter. In such a case, where system performance is much poorer than expected, user involvement is important both to prevent demoralization and to help implement either an alternative approach (less ambitious in selection of technology) or a mutual agreement to end the project.

The skills that lead to success in this type of project, however, are the same as those that make for effective administration of projects involving any kind of technical complexity. The leader needs a strong background in high technology projects (preferably, but not necessarily, in an IT environment) as well as administrative experience. The leader must also be effective in relating to technicians. By talking individually and collectively with the project team members at various times, the ideal manager will come to anticipate difficulties before the technicians understand that they have a problem. In dealing with larger projects in this category, the effective manager must establish and maintain teamwork through meetings, develop a record of all key design decisions, and facilitate subproject conferences as needed.

Project life-cycle planning methods identify tasks and suitable completion dates. Their predictive value is much less here than in the preceding category. The team will not understand key elements of the technology in advance, and consequently seemingly minor bugs in such projects have a curious way of becoming major financial drains.

Roughly once an hour an on-line banking system in one company generated "garbage" across the computer screen. Although simply hitting a release key erased this screen of zeroes and Xs, four months and more than $200,000 were spent eliminating the so-called ghost screen. The solution lay in uncovering a complex interaction of hardware features, operating system functions, and application traffic patterns. Correction of the problem ultimately required the vendor to redesign several chips. Formal results-control mechanisms have limits in monitoring the progress of such projects, and personnel controls become more important.

In summary, technical leadership and internal integration are the keys in this type of project, and external integration plays a distinctly secondary role. Formal planning and control tools give projections which intrinsically may contain major inaccuracies, and the great danger is that neither IT managers nor high-level executives will recognize this. They may believe they have precise planning and close control when in fact they have neither.

Low Structure–Low Technology Projects.   When low structure–low technology projects are intelligently managed they present low risk. Again and again, however, such projects fail because of inadequate direction. (In this respect they differ from the high structure–low technology project, where more ordinary managerial skills could ensure success.) The key to operating this kind of project lies in effective efforts to involve the users.

Developing substantial user support for *only one* of the thousands of design options and keeping the users committed to that design are critical. Essential aspects of this process include:

1. A user as either project leader or the number-two person on the team.
2. A user steering committee to evaluate the design.
3. Efforts to break the project into a sequence of very small, discrete subprojects.
4. Formal user review and approval on all key project specifications.
5. Distribution of minutes of all key design meetings to users.
6. Strong efforts to adhere to the key subproject time schedules. Low managerial and staff turnover in the user areas is vital in this respect, since a consensus on approach with the predecessor of a user manager is of dubious value.

The consumer-products company debacle described at the beginning of the chapter is an example of what can happen when this process does not take place. Soon after work started, under great time pressure, the project manager began reducing his liaison meetings with the key end users. He and his staff were geographically separate from the end users—their buildings were ten miles apart. The vice president of marketing was promoted to another division, being replaced by an individual from elsewhere in the company who had a very different background and different interests. Inadequately tuned into changes in priorities resulting from this move, the project team continued on a course that was inappropriate for the new direction of the company. The changing design made much of the programming obsolete. Tough, pragmatic user leadership throughout the design stages would have made a major difference in the outcome.

The importance of user leadership increases once the design is finalized. At that stage users almost inevitably will state some version of "I have been thinking . . ." Unless the alternatives they suggest are of critical strategic significance to the users (a judgment best made by a responsible, user-oriented project manager), the requests must be diverted and postponed until they can be considered in some formal change process. Unless this control is rigorous (a problem intensified by the near impossibility of distinguishing between the economies of a proposed alternative and those implicit in the original design), users may make change after change, with the project evolving rapidly to a state of permanent deferral, its completion forever six months in the future.

If the project is well integrated with the user departments, the formal planning tools will be very useful in structuring tasks and helping to remove any remaining uncertainty. The target completion dates will be firm as long as the systems target remains fixed. Similarly, the formal results-control devices afford clear insight into progress to date, flagging both advances and slippages. Personnel controls also are vital here. If integration with user departments is weak, for example, excessive reliance on these results controls will produce an entirely unwarranted feeling of confidence. By definition, the problems of technology management are usually less difficult in this type of project than in the high-technology ventures, and a staff with a normal mixture of technical backgrounds should be adequate.

In almost every respect, in fact, effective management of this type of project differs from that of the previous two. The key to success is close, aggressive management of external integration supplemented by formal planning and control tools. Leadership must flow from the user, rather than from the technical side.

Low Structure–High Technology Projects.   Because these projects are complex and carry high risk, their leaders need technical experience as well as the ability to communicate with users. The same intensive effort toward external integration needed for low structure–low technology projects is necessary here. Total user commitment to a particular set of design specifications is critical; and again, they must agree to *one* out of the many thousands of options.

Unfortunately, however, an option desirable from the user's perspective may turn out to be infeasible in the selected hardware/software system. In the last several years such situations have occurred, particularly with network designs, and they commonly lead either to significant restructuring of the project or to its elimination. It is clear that users should be well represented at both the policy and the operations levels.

At the same time, technical considerations make strong technical leadership and internal project integration vital. This kind of effort requires the most experienced project leaders, and they need wholehearted support from the users. In approving such a project, managers must decide if it can and should be divided into a series of much smaller subprojects and/or if less innovative technology should be employed.

While formal planning and results-control tools can be useful here, at the early stages they contribute little to reducing overall uncertainty and to highlighting overall problems. The planning tools do allow the manager to structure the sequence of tasks. Unfortunately, in this type of project new tasks crop up with monotonous regularity, and tasks that appear simple and small can suddenly become complex and protracted. Further, unsuspected interdependencies between tasks often become apparent. Time, cost, and resulting technical performance are almost impossible to predict simultaneously. In the *Apollo* moon project, for example, technical performance achievement was key, and cost and time were secondary, which in the private sector is usually unacceptable.

Relative Contribution of Management Tools

Table 10–3 shows the relative contribution that each of the four groups of project management tools makes to maximizing the possibility of project success. It reveals that quite different management styles and approaches are needed for managing the different types of projects

TABLE 10–3   Relative Contribution of Tools to Ensuring Project Success by Project Type

Project Type	Project Description	Contribution			
		External Integration	Internal Integration	Formal Planning	Formal Results Control
I	High structure–low technology, large	Low	Medium	High	High
II	High structure–low technology, small	Low	Low	Medium	High
III	High structure–high technology, large	Low	High	Medium	Medium
IV	High structure–high technology, small	Low	High	Low	Low
V	Low structure–low technology, large	High	Medium	High	High
VI	Low structure–low technology, small	High	Low	Medium	High
VII	Low structure–high technology, large	High	High	Low +	Low +
VIII	Low structure–high technology, small	High	High	Low	Low

effectively. Although the framework could be made more complex by including more dimensions, it would only confirm this primary conclusion.

SUMMARY

The usual corporate handbook on project management, with its single-minded prescriptive approach, fails to deal with the realities of the tasks facing today's managers, particularly those dealing with information technology. The right approach for managing a project flows from the specific characteristics of the project.

Additionally, the need to deal with the corporate culture within which both IT and the project team operate further complicates the project management problem. Use of formal project planning and results-control tools is much more likely to produce successful results in highly formal environments than in ones where the prevailing culture is more personal and informal. Similarly, the selection and effective use of integrating mechanisms is very much a function of the corporate culture. (Too many former IT managers have made the fatal assumption that they were in an ideal position to reform corporate culture!)

The past decade has brought new challenges to IT project management and new insights into the management process. Our conclusions are threefold:

1. We will continue to experience major disappointments as we push into new application areas and technologies. Today, however, the dimensions of implementation risk can be identified in advance, and this information can be considered in the decision process. Inevitably, if all we implement are high-risk projects, we will sometimes fail.
2. The work of the IT development department in aggregate may be thought of as a portfolio in the same way that financial fund managers calculate and manage the risks within their portfolios. The aggregate implementation risk profile of that portfolio is a critical strategic decision.
3. Project management in the IT field is complex and multidimensional. Different types of projects require different clusters of management tools if they are to succeed.

Chapter 11

Operations Management

A major investment banking firm operated all of its foreign exchange trading and other trading activities out of a large computing center containing $15 million worth of hardware, totally without backup. One Friday afternoon the water main that ran vertically through the building burst on the floor directly above the computing center. In a half hour the computing center floor was covered with three feet of water, and the entire $15 million worth of equipment was destroyed. The company went into the weekend with many of its key trading positions uncovered and, indeed, not even knowing what those positions were. Truly extraordinary efforts were made to replace all of the equipment in a 48-hour period in order to prevent massive balance-sheet erosion. Multiple sites, much tighter environmental measures, better controls, and new management were all parts of the solution.

As a result of software glitches in a new installation in January 1990, AT&T's long-distance phone system went down for 14 hours. One insurance company had to send home 500 people who were working on telephone follow-ups to direct mailings, losing a day's sales. The insurer now spreads its business over several carriers so as to avoid this type of vulnerability in the future.

The chief executive officer of an industrial products firm discovered that the delay in year-end financial closing was not due to reduced emphasis on close control of financial accounting, but to unexpected work and personnel problems in the IT department. Increased use (and associated problems) of an on-line query system to provide salespeople and customers with detailed delivery and cost information has absorbed all available system support personnel. Consequently, no time was left for revising the accounting system for mandatory changes in tax laws before year-end closing.

The IT director of a large aerospace firm is pondering whether to totally reorganize and consolidate the 10 operations centers in order to save more than $50 million. At present, each center is configured to provide total support to a business unit. Workloads are erratic, long response-time delays exist on some on-line systems, and the costs are high. A consolidated center offers the opportunity to address all three of those issues.

Unusual problems? Hardly! Historically, the "glamorous" part of the IT function has been the technology-oriented new systems development activity. Systems maintenance and day-to-day operations and delivery of service have been distinctly secondary. Failures in the operations function, however, increasingly jeopardize entire organizations. In this chapter the term *operations* is defined as the running of IT hardware and data input devices, equipment scheduling, and work forces associated with these activities. The chapter also deals with the movement toward outside-sourcing both software and development and operations, and the special challenges of security and privacy.

CHANGING OPERATIONS ENVIRONMENT

Both the management resources devoted to operations activities and the sophistication of management practices within the operations center have often been inadequate for the growth and change within companies' operations activities. Changing technology is now triggering major changes in the way these activities are managed.

Move to On-Line Systems and Networks. Greatly increased on-line technology applications and increased sophistication in operating systems in the past decade have transformed a batch, job-shop environment with heavy human control into, first, a process-manufacturing shop, and now, a largely self-scheduled and -monitored 24-hour-a-day utility. This change in manufacturing work flow has precipitated a total rethinking of both what appropriate scheduling is and how adequate service levels are defined. These systems support thousands of internal devices and in many cases must provide "seamless" 24-hour-a-day service links to customers and suppliers around the globe. Any problems in this area immediately reflect unfavorably on the firm as a whole.

Diversity of Performance Measures. There is no such thing as an ideal, standard IT operations management control system or an ideal measure of performance. Appropriate balancing of quality of service, response time of on-line systems, ability to handle unexpected jobs, costs, and ability to meet schedules on batch systems varies from one organization to another.

Efficiency–Effectiveness Balance. Different IT operations environments must strike different balances between efficiency (low-cost production) and effectiveness in responding to unplanned, uneven flows of requests. IT operations cannot be *all things* simultaneously to *all people;* instead, they must operate with the priorities of trade-offs established by corporate strategy. Implementing these priorities has caused the reorganization of some large IT operations into series of focused, single-service groups, each of which can be managed to serve quite different user service objectives.

Changes in Staffing Needs.   Many formerly valuable employees are unsuited for new tasks, and their relatively simple jobs have been automated away. Such dilemmas have been complicated by the unionization of this function in many parts of the world. This is a relatively transitory problem in many settings where operations centers are becoming "lights-out factories."

Continued Change in Technology.   Evolving technology, while offering potential benefits of lower cost and new capabilities, poses significant problems of change and introduction of new operating procedures. It is an unusual IT operations center that has the same hardware/software configuration from one month to the next.

The Trend toward Outside Sourcing.   The major shift toward more outside sourcing for both IT processing and software development requires substantial changes in the procedures of the operations and development functions of a firm's IT department. Firms such as Eastman Kodak that have made this shift successfully have attracted widespread national attention to out sourcing.

   These issues are similar to those involved in running a manufacturing facility characterized as utilizing *highly volatile technology* and *specialized labor,* serving *dynamic markets,* and operating within a *changing industry structure.* Consequently, much of the analysis in this chapter draws on work done in manufacturing management, particularly as it relates to efficiency–effectiveness trade-offs.

A Focused Service Organization Alternative—An Example

A key question stemming from this manufacturing analogy is how focused the department should be. Should it subdivide itself into sets of stand-alone services networked together as needed or be organized as a general-purpose IT service? The problem one company faced of either closing its books late or providing continuous on-line service for queries from the sales force stimulated the company to review the responsiveness of its operations to the demands of new services. They perceived that it was impossible for their single, monolithic unit to respond adequately to such very different user needs.

To address the problem, the IT development and maintenance group was reorganized into four independent systems groups, each operating independently of the others and reporting to the IT manager. One group supported the on-line query systems, with its goals being to provide 10-second response, one-day change implementation, and hourly refreshment of all data. This query system was moved to a stand-alone minicomputer in the corporate data center to keep its volatility of demand from disturbing the rest of the company's operations. The second group was devoted to the general ledger accounting system. Their goals were to keep the software up-to-date for month-end closing, to schedule work so as not to interfere with other systems, to ensure the quality and reliability of accounting data, and to close the books five days after the last working day of the month. This system ran on the data center's large mainframe computer. The third group was responsible for all material-management systems. Their objectives were to ensure that all desired changes to the system were made and that all production control persons were well trained in use of the system so as to reduce rerun time dramatically. The fourth group worked with the systems that supported new-product development. They were responsible for identifying system requirements of new products, maintaining the capacity simulator used in planning new-product development, establishing the data standards used to describe new products, and developing and performing analyses on new products as directed by the vice president of product development. Their systems also ran on the mainframe computer.

Each focused group included at least one user and two to three systems professionals, with the query group having their own computer as well. All worked full time on their respective services with the exception of the new-product group, which had spurts of work as new products hit the market and lulls after the market settled down. This structure has produced happier customers, significantly better perceptions of service, and increased employee morale.

Alternative Organizations

Historically, IT systems were developed to be run out of an integrated IT operations unit. As we have noted, some firms have reorganized IT development and operations in order to be more responsive to user needs. For example, many organizations have not only shifted application programmers to users, but have also allowed maintenance and operations to be decentralized around the local system. As IT's monopoly of system construction and make-or-buy decisions erodes to greater user control, the factory becomes fragmented into a series of focused services (for example, using a standard word processing system for customer mailings). For some users and applications this may be very effective. The services for other users, however, may be dependent upon an integrated set of data, in which case severe coordination problems are created by a focused factory concept. The challenge is to identify where focus in operations (either within the central unit or distributed to the user) is appropriate and where it is not. Implementation of this is discussed in the section on production planning and control later in the chapter.

These problems are further complicated by the fact that in all but the most decentralized corporations, central telecommunications networks have been developed for binding corporations' activities together. These include the capacity for electronic mail, document transfer, data file transfers, and so on. Including everything from local area networks to satellite links, many of the networks are both very large and highly sophisticated as they evolve links between fragmented services. For example, a large aerospace company recently initiated a total rearchitecturing of its network after a confidential E-mail message from the president to the financial vice president wound up on the desk of a production planner in another country.

To build on the manufacturing strategy theme and develop an appropriate range of make-or-buy plans, the operations management discussion in this chapter is organized around these topics:

- Development of an operations strategy.
- Technology planning.
- Measuring and managing capacity.
- Managing the IT operations work force.
- Production planning and control.
- Security.
- Privacy.

DEVELOPING AN OPERATIONS STRATEGY

As noted earlier, the management team of an IT operations activity is trying to stay on top of a utility that is radically changing its production system, customer base, and role within the company. Twenty years ago the manager and his staff could be described as monopolists running a job shop where the key issues were scheduling (with substantial human inputs), ensuring that telecommunications were adequate, managing a large blue-collar staff, and planning capacity and staffing levels for future workloads of similar characteristics. Today, on the other hand, they (1) operate an information utility that provides a 24-hour, 7-day-a-week service in support of thousands of terminals and PCs—perhaps located around the world—that must cope cost-effectively with uncertain short-term and long-term user demand; (2) manage a work force far more highly skilled, more professional, and much smaller in numbers; and (3) evaluate both internal and external competing services that in many cases offer the potential to solve problems more economically and more comprehensively. Key issues for the IT operations manager continue to include staff, capacity, and telecommunications. Prominent additions to this list, however, are appropriate assessment, assimilation, and integration of software and services emanating from outside the corporation.

Senior management must assess the quality of IT operations and—depending on how critical it is to the overall strategic mission of the corporation—must be involved in determining its structure and the standards for its quality of service. The central question for both senior management and IT management is whether the current IT operations organization effectively supports the firm.

In this context, an operations strategy must address four key issues:

1. Ensure that an architecture has been conceived and is being implemented.
2. Ensure that new systems are developed in ways that appropriately address their viability.
3. Ensure that internal/external sourcing decisions are carefully considered, both as to their outcome and as to who should determine operational characteristics of any outsourcing arrangement.
4. Determine the extent to which IT operations should be managed as a single entity or be broken into a series of perhaps more costly but more focused subunits that provide more customized user service than is possible with a single facility. (This topic is discussed in the Production Planning and Control section.)

The following paragraphs discuss these issues in more detail.

The Role of IT Architecture

In today's evolving technology, managing a firm's IT portfolio in order to gain a competitive advantage for the firm is akin to urban renewal. Great tensions are inherent in the need to meet today's needs while providing a platform that permits tomorrow's services to evolve. To balance these conflicting goals, many firms have attempted to develop an overall IT architecture. Architecture includes such technical items as the vision of an evolving network for linking the various parts of the corporation and the protocols for ensuring that wide-area networks and local-area networks can communicate seamlessly and cost-effectively. It includes data standards and dictionaries that ensure that files from different parts of the firm can be accessed and correlated appropriately and cost-effectively. It also includes standards for hardware/software vendors that ensure maintainability of uptime at a reasonable cost and easy interconnectivity between different parts of the organization. Standards on protocols like UNIX and Windows are crucial for the long-term growth and adaptability of the firm. This architecture (1) provides an operational vision, (2) is modified as an ongoing process, (3) allows concrete projects to be identified for the immediate future, (4) serves as a basis for establishing priorities and sequencing of IT projects, and (5) establishes a basis for organization change.

Vision.   The most celebrated operational vision was that of C. A. Smith (past CEO of American Airlines): the idea of a passenger name record for every reserved seat on American Airlines. Created in 1954, this idea drove the development of SABRE in the early 1960s and its subsequent modification. Such a vision encompasses the key business purpose of IT (examples: an active electronic link to every important customer for industrial wholesalers; a complete product sales history and demographic profile for all financial service customers to facilitate crossmarketing). The practical implications of the vision—such as seat selection, boarding passes, frequent flier programs, and personal marketing—will evolve through ongoing discussion and implementation.

Ongoing Process.   Successful architectures are not bound in a book, but rather, are present in ongoing discussions among the key decision makers; they are architecture in action. As an illustration of this process, let us step into the strategy status room of a multinational bank. On one wall are posted descriptions of the key strategy and service objectives for each decision-making unit, retail branch, and overseas office and lists of new, electronic-based products for each major business. In 1990 these new products included the consolidation of branch banks acquired in a recent merger into a single operating system; the final phase of a combined purchasing incentive program between the firm, an oil company, and an airline; the introduction of a new credit card product; and an expert-system project. On another wall is a chart that lists all sites and the services provided and planned maintenance at each site. On the back wall is a list of all the hardware and the main software that provide these services. Senior management meets in this room once a month to review progress and deal with new issues.

Project Identification.   A working architecture permits and encourages the planning of sound projects that can be justified and initiated within the existing organizations. These projects originate from both business and IT staffs, stimulated by ongoing dialogue. For example, in a large chemical business the R&D group initiated an experimental local-area network (LAN) as a means to improve R&D productivity (an objective of their architecture). Over time the LAN grew into a network that supported corporate headquarters. It started in R&D and was phased into IT as it became perceived as a useful general service. In a publishing company, a group of editors formed a steering committee to explore how PCs could better support the entire editorial process. This was stimulated in part by an earlier series of architectural discussions on the role of work stations in supporting specific editorial tasks that had led to some very high payoff projects.

Priorities. A prime purpose of IT architecture is to facilitate the establishment of priorities for meeting today's needs while providing flexibility to grow to tomorrow's competitive challenge. The recent simultaneous explosion of PC use, expansion of communication services, and massive reorganization of data structures exemplify the contrast in needed time and resources for implementing interdependent services. A network development and implementation program may take years to accomplish, while new local-area-network terminal systems can be implemented in a matter of weeks. Without an architecture, short-term tactical moves can insidiously postpone long-term projects. Further implementation complications are caused by both the shift to buying (rather than developing) software and services and the shift of responsibility for these activities to line managers. Both of these must be managed carefully. Finally, an IT architecture imposes a global perspective on priorities for IT projects, because the pieces must fit together.

Organization Change

As we have noted in earlier chapters, IT identifies opportunities for restructuring work and fundamentally altering the way work is carried out in organizations. Architectural development provides these opportunities and fosters discussion of how they can be achieved. Technologies can open up opportunities for these changes but cannot guarantee that positive changes will occur.

System Design and Operations

Effective IT operations hinge heavily on ensuring that the first step of the systems life cycle, the design phase, is well executed. The key operations discussions for a system often occur early in the design phase. Both user and IT operational personnel should be intimately involved in the early design of significant processing systems. Strong IT operational input ensures that operational feasibility issues are given high priority from the beginning. It is easy for a development group to overlook such issues as appropriate restart points in case of hardware failures, adequate documentation and support for operational personnel when a program abnormally ends, and so on. They further need to ensure that inappropriate shortcuts are not taken during development and that the details of the conversion from the old to the new system have been conceived appropriately. These issues are particularly complex if an external package is sourced.

Externally Sourced Services—Pressures and Challenges

The shift from in-house software construction managed by IT staff to today's great reliance on purchased software and service is not surprising. While the supply and performance of inexpensive hardware have been growing dramatically, the human resources devoted to developing corresponding software have remained relatively constant. Neither user-oriented programming languages nor programmer "workbench" and other efficiency aids have fully addressed the problem of resource shortage. Consequently, salaries for skilled people have increased significantly.

In response to these two trends, a large market has developed for software developed by outside firms. These firms are able to provide reliable products at significantly lower user cost by spreading their costs over many users. The industry was born when software vendors developed complex technical software to support the operation of computers (operating systems, database handlers, inquiry languages, etc.). Vendor software, however, has now effectively moved "downstream" to products such as standard user-oriented software services including payroll and accounting packages, report writers, procedural language, computer-aided software engineering (CASE), and so on. Finally as noted earlier, the out sourcing of the entire IT operations function is being widely discussed as a way of allowing firms to concentrate their energies on things they believe will make a real difference.

Challenges.   Purchased systems potentially generate special problems for IT operations management. These problems are particularly complex if the user has full authority to purchase and operate the new service while the IT operations department must maintain and operate other services and at the same time ensure their compatibility with the new service. Potential loss of sole control of operations poses four key challenges to IT operations management:

1. How to maintain existing services while building appropriate and necessary data bridges to the new ones in order to integrate them with existing services where needed.
2. How to evolve the IT operations organization from primarily an integrated data processing system to a series of services for the specific needs of various users and then to neutralize users' desire for independent operations in cases where it does not make sense.
3. How to educate the user about the real operational problems and issues associated with the systems under their control. (Early successful user independence has very often led to long-term operating problems.)
4. How to help users manage vendor relationships in order to protect the company against ill-advised changes to software that can hurt operations. (The 1986 announcement of the incompatibility of Lotus 1-2-3 Release 2.0 with the previous versions of Lotus 1-2-3 illustrates this type of problem.)

Individual skill levels and perspectives of IT operations managers further complicate these problems. Many of them are accustomed to exercising total control over operations while sharing control over selection and implementation of maintenance changes with users. They must now learn to share control of operations, and it has been very difficult for some. Evidence of this failure to adapt is provided by the many organizations that, because of senior management frustration over IT's unresponsiveness, have given users total authority for purchased services acquisition and operation.

External Facilities Management Firms. Out sourcing the entire operations activity to facilities management firms is an important trend. Companies such as Electronic Data Systems (EDS) for Blue Cross/Blue Shield and state and local governments and Computer Science Corporation (CSC) for General Dynamics (a $3 billion–10-year contract) have created major market positions in the past decade. Companies such as Eastman Kodak have turned over major pieces of their operation to IBM and Digital Equipment Corporation (DEC). The key reasons for this movement include:

1. A desire to concentrate the company's energy around core missions or critical technologies (such as chemical engineering for a chemical company) and delegate responsibility for managing and staying abreast of other technologies to outsiders.
2. The need to both reduce costs and implement mechanisms for controlling cost growth. Many internal charge-out systems have associated with them a flavor of "funny money" that arm's-length contracts between independent firms do not have. For example, imagine that an internal user has a sudden systems desire and is

told that it is feasible but will cost $50,000. This figure will be much more sobering if it comes from a third party.

3. The desire of professional staff for meaningful careers. Small and mid-sized firms, in particular, cannot provide the richness of job positions that make for interesting careers and opportunities for self-renewal. Facilities management firms have this capability.

4. The salary caps particularly prevalent in civil service positions often make it impossible to attract and maintain the staff skill sets needed. Out sourcing allows an organization to sidestep this issue.

5. Out sourcing is an attractive way to "shake up" a troubled or frozen IT organization. Organizations have used intelligently planned outsourcing approaches successfully to clean up and reprofessionalize their operation; after three to four years they have insourced.

6. Out sourcing can help a company work through a complex conversion scenario, where extraordinary skills are needed for a defined period of time.

Where these discussions are made in the corporation and the intensity of investigations brought to them depend critically on the strategic dependence on the technology and its future strategic impact. The chief information officer and the chief financial officer together can structure and approve the out sourcing for a predominantly "support" unit, as was done by a university for its back-office administrative activities. When a major bank recently out sourced a major piece of its operations activity, it was a matter of intense board-of-directors concern and CEO involvement. A critical part of the firm's daily operations and product innovation capability was being delegated to an outsider in the expectation that it could do a better job of controlling it.

Potential Problems.   The potential problems with these arrangements are similar to those with a marriage. It is easier to enter the relationship than to exit it. The critical issues revolve around the following:

1. *Vendor viability* and its ability to renew itself. Financial failure of the vendor or deterioration of its service may cause deep problems, in some cases triggering large emergency investment in an operation the firm had no desire to invest in.

2. *Cost* that becomes more aggressive each year. The cost of moving out of the out sourcing arrangement can be so traumatic and expensive that there is a tendency to "ride along" for a while. Good initial contracting can alleviate this problem.

3. A *relationship* that becomes confrontational over time. With cash always passing hands between two profit-making entities, extraordinary efforts are required to ensure that a feeling of partnership develops and is maintained. If small incidents are not carefully managed, they can become cause célèbres. An understanding of the operational culture of the party providing the service is crucial in

assessing whether it is likely to be successful. These are long-term relationships, usually ten years; three successful years do not guarantee seven more successful years.

4. *Dissolving* the relationship. This can take a long time. It is crucial that mutual obligations during this stage of the relationship be carefully spelled out in advance, as this is where things can really go wrong. Realistically, however, with no anticipated future revenues, the service firm's professionalism and its concern for its reputation will be what you are depending on.

In short, out sourcing is not a panacea. While solving one set of problems, another potential set will surely come trailing in its wake.

TECHNOLOGY PLANNING

Technology planning for operations is a process of ongoing review of potential obsolescence and of opportunities. The scope and effort of this review should be determined by the nature of the business and the state of IT: for a bank it should be across many technologies and be very extensive; a mail-order business may concentrate on office support technology; a wholesale distributor may primarily focus on computing and telecommunications technologies. To be effective, the review must involve high-caliber, imaginative staff. (The role of the emerging technologies department was discussed in Chapter 8.) It should regard today's IT possibilities in the context of the potential available two or three years in the future. This potential must be based on technological forecasting.

If a company is trying to distinguish itself from the competition with its application of information technologies, the resources focused on technological planning should be quite extensive. If a firm is trying to just stay even with competitors and sees its IT activity primarily as "support," simple comparison with the operations of competitors or leaders in particular fields may be sufficient. Some firms periodically solicit bids from different vendors to help ensure that their IT department is fully up-to-date. For example, a large insurance company whose IT department is dominated by the technology of one vendor has annually asked a competitor of the vendor to bid an alternative system, even though they have not perceived a need for change. As a result of these bids, however, they recently switched to another vendor's minicomputers, and on another occasion they installed a large machine purchased from a different vendor. These moves have kept the annual bidding process honest.

The objective of the review is to determine—relative to available and announced systems—how cost-effective and adequate for growth the existing installed technologies are. The review should generate an

FIGURE 11–1   Forces to Be Managed in IT Innovation

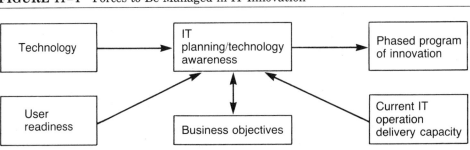

updated priority list of technologies to be considered as replacements. Such lead time is critical; technology replacements or additions that are planned two years in advance cause a small fraction of the disruption that those planned only six months in advance do. (Realistically, of course, breakthrough announcements limit the precision of advance planning.) In order to better define the architecture of the future information service, the planning activity should include field trips to vendors, education sessions, and pilot studies as vehicles for obtaining an understanding of emerging technologies.

A useful approach to a technology review is to categorize the applications portfolio of operations systems by length of time since development or last total rewrite of each system. The finding that a significant percentage of the IT systems were designed a decade or more ago often indicates that a major redesign and rewrite will offer great opportunities for reduced maintenance and improved operational efficiency.[1] When a large international bank recently performed such a review, it discovered that 60 percent of its CPU utilization and 50 percent of its systems effort were devoted to maintaining and running transaction processing systems constructed in the second era (Figure 1–1).

The implementation of new technology may be transparent to the user if it involves hardware replacement or new systems that use existing hardware more effectively. Other replacement technology, however, affects users consciously by providing different or improved service—as do report writers for databases or new terminals. These technologies basically support users, rather than change their operations style. Still other replacement technologies impact user habits so dramatically that if success is to be achieved, user leadership must

---

[1]Martin Buss, "Penny-Wise Approach to Data Processing," *Harvard Business Review,* July–August 1981.

drive the implementation effort. Each implementation situation requires careful planning to ensure that service is not interrupted and that the affected individuals understand how to operate with the new service. Figure 11–1 summarizes the tensions and forces that must be managed in IT innovation.

Good technology planning includes an ongoing appraisal of user readiness, an inventory of the uses of existing technology, an awareness of where technology is going, and a program of appropriate pilot technology projects. A large consumer products company, for example, has an IT unit with a very strong emerging-technology group. As part of their activity they maintain for each division and function an updated log of services in use and an assessment of current problems. They are currently introducing a program of office support that includes a large portfolio of applications in a pilot division. Their detailed program for this division, scheduled over 24 months, includes benchmarks and reviews for evaluating benefits, operating problems, and progress. Such pilot testing stimulates broader organizational awareness of the opportunities and operational issues associated with new technology and permits better planning for full-scale implementation in the other divisions.

MEASURING AND MANAGING CAPACITY

The less one knows about computer hardware/software/networking technology, the more certain one tends to be in matters of capacity. In reality, the various hardware/software/network elements tend to interact in such a complex way that diagnosing bottlenecks and planning long-term capacity require a high degree of skill. To understand capacity and its key changeability, we must consider these factors:

1. Capacity comes in much smaller, less-expensive increments than it did a decade ago. In many organizations this has created an "asymmetric reward structure" for capacity excesses versus shortages; that is, a shortage of capacity in critical operating periods is very expensive, while the cost of extra capacity is very low. For these organizations, a decision to carry excess capacity is sound.
2. A capacity "crunch" develops with devastating suddenness. During one six-month period a mid-sized sign manufacturer operated with few difficulties with a 77 percent load on the central processing unit (CPU) during peak demand. Senior management refused to listen to IT management's warning that they were on the edge of a crisis and would not permit IT management to order additional equipment. During the next six months the introduction of two new minor systems and the acquisition of a major contract brought the CPU

load during the first shift to 85 percent. This created a dramatic erosion in on-line systems response time and a steady stream of missed schedules on the batch systems. Working through weekends and holidays failed to alleviate the situation. To the untutored eye, the transition from a satisfactory to a thoroughly unsatisfactory situation occurs suddenly and dramatically.

3. There has been an explosion of diagnostic tools, such as hardware and software monitors, that assist in identifying systems' capacity problems. These tools are analytical devices and thus are no better than the ability of the analyst using them and the quality of the forecasts of future demands to be placed on the systems. In firms where operations play a vital role, these tools and their contributions have led to significant growth in both the number and quality of technical analysts in the IT operations group.

4. A dramatic increase has occurred in the number of suppliers of computer peripherals. This has sharply reduced the number of firms that are totally committed to a single vendor's equipment. Additional features, coupled with attractive prices of specialist manufacturers, have pushed many firms in the direction of IT vendor proliferation. Combined with the integration of telecommunications and office support, this phenomenon makes the task of capacity planning more complex and increases the need to referee vendor disputes when the firm's network fails.

5. Complex trade-offs must be made between innovation and conservatism. Companies in which IT offers *significant* (in terms of overall company profitability) cost reductions or the possibility of significant strategic competitive advantage should push innovation much harder than other firms. Similarly, firms that are very dependent on smooth minute-to-minute operation of existing systems must be more careful about introducing new technology into a network than other firms. Unanticipated interaction with existing systems could jeopardize reliable operation of key parts of the organization. (That was at the root of the AT&T network collapse noted at the beginning of the chapter. Inadequately tested switching software at one AT&T node interacted in an unexpected way with the rest of the network's software.)

6. The cost and disruption caused by change may outweigh the specific advantages associated with a particular technology. Therefore, skipping a generation of change is desirable in some circumstances. This must be examined carefully from two perspectives:

   a. The system design practices of the 1960s and early 1970s were quite different from those of today. Some firms, anxious to postpone investment, have stayed too long with the older systems and have exposed themselves to great operational risk when they have tried to implement massive change in impossibly short periods of time. In many cases the results have been disastrous. (These time pressures were triggered either by external vendor decommitment of key components of an operating hardware/software configuration *or* an urgent need to modify software drastically to meet new competitive needs.) Software, like a building, depreciates. Because industry accounting practices, except for those of software companies, do not recognize this, it is very easy for general managers to overlook the problems of this aging asset. Fundamentally, too many operating managers mistakenly think of IT development as an *annual* operating expense as opposed to a capital investment or asset maintenance activity.

b. Certain changes in the hardware/software configuration are critical if the firm is to be competitive; other changes cannot legitimately be considered essential. Investments in this latter category clearly can be postponed.

7. As investments in the products of small software and hardware vendors increases, the issues of vendor viability and product maintainability become important. The mortality rate among these small suppliers has been high since the early 1970s. In evaluating hardware vendors the issues are, If they go under, is there an acceptable, easily convertible alternative; Is it easy to keep existing systems going in both the short term and the long term; and, What are the likely costs of these alternatives? In evaluating software vendors the question is, Does the contract provide for access to source programs and documentation if the vendor goes out of business? An additional area of complexity is the vendor's posture toward program maintenance. This includes error correction and systems enhancements. How will these changes be charged? As noted earlier, experienced IT operations thinking is critical in these negotiations. Very unhappy outcomes have all too often ensued when either the user or the systems and programming department purchased software without understanding the long-term operating implications.

8. Finally, a hidden set of capacity decisions focuses on appropriate infrastructure backup—such as power, height above the flood plain, and adequate building strength for the weight of the equipment. The importance of the reliability of these items is often underassessed. For example, the temperature in a large metropolitan data center rose from 78 degrees to 90 degrees in a two-hour period, shutting down the entire operation. A frantic investigation finally found that three floors down a plumber had mistakenly cut off a valve essential to the cooling system room.

These points clearly show that capacity planning is a very complex subject that requires as much administrative thinking as technical thinking. Few organizations in the 1990s are building a new "factory" but, rather, they are implementing a continuous program of renovation and modernization on the factory floor while maintaining full production on the assembly line. This is a formidable and, unfortunately, often seriously underestimated task.

MANAGING THE IT OPERATIONS WORK FORCE

The personnel issues in the operations function have changed significantly in the past few years. Most dramatic has been the major reduction, and in *many* cases elimination, of the data input and preparation departments. The introduction of on-line data entry has not only changed the type of tasks to be done (keypunching, key verification, job-logging procedures, etc.), but has permitted much of this work to be transferred to the department that originates the transaction. Indeed the work is often transferred to the person who initiates the transaction or it is a by-product of another activity (such as cash register sales of bar-coded items). This is a desirable trend because it locates control firmly with the person most directly involved and it reduces costs. In some settings, however, it has been exceptionally difficult to implement, with users proving to be less enthusiastic than anticipated about taking over this accountability. In general, however, the large centralized data entry departments have faded into history.

At the same time, the jobs in the computer operations section are being altered significantly. For example,

1. Database-handling jobs are steadily being automated. The mounting of tapes and disks is automated and reduced. Many firms have successfully automated the entire tape library function. Further, as cathode-ray tubes (CRTs) have exploded in popularity, the amount of paper handling at the IT operations center has been reduced. It is likely that image processing will further impact this. The "lights-out factory" is becoming reality. (The wide use of facsimile machines and desktop printers is contributing to the good health of the paper industry.)
2. The formerly manual functions of expediting and scheduling have been built into the computer's basic operating system, eliminating a class of jobs.
3. Consolidation of data centers allows significant staff reductions as well as reductions in software site rentals. A recent consolidation of 10 large data centers reduced staff from 720 to 380.
4. The establishment of work performance standards in this environment has become less feasible and less useful. As the data input function disappears and the machine schedules itself rather than

being paced by the operator's performance, the time-and-motion performance standards of the 1960s and 1970s have become largely irrelevant. Inevitably, evaluating the performance of the remaining highly technical individuals has become more subjective. These people are either trouble-shooting problems or executing complex operating systems and facilities changes.

As these factors indicate, the composition of the operations work force has changed dramatically. The blue-collar component has been significantly reduced, while the technical and professional components have been increased significantly. In an environment of continuous technological change, the skills of these staff must continually be upgraded if they are to remain relevant.

Career Paths.   In this environment, career path planning is a particular challenge. At present, three major avenues are available for professionals. Those with technical aptitude tend to move to positions in either technical support or systems development. A common exit point for console operators is as maintenance programmers. As a result of operations experience, they have developed a keen sensitivity to the need for thorough testing of systems changes. The second avenue is a position as a manager in operations, particularly in large shops where management positions ranging from shift supervisors to operations managers are filled mostly through internal promotions. (The number of these jobs, however, is steadily decreasing.) Finally, in banks and insurance companies in particular there have been a number of promotions out of IT operations into other user positions in the firm. In the manufacturing sector this avenue of opportunity is especially rare. Any of these promotion paths, if given the proper attention, can make the operations environment an attractive, dynamic place to work.

Unionization.   Although the trade union movement has been relatively inactive in the U.S. IT environment, it has been quite active in Europe and portions of western Canada. Organizing this department gives the union great leverage in many settings, because a strike by a small number of individuals can virtually paralyze an organization. For example, strikes of small numbers of computer operations staff in the United Kingdom's Inland Revenue Service have caused enormous disruptions in its day-to-day operations in the past. Changes in the skill mix that favor highly professional and technical staff suggest that this concern will be less important in the future.

In thinking about the potential impact of unionization, these points are important:

1. The number of blue-collar jobs susceptible to unionization has dropped dramatically. IT shops were more vulnerable to being or-

ganized in the technology of the past generation than in the current or future generations.

2. The creation of multiple data centers in diverse locations tends to reduce a firm's vulnerability to a strike in one location. The networks of the future will reduce the risk even further. This has been a factor, although generally not the dominant one, in some moves toward distributed processing.

3. The inflexibilities that accompany unionization can pose enormous problems in this type of manufacturing organization given the frequency and unpredictability of operating problems and the need for high-technology skills. Further, the dynamics of technical change continuously transform IT operating functions and jobs. If the technology were ever to stabilize, the inflexibilities presented by organized labor would be of less concern.

Selection Factors for Operations Manager and Staff

Selecting the appropriate IT operations manager and key staff is crucial. Several factors generate the need for particular skills in different environments.

Scope of Activities. As scope widens from on-line satellite to knowledge-based systems, the IT activity demands greater diversity of staff, and the complexity of management increases dramatically. Significantly more sophisticated managerial skills are required.

Criticality of IT Operations Unit. Firms that are heavily dependent on IT operations ("factory" and "strategic") are forced to devote higher-caliber professional staff resources to this area. Uneven quality of support is very expensive for such companies.

Technical Sophistication of the Shop. A shop that is heavily devoted to batch-type operations (there are still some around) with a relatively predictable workload and a nondynamic hardware/software configuration requires less investment in leading-edge management than does a shop with a rapidly changing workload in a volatile technical environment. The latter type of shop requires staff who can effectively lead such efforts as upgrading operating systems.

These factors suggest the impossibility of describing a general-purpose IT operations manager. Not only do different environments require different skills, but over time the requirements within an individual unit shift. The overall trend of the last decade is toward demand for an even higher quality of manager. The tape handler or console operator of the early 1970s has often proven inadequate for the job.

Human Issues in Managing the Work Force

A series of long-term human issues must be dealt with in managing the work force effectively.

1. The problem of staff availability and quality is a long-term challenge for IT operations. In an environment where small numbers of highly skilled workers are needed, intensified efforts are needed to attract quality individuals to the IT operations group. Career paths and salary levels require continuous reappraisal. In "factory" and "strategic" companies, IT operations must not be treated as an unwanted "stepchild" of the development group.

2. IT operations must develop appropriate links to both the users and the development group. The linkage to development is needed for ensuring that standards are in place so that both new systems and enhancements to existing ones are operable (without the development staff being present or on call every time the system is run) and that no unintended interactions with other programs and data files occur. Establishing a formal IT operations quality assurance function is a common way to deal with this. No system is allowed to run on the network until it has been certified by the IT operations unit as meeting the company's standards. The user linkage is critical for ensuring that when an operating problem occurs the user knows who in the IT operations unit can solve it—and for avoiding endless rounds of finger pointing.

3. A long-term IT operations staff development plan that includes specific attention to training needs needs to be generated.

4. Issues concerning the quality of work life must be addressed continuously. These include such items as flexible time, three- or four-day workweeks, shift rotation, and so on.

No single ideal policy or procedure can address these issues. Rather, a continuous reassessment must occur to ensure that the best of current practice is being examined and that the unit does not inadvertently become frozen in obsolete work practices.

PRODUCTION PLANNING AND CONTROL

Setting Goals

Operations production planning is complicated by the multitude of goals an IT operations function may have. Among the most common goals are these:

- To ensure a high-quality, zero-defect operation. All transactions will be handled correctly, no reports will be lost or missent, and so forth.

- To meet all long-term job schedules (or to meet them within some standard).
- To be able to handle unanticipated, unscheduled jobs, processing them within x minutes or hours of receipt provided they do not consume more than 1 percent of the CPU resource.
- To provide an average response time on terminals for key applications during the first shift of x seconds. No more than 1 percent of transactions will require more than y seconds.
- To limit day-to-day operating costs to specified given levels. Capital expenditure for IT equipment will not exceed the budgeted levels.

Establishing Priorities

By and large IT operations goals are mutually conflicting, in that all of them cannot be optimized simultaneously. For companies where IT operations support is critical to achieving corporate missions ("factory" and "strategic"), establishment of priorities requires senior management guidance. In environments where it is less critical, these goals can be prioritized at a lower level. Failure to set priorities in a manner that makes for widespread concurrence and understanding of the trade-offs to be made has been a primary cause of the poor regard in which some operations units have been held. When their goals were not prioritized, their task has been impossible.

A firm's priorities give insight into how the firm should address two other items, organization of the capacity and ensuring consistent operating policies.

Organization of Capacity. Whether to have a single, integrated computer configuration or a series of modular units either within a single data center or in multiple data centers is an important strategic decision—assuming the nature of the workload allows a choice. Setting up modular units ("plants within a plant," at some cost) allows specialized delivery of service for different applications and users. These multiple factories also allow for simpler operating systems and for quite different types of performance measures and management styles to be implemented for each. This focused factory concept has been too often overlooked in IT operations.

Consistent Operating Policies. Uncoordinated management specialists, each trying to optimize his or her own function, may create a thoroughly inconsistent and ineffective environment. For example, in a large insurance company the following policies were simultaneously operational:

- An operator wage and incentive system based on meeting all long-term schedules and minimizing job setup time.

- A production control system that gave priority to quick-turnaround, small-batch jobs that met certain technical characteristics.
- A quality control system that focused on zero defects, ensuring that no reruns would have to take place.
- A management control system that rewarded both low operating budgets and low variances from the operating budgets. Among other things, this control incentive had pushed the company toward a very constrained facilities layout as a means of minimizing costs.

While each of the policies could have made sense individually, collectively they were totally inconsistent and created tension and friction within the IT operations group. Not surprisingly, the key users' perceptions of service varied widely.

Strategic Impact of IT Operations

The management focus brought to IT operations depends on the IT function's role in the firm. IT operations in the "support" and "turnaround" categories can appropriately be oriented toward cost-efficiency. Deadlines, while important to meet, are not absolutely critical to these organizations' success. Quality control, while important on the error dimension, can be dealt with in a more relaxed way. It is appropriate to take more risks on the capacity dimension for both job-shop and process-type IT operations in order to reduce the firm's financial investment. Less formal, less expensive backup arrangements are also appropriate. Finally, corners can safely be cut in user-complaint response mechanisms.

The "factory" type of operation poses very different challenges, because IT is integrally woven into the ongoing fabric of the company's operations. Zero-defect accuracy, fast response time, and prompt schedule meeting are absolutely critical. Capacity to meet various contingencies is critical, because severe competitive damage may occur otherwise. Consequently, the issue of capacity needs to be managed more carefully and more reserve capacity for contingencies usually needs to be acquired. New operating systems and hardware enhancements must be very carefully evaluated and managed to avoid the danger and financial damage of downtime. These factors cause a company to make any necessary cost-reduction decisions more carefully than in organizations less dependent on IT service.

The "strategic" operation faces all the issues of the "factory" operation plus several others. Capacity planning is more complicated because it involves major new services, not simply extrapolating figures for old services with new volume forecasts. A stronger liaison must be maintained with users in order to deal with the potential service disruptions associated with adding new technology and new families of applications. These factors suggest the need for more slack in both capacity and budget to protect vital corporate interests.

Implementing Production Control and Measurement

The issues raised in the previous section show why only an evolutionary, adaptive control and reporting structure will work. The indexes, standards, and controls that fit one organization at a particular time will not meet their own or other organizations' needs over an extended period of time as both the technology and the organization evolve more toward on-line systems.

Within the appropriate goals for the operations department, there is a critical need to establish both performance indexes and performance standards. This allows actual data to be compared against standards. Performance indexes should include items in the following areas:

- Cost performance, both aggregate performance and the performance for different IT services.
- Staff turnover rates.
- Average and worst 5 percent response times for different services.
- Quality of service indicators, such as amount of system downtime, by service.
- Number of user complaints, by service.
- Number of misrouted reports and incorrect outputs.
- Usage of services—such as word processing, electronic mail, and computer utilization—and peak hours.
- Surveys of user satisfaction with service.

While the data generated may be quite voluminous, the data (including trends) should be summarizable in a one- to two-page report each week or month. Such quantitative data provide a framework for making qualitative assessments of performance against the standards that reflect the department's goals.

SECURITY

One of the emotional topics related to IT operations is how much security is needed for protecting the site and how much actually exists. This complex subject is discussed only briefly here in order to call attention to the nature and importance of security. Exhaustively covered in other sources, the breadth of the issue is defined by the following points:

1. Perfect security is unattainable at any price. The key need is to determine the point of diminishing returns for an organization's particular mission and geography. Different units in the organization and different systems may have distinctly different security requirements.

2. Smaller organizations for which the IT activity is critical have found it desirable to go to something like the SUNGUARD solution, by which consortium of firms has funded the construction and equipping of an empty data center. If a member firm incurs a major disaster, this site is available for use.

3. Large organizations for which IT activity is fundamental to their functioning and existence appropriately will think about this differently. Such firms will be strongly motivated to establish multiple remote centers (to avoid the investment bank's experience explained in the first example at the beginning of the chapter). Duplicate data files, extra telecommunications expense, and duplicate staff and office space all make this an expensive (although necessary) security measure. These firms have come to the conclusion that if they do not back themselves up, no one else will. The architecture of these networks is extraordinarily complex to design in an efficient yet responsive fashion.

4. For organizations in which the IT operation is less critical, appropriate steps may include arranging backup with another organization. (This sounds simpler in theory than it is in reality.) Another alternative is to prepare a warehouse site with appropriate wiring, telephone lines, air conditioning, and so on. (In a real emergency, locating and installing the computer is the easiest thing to do. Locating and installing all the other items consumes much more time.) Backing up the network is much more complex than just data centers. The insurance company in the example at the beginning of the chapter now has two entirely separate networks with two carriers and carefully allocates work between them in order to reduce their operational vulnerability. Reuters news service has processing nodes around the world with multiple paths out of each node. If one path fails, the network is unimpacted; if a node fails, the network degrades but does not fail in all respects.

5. Within a single site, a number of steps can be taken to improve security. Listed here are some of the most common, each of which has a different cost associated with it.

   a. Limiting physical access to the computer room. Methods from simple buzzers to isolated "diving chamber" entrances can be used.

   b. Complex access codes that serve to deny file and system entry to unauthorized personnel. External Hackers have successfully penetrated a large number of organizations who have not paid attention to this item.

   c. Surrounding the data center with chain-link fences, automatic alarms, and dogs. Monitoring access to inner areas by guards using remote TV cameras.

   d. Ensuring an uninterrupted power supply, including banks of batteries and stand-alone generators.

   e. Storing a significant number of files off-site and updating them with a high level of frequency.

   f. Use of a Halon inert gas system to protect the installation in case of fire.

   g. Systematic rotation of people through jobs, enforcement of mandatory vacations (with no entry to building allowed during vacation time), and physical separation of IT development and operations staff.

This is merely an illustrative list and in no sense is intended to be comprehensive. Sadly, it is extremely difficult to fully secure files in a world of PCs, viruses, and floppy disks that go home at night.

PRIVACY

An explosive issue that cuts across the IT applications world of the 1990s is that of the increasingly intrusive role of IT on individual privacy. This issue transcends all aspects of the field of information technology and is included in this chapter only as a matter of organizational convenience. Consider the following examples.

- A consumer foods company uses information from redeemed coupons and rebate forms to create a database for targeted marketing. It is assailed in a national consumer-advocacy publication with the headline "Smile—You're on Corporate Camera!"
- An entrepreneur realizes that he can easily tie together several credit-bureau databases and some other sources of information (such as motor vehicle records) about individuals. When he begins to market this service to small businesses for credit checking and pre-employment screening, the state assembly passes a bill that would significantly regulate his activities.
- Many credit bureaus offer services in which mailing lists are "pre-screened" according to a customer's stated criteria. In addition, some credit bureaus transfer selected information from their credit files to marketing databases, from which mailing lists are sold for targeted marketing. These policies became major topics of discussion in a House of Representatives subcommittee hearing, where there were many calls for additional federal legislation.

These examples—all of which occurred in 1990—demonstrate an increasing challenge to managers for the 1990s. Societal concerns about information privacy—the belief that limits are needed on access to information about individuals—are increasing, and these concerns could erupt in the next decade with considerable force. Unless proactive steps are taken, firms will find themselves grappling with these societal anxieties in two forms: public-opinion backlash against various computerized processes, and a tightened legal environment with additional governmental control.

The Roots of the Privacy Issue

Two forces are behind this focus on privacy in the 1990s: the new technology capabilities that allow these new applications and the vacuum surrounding the distinction between "right and wrong."

Technological Capabilities.   Much more information is in computer-processable form today. Information that was previously stored in hand-written or typed paper files is now digitally encoded and electronically accessible from thousands of miles away.

Owing to less-expensive storage devices, faster processors, and the development of relational database techniques and structured query languages, it has become both more feasible and vastly more economical to cross-classify information. Likewise, passing and correlating information between organizations is now relatively inexpensive and easy to accomplish. As networks become commonplace, new strategic applications pool data from different sources.

In addition to the problem of potential intrusiveness of this pooling, there is also the almost unsolvable issue of correcting errors in information. In many cases, it is virtually impossible to stop the trickle of errors as data pass from firm to firm.

Not only have the speed and cost of computing undergone phenomenal improvements in the last decade, but the trend is accelerating. Thus, in the future it will be even easier and more economical to search for information and store it. As personal computers and local-area networks proliferate across organizations in the hands of nonsystems personnel, people will propagate uncontrolled databases (on personal hard disks and file servers), and the number of people accessing networks will increase.

Add to this the growing use of artificial intelligence. As more decision rules are automated in expert systems, perceptions of these problems may be amplified as mistakes are inexorably carried to their logical conclusion in a documented form.

Taken together, these technological trends could easily and inexpensively lead to applications that would create unacceptable intrusions into people's privacy.

Ethical Concerns.   The technological forces operate in a large vacuum regarding right and wrong. Situations have been created for which the rules of behavior that worked well in earlier decades do not offer meaningful guidance. We are confronting a new set of policy decisions. While it is true that individuals and organizations may be inappropriately harmed by certain applications and activities, the degree of the impact is uneven. Some practices can be deeply damaging to people, while many others lie in the category of "merely inconvenient." Some inconvenient results of increased information gathering—such as mailbox clutter—are accepted by many as the "cost of progress," but society will eventually draw a line to protect against other applications that are recognized as more damaging.

For example, tenant-screening services, which allow landlords to exchange information about problems with former tenants, can lead to the unjust refusal of an individual's rental application if incorrect information is in the database or if mistaken identification occurs.[2] More often than not, however, such services protect landlords from losses incurred in renting to tenants who have already proven to be bad risks, and they thereby facilitate lower rents. Will society demand that such screening services be restrained?

The Implications

Questions for Organizations.   Firms must anticipate potential privacy problems as they make decisions and take action to avoid negative public opinion and extreme legislative responses to inflammatory charges. Good planning may help your firm avoid the cost of adapting to new rules. Some critical questions regarding privacy issues are discussed here.

Storage of Information.   Is there any information in the organization's files that should not be there? If it were brought to light that such information was being collected and stored, would there be a public backlash? For example, several insurance firms have recently struggled with this issue as it applies to AIDS test results, and where and how this information should be disseminated. Some advocates became outraged when they learned that individuals' files contained notations about positive test results. Lawsuits and numerous pieces of legislation (mostly at a state level) followed quickly.

Use of Information.   Is information being used for the purposes individuals believed it was being collected to serve? Many individuals who provide information for what they believe is one purpose become angry when they learn it has been used for a different purpose. For

---

[2]Some of the examples used here are adapted from *The Privacy Journal,* an independent monthly newsletter based in Washington, D.C.

example, a credit-card issuer came under legal scrutiny when it installed a computer system that could evaluate cardholders' purchasing histories for the purpose of enclosing targeted advertising material with their monthly statements. In another example, a car dealership installed an interactive computer system that asked potential customers to answer questions about their personalities and attitudes. The computer printed a "recommended car profile" for each customer. It *also* printed—with a different printer, in a back room—suggested sales strategy for the salesperson based on the customer's answers. Had the potential customers known about this back-room printer, they might never have entered the dealer's showroom.

Sharing of Information. *Are pieces of information about individuals being shared electronically with other organizations? If so, would individuals approve of this sharing if they knew about it?* Certainly, extraordinary opportunities for gaining strategic advantage have come through such sharing activities (micromarketing strategies). However, some individuals object when a company with which they do business sells their names and addresses, purchasing histories, and other demographic details to other companies. If the shared information is highly sensitive—if, for example, it concerns individuals' medical or financial histories—the reaction to having it shared—sold even—is dramatically exacerbated.

Human Judgment. *Are decisions that require human judgment being made within appropriate processes?* Individuals legitimately become upset and request governmental protection when decisions that they feel require human judgment are being made without it. For example, an insurance company's decisions on whether to accept or reject new applicants—made within prescribed formulas and without direct human involvement—caused considerable difficulties when blindly applied in extraordinary situations that had not been contemplated when the rules were formulated.

Combining Information. *Are pieces of personal information from different sources combined into larger files?* The concerns of individuals and lawmakers are heightened when disparate pieces of information—even if innocuous in themselves—are pulled together. The possibility of creating a single profile of an individual's life is, to many, a threatening prospect. The entrepreneur who tied together several databases in order to provide "one-stop shopping" for several types of information through one vehicle faced this perception.

Error Detection and Correction. *Are appropriate procedures in place for preventing and correcting errors?* At issue here are both deliberate and inadvertent errors. Deliberate errors, which include unauthorized intrusions into databases, are often subject to audit controls. Inadvertent errors, on the other hand, are much more subtle and stubborn. They include misclassifications, data-entry errors, and the sorts of errors that arise when information is not updated as circumstances in people's lives change. It is impossible to achieve 100 percent error-free operation, but observers may reasonably ask whether the trade-offs a company makes for assuring accuracy are reasonable. *If your organization were examined by lawmakers or consumer advocates, would you appear to be making the "correct" trade-offs?*

An example from the public sector centers on the National Crime Information Center, a nationwide computer system that is linked to many state criminal-justice information systems. Outstanding warrants, parole violations, and other criminal data are often entered into local systems and are later "uploaded" to the national system. Law-enforcement agencies can then query the system to learn if individuals are wanted in other areas. Unfortunately, for a long period of time, problems with inaccurate data and mistaken identities were not uncommon. These problems led to improper arrests and incarcerations, and a number of lawsuits were filed.

Other Issues.   An audit of the questions we have enumerated often reveals several items for action in the organization. Additional issues to be considered by firms include the following:

Long Term versus Short Term.   Line management should carefully think through each new use of information before they embrace it. In some cases, a "quick hit" for short-term profitability can yield disastrous results later. For example, an insurance company sold a list of its policyholders to a direct-marketing firm, earning a healthy fee. However, many policyholders determined that the company had done this—because of unique spellings of their names and other peculiarities—and were unhappy about it. The company received an avalanche of mail complaining about this use of their names and addresses, as well as a nontrivial number of policy cancellations, which brought the CEO to vow "never again." The short-term gain was not worth the long-term fallout.

Education.   Problems can be avoided through appropriate education initiatives. An organization's clients (customers or other individuals about whom information is stored) should be informed regarding the corporation's use of information about them when it strays from the narrow purpose for which it was collected. Clients should be told (1) the type of information about them that is permanently stored in the corporation's files, (2) what is done with the information they provide, and (3) whether additional information from external sources is added to their files. This education process can take place in several forums, including inserts with monthly statements, special letters, and press releases. Corporations in particularly sensitive industries might provide toll-free telephone lines for clients' questions about information use.

Organizational Mechanism.   Through both an initial audit and on a continuing basis, the internal and external uses and distribution of data should be given close scrutiny—especially if the firm is in an industry where such data sharing is likely to occur, such as consumer marketing or financial services. In very sensitive situations, a standing "Data Distribution Committee" can provide a forum for evaluating these issues. Such a committee should have high visibility and comprise senior executives. It could also be augmented by outside advisers (such as corporate directors) to ensure that objective viewpoints are provided and that problems are approached with sufficient breadth.

As laws and public opinion change in the next decade, it will be necessary to check current and planned applications against evolving policies and attitudes. Data files should be organized in ways that facilitate such ad hoc evaluations. For example, one might be called upon to list all data elements that are exchanged between internal organizational entities and with external entities. Could your organization construct this list in a quick and credible way?

Conclusions. Our discussion of these issues indicates the complexity of the privacy concerns growing up around IT use. Chief information officers and other members of senior management should brace themselves for intense scrutiny of their activities by both legislators and privacy advocates. No doubt, there will be more focus on commercial IT activities than on governmental ones in the 1990s. The tension between the effective functioning of commerce and individuals' rights to privacy will certainly become more pronounced. It is far better for the business community to be taking a voluntary, proactive stance now than to have to adopt a reactive posture later.

SUMMARY

IT operations management is a complex, evolutionary field. This is partly due to a changing technology that continually makes obsolete existing IT service delivery processes and controls, partly due to the continuing questions related to in-house versus out sourcing of the service, and partly due to the changing profile of the IT work force. Major insights for dealing with these issues come from applying the understandings gained in managing technological change and manufacturing to this very special type of high-technology endeavor. Most large firms now know how to schedule and control multiprocessing batch computer systems working on numerical data from decentralized input stations. Building upon this base to include word processing, electronic mail, CAD, image processing, links to outside customers and suppliers, and a host of more decentralized IT activities is an extraordinarily challenging task. Underlying this, the most critical need for operations success is for recruiting, training, and retaining knowledgeable people to operate, maintain, and develop IT services. Finally of course, is the issue of privacy, what forms of Data Files should be kept, what forms of cross correlation are acceptable and who should have access to them.

Chapter 12

Transnational IT Issues

The head of Management Information Systems (MIS) of a major European research company suddenly discovered that three of its largest foreign subsidiaries had recently ordered medium-sized computers and were planning to move their work from the corporate IT department to installations in their respective countries. This would reduce the workload in the corporate data center by 45 percent. The reasons cited for the decision were that it would provide better control over day-to-day operations, offer more responsive service, and reduce costs. Located in a country with a small, high-cost labor pool, the MIS head was unsure of how to assess the risks this change posed to his operation and to the company as a whole.

A large pharmaceutical company's head of corporate IT recently held a three-day meeting of the IT heads of the company's 15 largest foreign subsidiaries. A major unresolved issue discussed at the meeting was the appropriate relationship of corporate IT to the more than 50 smaller foreign subsidiaries that also have computing equipment. Historically, the department has responded to requests for assistance (five to eight requests per year) but has not gone beyond that. The head of corporate IT is increasingly doubtful that this level of involvement is appropriate.

These stories are representative of a major, largely unreported, unstudied IT story; namely, that management of transnational IT support for any company is very complex and that its issues go well beyond legislation relating to transborder information flows. These issues have become more significant in the past decade as the post–World War II explosion of transnationals, in both numbers and scope, has continued. This growth has sparked the need for development and expansion of management systems that permit appropriate coordination of geographically distant business activities.

In the past, investigation of these issues has been neglected by two schools of thought. On the one hand, the area has seemed too specialized and technical to the scholars of international business. On the other hand, the scholars of information technology management have been highly national in their orientation, and so they, too, have tended to avoid transnational IT issues.

Transnational IT management is a major challenge today, and the need to resolve its issues is likely to grow rapidly in the coming years. Managing the forces (described as six "trends" in Chapter 2) driving transition in IT is complicated in the international arena by the wide diversity in national infrastructures (for example, those of Germany versus those of Sri Lanka), corporate manufacturing and distribution technologies, and scope and sophistication of IT applications. Building on the concepts of strategic relevance, culture, contingent planning, and managing diffusion of technology, this chapter focuses on aspects of transnational business that influence IT.

IT support coordination issues for international operations are vastly more complex than purely domestic ones, because they involve all the issues of domestic operations plus many additional difficulties. During the coming decade, IT will continue to be challenged by the opening of Eastern Europe to private enterprise, the need to share technologies within a firm for common problems around the world, and the continued evolution of transnational firms in both products and structure. The cross-border flows of goods and materials are accelerating, requiring new and complex information infrastructures. Financial and human resources for global operations require extremely coordinated management. Many firms have growing pools of staff that require extensive global coordination and development and their electronic support. Finally, technology skills, expertise, and intelligence all require much tighter coordination in the multinational realm. Information technology is central to accomplishing this.

Additional complexity is provided by the wide differences in culture, labor/technology costs, products, and need/viability of IT support in different areas of the world. A subsidiary in India, for example, with its cheap labor and marginal telecommunications, realistically poses fundamentally different integration issues than one in Singapore with its high-cost labor, high-quality telecommunications, and small geography. Additionally, recent technology advances that have impacted firms' overall organization structures now permit moving tasks around the globe while maintaining tighter control and facilitate new ways of defining and doing work.

The first section of this chapter describes the impact of IT on transnational firms. The second section deals with national characteristics that determine what type of IT support is both possible and appropriate for a firm's operations in a country. The third section explains IT environmental issues that influence how a firm can develop IT support in another country. The fourth section discusses company-specific issues that can help corporations develop and coordinate IT activity internationally. The final part describes some IT policies that firms have adopted and discusses the factors of their appropriateness in particular settings.

INFORMATION TECHNOLOGY IMPACT ON TRANSNATIONAL FIRMS

The new technologies of the past decade have affected the ways and places where firms do work in many ways, and their impact will be even greater in the coming decade, as the technologies evolve and firms gain experience in implementing the changes enabled by the technologies. Organization structures, control procedures, and tasks are being altered, albeit with great effort and expense.

Geographic Transfer of Work

The new technologies have facilitated the physical movement of work from areas with high-cost labor pools to areas where labor pools are both high quality and low cost. A domestic U.S. example of this is Citibank's move of its credit card operation from high-cost New York City to Sioux Falls, South Dakota. (Citibank achieved enormous savings.) In the same vein, American Airlines has moved a significant amount of its data entry work out of Dallas. Documents are now keyed in Barbados. The resulting outputs are transmitted electronically back to Dallas. Several years ago a U.S. insurance company developed a significant systems development and programming unit in Ireland. This allowed them to access the much less expensive, high-quality Irish labor pool, effecting important savings. An added bonus was that the firm was able to use the third shift of the domestic computer operations for debugging because of the five-hour time difference between Ireland and the United States. Similarly, a number of programming organizations have developed in the "free trade" zones of India that compete cost-effectively with Western Europe and American systems development activities, particularly for highly structured tasks.

In a world where the economy is increasingly service-oriented and where telecommunications costs continue to drop, these trends will accelerate. In this new transportable business world local tax authorities must avoid becoming too greedy lest big pieces of the economy will disappear overnight. Clerical and knowledge-based work is movable; office buildings and factories are not.

Global Networking and Expertise Sharing

Firms like IBM and Digital Equipment Corporation (DEC) have developed very sophisticated international electronic mail and conferencing procedures. Tens of thousands of professional support staff around the world now have direct electronic access to each other. Global sources of knowledge can be quickly tapped, the barriers of time zones swept away, and the overall response time to problems sharply altered. (Recall the example cited in an earlier chapter of a marketing representative assembling documentation from around the world and preparing a 200-page, multimillion-dollar project proposal in 48 hours.) As overseas markets, manufacturing facilities, and research facilities proliferate, these coordinating mechanisms become vitally important in a world where competition is time-based. Inexpensive, broad-band, global communication provides important opportunities for sharing and managing designs, manufacturing schedules, and text. Identifying expertise and then sharing it globally will allow some transnational firms to distinguish themselves in the 1990s. The new capabilities made possible by optical fiber will only accelerate this.

Global Service Levels

The standards of what constitutes world-class service are sharply increasing. For example, several years ago a major U.S. trucking company could tell you where every one of their trucks was and what was on it. That is, it could tell you a truck had just left the depot in Kansas City and that it should arrive in San Francisco in 36 hours. The truck's location at the moment was unknown, and there was no way to direct the driver to cities in between for emergency pickups. (This was as good as any of its competitors could do.) Today, on top of each of the company's trucks is a small satellite dish with a computer in it. The firm now knows exactly where each truck is (within a city) and at any time can send instructions to drivers to alter their routes as customer needs emerge and change. In the overseas transportation business, global information links have allowed U.S. carriers such as American President Lines to survive in a world dominated by low-cost competitors. Since the 1970s they have used IT to provide a highly customized and differentiated electronic-based service for their customers around the world. In so doing they have neutralized the significant labor cost advantage of their competitors by providing a highly valuable customer service. This service includes up-to-the-minute cargo locations, reliable delivery promises, and flexibility in handling emergencies.

Such advantages, of course, do not endure forever, and there is constant pressure to innovate to maintain this edge.

Time-Based Competition

The required response time in the global community is dramatically shrinking. Automobile manufacturers and large construction firms, for example, have been able to shave months and years off the design cycle as local computer-assisted-design equipment is linked internationally to CAD equipment owned by them, their suppliers, or their customers. In financial services, the question repeatedly arises, "Is two-second response time enough, or are we at a significant competitive disadvantage?" A speaker at a telecommunication conference recently noted that within a week after the opening of the new London stock exchange, which allows automatic electronic tracking, firms using satellites had shifted to optical fiber because the 50-millisecond delay put them at a distinct competitive disadvantage. In between these extremes, of course, are situations where we talk about taking weeks off order entry, order confirmation, and manufacturing cycles. A U.K. chemical company's $30 million investment in manufacturing and information technology recently transformed what had been a ten-week order entry and manufacturing cycle to one or two days. Needless to say, this changed the rules of competition in the industry and put unbearable pressure on some competitors. In the words of one of our colleagues, "competing on the basis of time may be done not just by speeding up the mess, but by enabling the construction of very different infrastructures that challenge every aspect of the firm's procedures." Global time-based competition will be a major item for world business in the next decade.

Cost Reduction

The much tighter information links between overseas operations, customers, and suppliers allows a firm to eliminate significant slack from their manufacturing systems. This results in significant reductions in buffer inventories and staffing levels and a general acceleration in asset utilization. At the extreme, it enables the creation of "hollow" global corporations such as Benetton, which owns virtually nothing but a sophisticated global information system that links the activities of its franchises with its suppliers.

The sum of these observations is that IT has transformed the very structures of transnational organizations, the type of work they do, and where they do the work. More importantly, the new technologies assure continued evolution in this impact. The dark side of this, of course, is a huge increase in the operational dependence of firms on their networks, central processors, and so on. This has forced them to build high levels of redundancy into their networks, creating alternative paths for information flow to back up their computing centers and so on. As noted earlier, Reuters, for example, provides more than a dozen electronic information paths from one part of the world to others. For a number of firms, these issues are so fundamental and of such potential impact that the IT activity is positioned near the top of the firm and is intimately involved in all strategic planning activities in order to ensure a fit between IT and the firm's plans.

DIVERSITY OF COUNTRIES

A number of factors inherent in a country's culture, government, and economy determine which IT applications are feasible in that country, how they should be implemented, and how they should be directed by a corporate IT function located in another country. The most important of these factors are discussed here.

Sociopolitical

A country's industrial maturity and form of government are particularly important factors when considering the use of information technology. Developing countries with high birth rates have views and opportunities far different from those of mature industrialized nations with their shrinking labor populations. Mature industrial societies have well-established bureaucracies that provide the necessary stability for development of communication systems. In some countries investments in technical infrastructure are made at the expense of such other national priorities as food and medical care.

Language

A common language facilitates technical communication and the sharing of relevant documentation. When this is lacking, the potential for errors, mishaps, or the like is greatly increased. Frequently senior managers of international subsidiaries are fluent in the language of the parent company, but lower-level managers and staff technicians are not. N.V. Philips, the large Dutch electronics company, has made a major effort to develop English as the companywide language, but realistically full fluency lies only at the senior management and staff levels.

Local Constraints

A multitude of local cultural traditions can inhibit the development of coordinated systems and orderly technology transfer between countries. Differing union agreements, holidays, tax regulations, and customs procedures all force major modifications of software for applications such as accounting and personnel. Further, differences in holidays, working hours, and so on, complicate coordination of reporting and data gathering.

Also important are issues relating to geography and demographics. For example, a large phonograph record company has centralized its order-entry and warehouse management functions for France in Paris, because it fits the structure of that country's distribution system. In Germany, however, the company had to establish multiple factories and distribution points and a quite different order-entry system for serving the German market, because that structure reflects the realities of German geography and prevailing distribution patterns. Unfortunately, as a result the software and procedures used in the French subsidiary are inappropriate for German operations.

Economic

A mature industrial economy normally has an available pool of well-trained, procedurally oriented individuals who are well paid relative to world standards. Further, the economic incentive to replace clerical people with IT systems is complemented by the limited availability of well trained clerical staff. It is a sensible economic decision. In countries with low wage rates, many of them dependent on one or two main raw-material exports for currency, there is typically a lack of both talent and economic incentive toward IT. (In many such countries this is changing fast, however.) They need to develop a reliable source of available information—a noneconomic decision. Implementing this new system, however, may move against both economic and cultural norms in the country. Trying to serve the interests of different national cultures in a transnational IT organization often means developing different solutions for each country.

Currency

The operation of international data centers is complicated by currency restrictions and the volatility in exchange rates. A change in exchange rates may make a location that was cost-effective for providing service to neighboring countries suddenly quite cost-ineffective. This happened with several Swiss data centers between the early 1970s and the late 1970s as a result of the heavy appreciation of the Swiss franc against other currencies.

Autonomy

Also important are the universal drive for autonomy and feelings of nationalism. The normal drive for autonomy in units within a country is intensified by differences in language and culture as one deals with international subsidiaries. In general, more integration effort is needed for coordinating foreign subsidiaries than for domestic ones. Coordination difficulties increase with the subsidiary's distance from corporate headquarters, as its relative economic importance to the corporation decreases, and with different spoken languages.

National Infrastructure

The cost and availability of utilities, particularly telecommunications utilities, and a transportation system can place important constraints on feasible alternatives. On the other hand, their absence can serve as an opportunity to experiment with certain emerging technologies. For example, to overcome one country's unpredictable transportation and communication systems, a South American distributor developed a private microwave tower network to link the records of a remote satellite depot with the central warehouses. Direct ground links to satellites promise to by-pass the need for expensive ground line installation in some developing areas.

Summary

All of these factors make coordination of international IT activities more complicated than coordination of domestic IT activities. As noted above, the factors leading to these complications are so complex and deep-rooted as to provide enduring challenges. Consequently, some companies have found it necessary to develop special staff and organizational approaches for handling these issues.

NATIONAL IT ENVIRONMENT ISSUES

In addition to the many differences between countries, some specific IT issues make coordinating and transferring information technology from one country to another particularly challenging. These are due in part to the long lead times necessary for building effective systems and in part to the changing nature of the technology. The most important of these issues are discussed in this section.

Availability of IT Professional Staff

Inadequate availability of systems and programming resources, a worldwide problem, is more severe in some settings than others. Further, as soon as people in some English-speaking countries develop these skills, they become targets for recruiters from more industrialized countries where salaries are higher. This is a particular problem in the Philippines, for example.

This personnel shortage has led to the growth of India-based software companies, which take advantage of India's high skill levels and very low wage rates to bid effectively on overseas programming jobs. Obviously, geographic distances limit the types of work these companies can bid on. Highly structured applications are much easier to develop in these ways than ones that have less structure and thus require much closer interaction between end user and developer.

When an attempt is made to supplement local staff with individuals from headquarters, the results may not be totally satisfactory. There is usually an initial outburst of productivity by the expatriates and an effective transfer of technology. Later, however, this may result in resentment by the local staff (whose salaries and benefits are usually much lower) and broken career paths for the expatriates, who find they have become both technically and managerially obsolete when they return to corporate headquarters. Management of IT expatriates' re-entry has generally been quite inadequate.

Central Telecommunications

The price and quality of telecommunications support vary widely from one country to another. On both dimensions the United States sets the standard. In many European countries the tariffs on these services are an order-of-magnitude higher than those in the United States. Also, lead times to get extra land lines, terminals, and so forth, can stretch to years instead of weeks in many countries—if they are available at any price. Finally, communication quality, availability, and cost differ widely among countries. Varying line capacity, costs, and uptime performance can make profitable home-country on-line applications cost-ineffective, inadequate, or unreliable in other countries.

National IT Strategy

In some countries development of a local computer manufacturing and software industry is a key national priority. This is true of France, Germany, Singapore, and the United Kingdom, for example. In these situations subsidiaries of foreign companies often view buying the products of the local manufacturer as good citizenship and as an opportunity to build credit for later dealings with the government. This creates a legitimate need for local deviation from corporate hardware/software standards.

Some countries, such as India and Nigeria, require that computer vendors sell a majority share of their local subsidiary to local shareholders in order to do business in the country. IBM and some other vendors have preferred to withdraw from a market rather than to enter into such an arrangement. Complying with such a requirement also may force a deviation from corporate-mandated IT standards. In the 1990s, however, both computer vendors and manufacturers are proving to be more adaptable and flexible in working around this difficulty.

Finally, concern may exist about whether the country exporting the hardware will continue to be a reliable supplier in a world of turbulent national politics and shifting foreign policies. A number of South African companies, for example, unsure of their ability to get a sustained flow of products from any one country, moved to prevent potential disruptions of equipment delivery by dealing with vendors of several countries. In making this move they committed themselves to significant additional costs.

General Level of IT Sophistication

The speed and ease with which companies can implement or develop an IT activity in another country are linked to the general level of IT activity in the country. A firm located in a country with a substantial base of installed electronic-based information systems and well-trained, mobile labor can develop its IT capabilities more rapidly and effectively than if none of these conditions exist. Countries with limited installed electronic-based information systems require substantially more expatriate labor to implement IT work, as well as great effort and time to educate users in the idiosyncrasies of IT and how best to interface with it. Careful investigation of the staff mobility factor is particularly important, because bonding arrangements and cultural norms may place considerable rigidity on what appears to be a satisfactory labor supply.

Size of Local Market

The size of the local market influences the number of vendors who compete for service in it. Thus in small markets a company's preferred international supplier may not have a presence. Further, the quality of service support often varies widely from one setting to another; vendors who provide good support in one country may give inadequate support in another. Another important issue is the availability and quality of local software and consulting companies (or subsidiaries of large international ones). A thriving, competent local IT industry can do much to offset other differences in local support and availability of staff.

Data Export Control

A topic receiving significant publicity since the mid-1980s is legislation that would dramatically reduce the amount of information relating to people and finances that may be transmitted electronically across national boundaries. This is driven both by concerns about individual privacy and the often weak security and low quality controls over these data.

A relatively benign topic in the 1980s, it will rear its head much more vigorously in the 1990s. The use of personal data generates a wide range of sensitivities in different societies. In general, it is of most concern in Western Europe today, particularly in the Scandinavian countries, and is of less concern in the United States. Existing legislation and practice varies widely among countries, as do criteria for evaluating and resolving these issues. The current apparent lack of interest in these issues in many countries should not be misread by the business community. The issues are deep and emotional, and the spotlight will surely make this a burning issue in the 1990s. What is seen in one environment as a sharp consumer micromarketing implementation may be seen as deeply intrusive and immoral in another. The word *Orwellian* is increasingly being used in describing some new IT applications that use personal data. (See the material on privacy in Chapter 11.)

Technological Awareness

Awareness of contemporary technology spreads very rapidly around the globe because IT magazines and journals are distributed internationally. This awareness poses problems in terms of orderly development of applications in less IT-sophisticated countries, because it leads subsidiaries to promote technologies that they neither understand nor need and that they are incapable of managing. Conversely, starting with a high degree of IT awareness has advantages, because distinctly different paths may be implemented for exploiting information technology in the subsidiaries than are used in home offices.

Border Opportunities

In periods of fluctuating exchange rates, significant discontinuities often appear in vendor prices for the same equipment in different countries. In 1980, for example, there was a period when a 15 to 20 percent savings could be achieved by buying equipment in Italy for use across the border in Switzerland, as opposed to buying it in Switzerland.

Summary

For the transnational firm the practical implication of these factors is severe restraint of the degree to which standard policies and controls can be placed on diverse international activities. Rigid policy on many of these issues cannot be dictated effectively from corporate headquarters, often located a vast distance from the subsidiary's operating management. There are many legitimate reasons for diversity, and considerable *local* know-how must be brought to the decisions.

CORPORATE FACTORS AFFECTING IT REQUIREMENTS

Within the context of the different national cultures and the current state of the IT profession in different countries, a number of factors inside a company influence how far it can move to manage the transfer of information technology and how centralized its control of international IT activity should be. Because of the many factors discussed in the previous sections, more control must be delegated in an international environment than in a domestic one. However, important opportunities exist for technology transfer, and potentially important limitations in service will occur if these opportunities are not managed. The more important company-specific factors are discussed here.

Nature of Firm's Business

Some firms' businesses demand that key data files be managed centrally so that they are accessible, immediately or on a short delayed-access basis, to all units of the firm around the world. Airline reservation files for international air carriers require such access. A United Airlines agent in Boston confirming a flight segment from Tokyo to Hong Kong needs up-to-the-minute access to the flight's loading to make a valid commitment, while other agents around the globe need to know that seat is no longer available for sale. Failure to have this information poses risks of significant loss of market share as customers perceive the firm to be both unreliable and uncompetitive.

American President Lines, an international shipping company, maintains a file, updated every 24 hours, as to the location of each of its containers, its status, and its availability for future commitment by regional officers in 20 countries. Without this data the firm would most likely make unfulfillable commitments, which would present an unreliable image to present and potential customers. In another example, the standards of international banking have evolved to where the leaders provide customers with an instantaneous worldwide picture of clearances, and so on, thus opening the door for more sophisticated cash management—for which the banks charge significant fees. Those firms not providing such services find themselves increasingly at a competitive disadvantage.

Other firms require integration and on-line updating of only some of their files. A European electronics firm attempts to provide its European managers with up-to-date, on-line access to various key operational files on items such as production schedules, order status, and so forth. This is done for its network of 20-plus factories in order to manage an integrated logistics system. No such integration, however, is attempted for their key marketing or accounting data, which essentially are processed on a batch basis and organized by country. While developing such integration is technically possible, at present the firm sees no operational or marketing advantage in doing so.

Still other firms require essentially no integration of data, and each country can be managed on a stand-alone basis. A U.S. conglomerate, for example, manages each division on a stand-alone basis. Eight of its divisions have operations in the United Kingdom, and by corporate policy they have no formal interaction with each other in IT or any other operational matters. (A single tax specialist who files a joint tax return for them is the sole linking specialist.) The company's staff generally perceives that this is an appropriate way to operate and that nothing of significance is being lost. These examples suggest the impossibility of generalizing about how transnational IT activities should be organized.

Strategic Impact of IT

If IT activity is strategic to the company, tighter corporate overview is needed to ensure that new technology (with its accompanying new ways of operating) is rapidly and efficiently introduced to outlying areas. One of the United States' largest international banks, for example, has a staff of more than 100 at corporate headquarters to develop software for their international branches and to coordinate its orderly dissemination to them. The bank feels the successful use of IT is too critical to the firm's ultimate success to be managed without technical coordination and senior management perspective. At the other extreme is a reasonably large manufacturer of chemicals that sees IT as playing an important but clearly a *support* role. At least twice a year the head of the European IT unit and the head of corporate IT exchange visits and share perceptions with each other. The general consensus is that there is not enough potential payoff to warrant further coordination.

Corporate Organization

As its international activity grows, a firm adopts different structures, each of which requires quite different levels of international IT support and coordination. In the earliest phase of an export division there are only limited numbers of overseas staff, who require little if any local IT processing and support. As the activity grows in size it tends to be reorganized as an *international* division with an increasing number of marketing, accounting, and manufacturing staff located abroad. At this stage an increasing need may arise for local IT support. A full-blown level of international activity may involve regional headquarters (in Europe, the Far East, and Latin America, for example) to coordinate the activities of the diverse countries.

Coordinating such a structure is very complex, because not only are there vertical relationships between corporate IT and the national IT activities, but cross-border marketing and manufacturing integration requirements create the need for relationships between individual countries' IT units. Appropriate forms of this coordination, of course, vary widely among organizations. A multibillion dollar pharmaceutical firm was discovered to have very close links between corporate IT and its major national IT units (defined by the firm as those with budgets in excess of $5 million). None of the IT unit managers, however, knew the names of their contemporaries or had visited any of the other units. Since there was little cross-border product flow and none was planned for the near future, this did not appear to present a significant problem.

At the most complex, firms are organized in a matrix fashion—with corporate IT activity, divisional IT activities (which may or may not be located at corporate headquarters), and national IT activities. Here, balancing relationships is a major challenge. Divisions that have substantial vertical supplier relationships with each other and substantial integration of activities across national borders have even more complicated relationships. In such cases the policies that work for the international divisions are too simplistic.

Company Technical and Control Characteristics

Level of Functional Control.   An important factor in effective IT control structures is the corporation's general level of functional control. Companies with a strong tradition of central control find it both appropriate and relatively easy to implement line IT control worldwide. A major manufacturer of farm equipment, for example, has for years implemented very strong management and operational control over its worldwide manufacturing and marketing functions. Consequently it found considerable acceptance of similar controls for the IT organization. Most of the software that runs their overseas plants has been developed and is maintained by the corporate IT headquarters group.

At the other extreme is a 30-division, multibillion-dollar conglomerate with a corporate staff of approximately 100 people who are involved mostly in financial and legal work associated with acquisitions and divestitures. This company has totally decentralized operating decisions to the divisions, and the number of corporate staff is deliberately controlled as a means of preventing meddling. At present a two-person corporate IT "group" works on only very broad policy and consulting issues. Effective execution of even this limited role is very challenging, and its expansion is very difficult to visualize.

Technology Base.   Another element of significance is the technology base of the company. High-technology companies with traditions of spearheading technical change from a central research and engineering laboratory and disseminating it around the world have successfully used a similar approach with IT. Their transnational managers are used to corporately initiated technical change. Firms without this experience have had more difficulty assimilating information technology in general as well as more problems in transplanting IT developed in one location to other settings.

Corporate Size.   Finally, corporate size is also relevant. Smaller organizations, because of the limited and specialized nature of their application, find transfer of IT packages and expertise to be particularly complex. As the scope of the operation increases, finding common applications and facilitating transfer of technology becomes easier, perhaps because the stakes are higher.

Other Considerations

Other factors also influence IT coordination policies. Is there substantial rotation of staff between international locations? If so, is it desirable to have common reporting systems and operating procedures in place in each subsidiary to ease the assimilation of the transfers? Do the firm's operating and financial requirements essentially demand up-to-the-week reporting of overseas financial results? If not, consolidation of smaller overseas operations on a one-month, delayed-time basis is attractive.

TRANSNATIONAL IT POLICY ISSUES

As the preceding sections explain, great diversity exists in the policies for coordinating and managing international IT activities. This section identifies the most common types of policies and relationships and briefly focuses on key issues associated with the selection and implementation of each. The scope of these policies and the amount of effort needed to implement them are influenced by the degree of needed central control, corporate culture and policies, strategic importance of information technologies, and other factors.

Guidance on Architecture

The most important central IT role is to facilitate the development and implementation of a view on appropriate telecommunications architecture and database standards. The firm must pragmatically move to ensure that these standards are installed in all of its operations. There are no substitutes in this task for travel, pragmatism, and the ability to listen. Ideas that make perfect sense in Detroit often need selective fine tuning in Thailand, if indeed they are even viable there.

The opportunity to transmit data electronically between countries for file updating and processing purposes has created the need for a corporate international data dictionary. Too often this need is not addressed, leading to clumsy systems designs and incorrect outputs. Where data should be stored, the form in which it should be stored, and how it should be updated are all considerations that require centrally managed policy—operating, of course, within the framework of what is legally permissible.

Similarly, central guidance and coordination in the acquisition of communication technology are needed. At present, communication flexibility and cost vary widely from country to country and they are shifting rapidly.

Effective anticipation of these cost and flexibility changes requires a corporate view and broad design of telecommunications needs for meeting the demands of growth and changing business needs over the coming decade. It must be specific in terms of service levels that will be needed and the technologies to be utilized. Such a plan requires capable technical inputs and careful management review. An important by-product of the plan is guidance for corporate negotiation and lobbying efforts on relevant items of national legislation and policies regarding the form, availability, and cost of telecommunication.

Central Hardware/Software Concurrence or Approval

The objectives of a central policy for acquiring hardware and software are to ensure that obvious mistakes in vendor viability are avoided and that economies of scale are achieved in purchasing decisions. Other benefits include the bargaining leverage a company achieves by being perceived as an important customer, the reduction of potential interface problems between national systems, and the enhancement of applications software transferability between countries. Practical factors that require sensitive interpretation and execution of central policy include the following:

- Degree of awareness at corporate headquarters of the vendor's support and servicing problems in the local country.
- Desire of the local subsidiary to exercise its autonomy and control of its operations in a timely way. The Korean subsidiary of a large bank wanted to buy a $25,000 word-processing system. Its request for approval took six months to pass through three locations and involved one senior vice president and two executive vice presidents. Whatever benefits standardization might have achieved for the bank in this situation seemed to be more than offset by the cost and time of the approval process.
- Need to maintain good relationships with local governments. This may involve patronizing local vendors, agreeing not to eliminate certain types of staff, and using the government-controlled IT network.
- Level and skill of corporate headquarters people who set the technical and managerial policies. A technically weak corporate staff dealing with large, well-managed foreign subsidiaries must operate quite differently from a technically gifted central staff dealing with small, unsophisticated subsidiaries.

Central Approval of Software Standards and Feasibility Studies

Central control of software standards can ensure that software is written in a maintainable secure way so that the company's long-term operational position is not jeopardized. Control of feasibility studies can ensure that potential applications are evaluated in a consistent and professional fashion. Practical problems with this policy of central approval revolve around both the level of effort required and the potential erosion of corporate culture.

Implementation of such standards can be expensive and time-consuming in relation to the potential benefits. The art is to be flexible with small investments and to review more closely the investments that involve real operational exposure. Unfortunately, this approach requires more sensitivity than many staffs possess.

Further, directly counter to central control may be a decentralized company's prevailing management control system and the location of other operating decisions. The significance of this conflict depends on the size and strategic importance of the investment. Relatively small, distinctly "support" investments in decentralized organizations should clearly be resolved in the local country. Large, strategic investments, however, should be subject to central review in these organizations, even if time delays and cost overruns result.

Central Software Development

In the name of efficiency, reduced costs, and standard operating procedures worldwide, some firms have attempted to develop software centrally, or at a designated subsidiary, for installation in subsidiaries in other countries. The success of this approach has definitely been mixed. Most companies that have succeeded with this have well-established patterns of technology transfer, strong functional control over their subsidiaries, substantial numbers of expatriates working in the overseas subsidiaries, and some homogeneity in their manufacturing, accounting, and distribution practices. Success has also been fostered when the IT unit assigned responsibility for the package's development and installation has carried out very intensive marketing and liaison activities.

When these preconditions have not been present, however, installation has often been troubled. The reasons most commonly cited by IT managers for the failure include:

- The developers of the system did not understand local needs well enough. Major functions were left out, and the package required extensive and expensive enhancements.
- The package was adequate, but the efforts needed to train people to input data and handle outputs properly were significantly underestimated (or mishandled). This was complicated by extensive language difficulties and insensitivity to existing local procedures.

- The system evolution and maintenance involved a dependence on central staff that was not sustainable in the long run. Flexibility and timeliness of response were problems.
- Costs were significantly underestimated. The overrun on the basic package was bad enough, but the fat was really in the fire when the installation costs were added.

These statements seem to reflect the importance of organizational and cultural factors. In reality, an outside software house, with its marketing orientation and its existence outside the corporate family, often does a better job of selling standard software than an in-house IT unit in a decentralized transnational environment. Finally, in many settings the sheer desire on both sides for success is the best guarantee of that success occurring.

IT Communications

Although they are expensive, investments in improving communications between the various national IT units have paid big benefits. Several devices have proven useful:

Regular Interunit Meetings.   An annual or biannual conference of the IT directors and the key staff of the major international subsidiaries. For organizations in the "turnaround" or "strategic" categories, these meetings ought to take place at least as frequently as meetings of international controllers. Small subsidiaries (IT budgets under $1 million) probably do not generate enough profitable opportunities to warrant inclusion in this conference or to have a separate one.

The agenda of the conference should combine planned formal activities—such as technical briefings, application briefings, and company directives—with substantial blocks of unplanned time. The informal exchange of ideas, initiation of joint projects, and sharing of mutual problems are among the most important activities of a successful conference.

Corporate–Subsidiary Exchange Visits.   Regular visits of corporate IT personnel to the national organizations, as well as of national IT personnel to corporate IT headquarters. These visits should take place at planned intervals, rather than only when there is an operational crisis or technical problem. Less contact is needed with the smaller units than with the larger ones.

Newsletters.   Preparation and circulation of a monthly or bimonthly newsletter to communicate staffing shifts, new technical insights, major project completions, experience with software packages and vendors, and so forth.

Education. Organization of joint education programs where possible. This may involve the creation and/or acquisition of audiovisual materials to be distributed around the world. A large oil company recently supplemented written communications about a radically different IT organization structure with the preparation of a special film, complete with sound track in five languages.

One of the largest U.K. chemical companies has literally a one-person corporate IT department. The individual continuously travels the world, helping to facilitate education and training sessions and identifying appropriate topics and sources of expertise for IT staff in far-flung places. This individual is a member of the most senior general management of the firm and clearly adds substantial value. General-management and middle-management staff awareness programs remain a central 1990's challenge for this leader.

A fundamental need is for developing stronger psychological links between the national IT units. These links can be as important as the formal ties between the national IT units and the parent company's IT unit.

Facilitating the development of centers of systems expertise in many parts of the world is another important need. It is not obvious that a single-system unit in the parent company's home country is the best way to operate. Many jobs can usefully be split over three or four development centers. One of the large entertainment companies recently assigned large portions of its financial systems, marketing systems, and production systems to its U.K., German, and French development units, respectively. While each unit was enthusiastic about leading their part of the effort, they also knew that if they did not cooperate with the other units, they would not receive the cooperation necessary to assure that their unit's output would be successful. This approach tapped new sources of expertise and was successful because of the *shared* interdependencies of *leadership* and innovation.

Staff Rotation

An important way of addressing the issue of communications is by rotating staff between national IT units and corporate IT.

Advantages. Key advantages that stem from this include:

• Better corporate IT awareness of the problems and issues in the overseas IT units. As a corollary, the local IT units have a much better perspective on the goals and thinking at corporate headquarters because one of their members has spent a tour of duty there.

- More flexibility in managing career paths and matching positions with individual development needs. Particularly to someone working in a crowded corporate IT department, an overseas assignment could seem very attractive.
- Efficient dispersion of technical know-how throughout the organization.

Disadvantages.   On the negative side of staff rotation, practical problems can occur:

- As pointed out earlier, people can jeopardize their career paths by moving from corporate headquarters to less-IT-developed parts of the world. The individuals bring leading-edge expertise to the overseas installation and have a major positive impact for several years. When they return to corporate headquarters they may find themselves completely out of touch with the contemporary technologies being used. Also, some of these people have been dropped out of the normal progression stream through oversight.
- Assignment of individuals overseas is not only expensive in terms of moving allowances and cost-of-living differentials, but it also raises a myriad of potential personal problems. These problems, normally of a family nature, make the success of an international transfer more speculative than a domestic one.
- Transfers from corporate to smaller overseas locations may cause substantial resentment and feelings of nationalism in the overseas location: "Why aren't our people good enough?" Such problems can be tempered with appropriate language skills and efforts on the part of the transferred executive, corporate control over the number of transfers, local promotions, and clearly visible opportunities for local staff to be transferred to corporate.

Appropriately managed within reasonable limits, the advantages far outweigh the disadvantages.

Consulting Services

Major benefits can come from a central IT group providing foreign subsidiaries with consulting services on both technical and managerial matters. In many cases corporate headquarters is not only located in a technically sophisticated country, but its IT activities are bigger in scope than those of individual foreign installations. Among other things, this means that:

1. Corporate IT is more aware of leading-edge hardware/software technology and has had firsthand experience with its potential strengths and weaknesses.
2. Corporate IT is more likely to have experience with large project management systems and other management methods.

In both cases the communication must be done with sensitivity in order to move the company forward at an appropriate pace. All too often the corporate group pushes too fast in a culturally insensitive fashion, creating substantial problems. Movement through the phases of technology assimilation can be speeded up and smoothed, but no phase should be skipped.

As an organization becomes more IT intensive, effective IT auditing becomes increasingly important for shielding the organization from excessive and unnecessary risks. As mentioned earlier, IT auditing is a rapidly evolving profession that faces a serious staff shortage. The shortage is more severe outside the United States and Europe. Thus the corporate audit group of a transnational frequently must take responsibility for conducting international IT audits and for helping to develop national IT audit staffs and capabilities.

Central IT Processing Support

Whether IT should be pushed toward a central hub or a linked international network depends on the firm's type of industry and the dimensions along which it chooses to compete. At one extreme is the airline industry, where it is a significant competitive disadvantage to be unable to confirm seats on a global basis. Originally, international airlines were driven to centralize as an offensive weapon; now it is a defensive one. At the other extreme is a company that has a network of operations for converting paper (a commodity). Transportation costs severely limit how far away from a plant orders can profitably be shipped. Thus the company handles order entry and factory management on a strictly national basis, and there is little interchange of data between countries.

Technology Appraisal Program—An Example

An international appraisal can provide perspective that allows greater coordination of overseas IT efforts. A U.S.-based transnational company with a long history of European operations discovered that their operations in the Far East and South America were posing increasingly complicated information problems. General management initiated a three-year program for bringing the overseas operation under control. The first step was to appraise the condition of each national IT unit and its potential business. This appraisal was conducted by a three-person IT team with multilingual abilities. It was followed by a formulation of policies and appropriate action programs at the annual meeting of company executives.

Originally planned as a one-time assessment of only 11 national IT units, the effort was considered so successful that it was reorganized as an established audit function. The team learned to appraise locally available technology and to guide local management's attention to judging its potential. This required at least one week and often two weeks in the field, typically in two trips. The first visit appraised existing services and raised general concerns that could be pursued effectively by the local management. The second visit assessed problems of:

1. Government restrictions.
2. Quality and quantity of available human skills.
3. Present and planned communications services.

Alternatives to the present means of service were examined further, and economic analyses of at least three standard alternatives were prepared. The three standard alternatives were:

1. Expansion of present system.
2. Transfer of all or portions of IT work to a neighboring country.
3. Transfer of all or portions of IT work to regional headquarters.

The enthusiasm of local managers for this review was not universal, and in several countries long delays occurred between the first and second visits. However, in 7 of the original 11 units the appraisals succeeded in generating appropriate change by bringing better understanding of the potential impact of uncertainties—such as changing import duties, planned market introduction of new technologies by U.S. suppliers, and a new satellite communications alternative. This organized appraisal significantly increased senior management's awareness and comfort concerning IT. The activity became an ongoing effort for the company, and several persons were added to the appraisal team.

SUMMARY

Coordinating international IT is extraordinarily complex. Corporate IT management may have maximum responsibility but only limited authority over distant staff and technologies. Leadership demands persuasion and cajoling plus being well informed on new technologies, the corporate culture, and the wide diversity that exists in the world. The job requires very high visibility and a sound reporting structure inside the firm. This is particularly important because of the need to lead through *relationships*. The IT leadership must be represented at the very top of the firm, where acquisition, divestiture, and other components of changing corporate strategy are developed. The IT department's effectiveness crucially depends on being heard in this forum. Further, the function varies widely by industry, global reach, and size of firm. For example, the nature of the international airline business requires a large central hub. The IT leadership role in this industry consequently has a very strong line management component. The earlier described chemical company's operations, on the other hand, are contained within individual, autonomous national units. Hence an entirely different structure of central IT is appropriate for that company, and IT leadership involves little line responsibility but high-placed coordination.

International IT development must be managed actively in order to avert major, long-term difficulties within and between national IT activities. This is complicated, because assimilation of information technology in other countries is often more heavily influenced by local conditions than by the current state of the technology. Overcoming obstacles presented by the local conditions demands much more than simply keeping abreast of technology. Thus a long view is required to succeed.

Chapter 13

IT Planning:
A Contingent Focus

A manufacturing company has just eliminated its five-person IT planning staff, reassigning three persons to other jobs in the IT organization and letting two go. In commenting on this the vice president of finance states, "We just didn't seem to be getting a payoff from it. After three years of trying we thought we could find a better place to spend our money."

A financial institution's executive vice president of operations is overheard speaking of a recently completed business systems planning effort. She says, "This has given us a whole new picture of how much we need to devote to IT expenditure and where we should spend it over the next five years. We would be lost without it."

The head of IT planning for a major financial services organization is discussing his disillusionment with planning. He notes, "When we started IT planning two years ago we were very enthusiastic about its potential for invigorating the company. It worked for a while, but now it seems to have gone flat."

These comments are typical. Organizations launch IT planning efforts with great hope and often positive early results. Subsequently, however, many of the these efforts run into difficulty. This chapter explores key managerial issues surrounding IT planning and provides guidelines that can help to assure success.

As information technology applications have grown in size and complexity over the past two decades, the development of a strategy for assimilating these resources into firms' operations has grown steadily more important. A key vehicle for strategy development is a sensitively architected planning process. To be effective, such a planning process must deal simultaneously with the realities of the firm's organizational culture, corporate planning culture, various technologies, and the importance of IT activities to the corporate goals.

Many studies have shown a positive correlation between user *perception* that IT activities are effective and a focused, articulated, appropriate planning process.[1] However, since good standards do not exist for measuring the overall effectiveness of the IT activity, the evidence linking its effectiveness with planning processes is necessarily diffuse and fragmentary.

This chapter is organized around four topics:

1. External and internal pressures that generate the need for an articulated IT planning process.
2. Pressures that limit the value that can be derived from IT planning.
3. The relationship between IT planning and corporate strategy formulation.
4. Corporate factors that influence the effectiveness of IT planning—tailoring the IT planning process to a specific firm.

PRESSURES TOWARD IT PLANNING

External (Corporate) Pressures

A variety of external pressures define the need for IT planning. The more important ones are discussed here.

Rapid Changes in Technology. Hardware and software continue to evolve rapidly, providing substantially different and potentially profitable IT applications from year to year. This requires continual interaction between IT staff and management groups to ensure that they have properly identified the technology changes that are significant to the company and have developed appropriate plans and pilot projects. IT staff must make potential users, such as office managers and analytical staffs, aware of the implications (including the potential problems) of these new technologies so that they can identify potential new applications in their areas of responsibility that the IT staff might not recognize.

As the technology changes, planning becomes increasingly important in order to avoid the problems of incompatible systems and inac-

---

[1]Philip Pyburn, "Information Systems Planning—a Contingency Perspective," DBA thesis, Harvard Business School, 1981.

cessible data files. The networked organization is becoming reality, and developing network linkages frequently requires implementation schedules of up to four years.

For example, an insurance company has instituted a two- to three-year program for placing a portable PC with expert financial counseling software in it into the hands of each of its more than 5,000 agents. A detailed plan was absolutely critical to maintaining senior management's confidence in the integrity of the program and the sales force's effectiveness and good morale during the implementation.

Personnel Scarcity.   The scarcity of trained, perceptive analysts and programmers, coupled with their long training cycles, continues to restrain IT development and to demand that planning priorities be established. As discussed earlier, these appear to be long-term difficulties rather than cyclical problems. This is forcing increasing amounts of software and electronic data to be sourced from outside the firm and necessitating tough internal resource allocation decisions. Indeed despite the proliferation of IT productivity tools and software tools for distributing work to users, an increasing number of U.S. firms are looking overseas for English-speaking technical personnel to meet staff shortages at attractive U.S. salaries. Firms have also outsourced portions of software development to such countries as India and Ireland, where the labor costs for comparable skills are dramatically lower.

Scarcity of Other Corporate Resources.   Limited availability of financial and managerial resources is another planning pressure. IT is only one of many strategic investment opportunities for a company, and the potential financial returns of investments in it must be weighed against those of alternative investments. This problem is intensified by the financial accounting practice in most U.S. companies of charging IT expenditures against the current year's earnings even though much of it is actually a capital expenditure. Review of the effectiveness and the efficiency of these expenditures is of great importance, as resource availability is a critical limiting factor for new projects—particularly in companies that are under profit or cost pressures.

Scarcity of IT middle-management personnel, particularly in the area of systems development, is also a significant constraint. The inability of some companies to train sufficient project leaders and supervisors has significantly restrained those firms' IT development. This has forced significant reductions in their systems development applications portfolios and the undertaking of projects that pose very high risk solely because of inadequate human resources.

Trend to Database Design and Integrated Systems.   An increasing and significant proportion of the applications portfolio involves the design of relational data architecture for supporting sophisticated applications that link different parts of the firm as well as its customers and suppliers. A long-term view of the evolution of applications is critical in order to appropriately select database contents, the methods for interrelating them, and the protocols for updating them.

Validation of Corporate Plan.   In many organizations new marketing programs, new-product design, and introduction and implementation of organizational strategies depend on the development of IT support programs. Understanding these points of dependency is critical. If the corporate strategy is infeasible due to IT limitations, that message needs to be highlighted for corporate management, because the problem must be faced and resolved while alternatives are still available.

As we have pointed out many times, in organizations where IT products and processes are integral to elements of the corporate strategy, this linkage is very important. A large paper company, for example, was forced to abandon its planned new billing discount promotions—a key part of its marketing strategy—because its IT function was unable to translate the very complex ideas into the existing computer programs with the present level of staff skills. Advance coordination between IT and marketing management would have identified the problem much earlier and permitted satisfactory solutions to be identified.

Internal (IT Process) Pressures

At various points in the evolution of an information technology the balance between pressures shifts and planning serves substantially different purposes. Reflecting upon the advent and growth of business data processing, databases, distributed systems, fiber optics, image processing, and other new technologies (as noted in earlier chapters) one can identify four distinct phases of technology assimilation, each of which poses different pressures.

Phase 1: Technology Identification and Investment.   The basic focus of planning in the initial phase of a new technology is oriented toward both technology identification and the need for new human resource skills. Key IT planning problems include identifying the appropriate technologies for study, preparing the site, developing staff skills, identifying potential product champions, and managing development of the first pilot applications of the technology.

In this phase short-term technical problem resolution is so critical and experience is so limited that effective long-term strategic thinking about the implications of the technology is often precluded. This is not bad, since those involved usually do not yet have a strong enough background in the technology to think long term about its implications for the company. As the organization gains experience with the technology through pilot projects, selecting appropriate new applications for the technology becomes a topic of interest. This signals the evolution to the second phase. (As noted earlier, in some IT organizations, "Emerging Technologies" departments have been established to ensure that appropriate technologies are identified and streamed through Phases 1 and 2.)

Phase 2: Technological Learning and Adaptation.   The basic thrust of planning in this phase is to develop potential users' consciousness of the new technology's existence and to communicate the ways it can be useful to them. Sequencing projects and ensuring that there is good coordination between team members is also important as the company continues to master the technology's nuances. The initiation of a series of user-supported pilot projects is a measure of the effectiveness of the planning.

As a secondary output, the planning process for technologies in this phase focuses on identifying the number of staff and the skills that must be acquired. The direction that comes out of Phase-2 planning is not necessarily an accurate indicator of the pace of future events. This is because individuals are still learning and do not yet have sufficient insight to be concise and accurate about the real implications of the technology in their operations and about how hard it will be to achieve the desired results.

Since technology will continue to evolve for the foreseeable future, there will normally be a Phase-2 flavor to some part of a company's IT development portfolio. Our observations of successful planning in this phase suggest clearly that:

1. A new technology is best introduced by starting with a pilot test to generate both IT staff and user learning, rather than by spending years on advance introspection and design without any practical hands-on experience.
2. Attracting the interest of potential users on *their* terms and stimulating their understanding about what the technology can do for them is critical to success. Success here leads to later requests for service, and the pilot users are your most important allies.
3. Planning during this phase (and Phase 1 as well) involves a program of planned technological innovations, encouraging users to build upon their past experience, and organizational receptivity to change. There is a desirable "softness" in specificity of the tangible and intangible benefits associated with these projects.

Phase-2 planning has a heavy strategic focus. However, as is true of companies that are in a rapid growth phase in new industry sectors,

precision of the plan is limited by user's and developer's lack of familiarity with the technology and its implications. Therefore, planning for
technologies at this phase does not have the same predictive value as
planning for technology in the later phases. What the technical developer initially envisions as the implications of a new technology are
often quite different from the ultimate actual applications.

Phase 3: Rationalization/Management Control. Effective planning for technologies in this phase has a strong efficiency focus; the
emphasis shifts to get the results of the successful pilot projects implemented cost-efficiently. Whereas planning for technological learning and adaptation (Phase 2) has a long-range (though not terribly
accurate) perspective, planning for Phase-3 technologies has a short-
term—one- to two-year—efficiency focus. This includes getting applications identified and completed, upgrading staff to acceptable knowledge levels with the new technology, reorganizing to develop and
implement further projects using the technology, and efficiently utilizing the technology. For technologies in this phase, planning's objective
is to set appropriate limits on the types of applications that make sense
and to ensure they are implemented cost-efficiently. In terms of Robert
Anthony's framework,[2] effective planning for Phase-3 technologies has
a much stronger management and operational control flavor and a
weaker strategic planning thrust.

Phase 4: Maturity/Widespread Technology Transfer. The final
phase is one of managed evolution in which the technology is transferred to a wider spectrum of applications within the organization.
With organizational learning essentially complete and a technology
base that has appropriate controls in place, it is appropriate to look
seriously into the future and to plot longer-term trends in exploitation
of the technology. If one is not careful, such planning—based on the
business and technology as they are now understood—can be too rigid.
Unexpected quirks in the business and evolution of technology may
invalidate what has been done during Phase-4 planning as the technology is superseded by a still better one.

Given the current dynamic state of information technology, technologies in all four planning phases are normally present simultaneously
in a typical firm. Planning for business batch data processing for most
companies in 1991, for example, was in Phase 4, while electronic mail
was in Phase 3, and image processing was somewhere between Phases

---

[2]Robert Anthony, *Planning and Control Systems: A Framework for Analysis* (Boston:
Division of Research, Harvard University Graduate School of Business Administration,
1965).

1 and 2. This suggests that uniformity and consistency in IT planning protocols throughout the firm are inappropriate, because the organization is dealing with a portfolio of technologies, each of which poses a different planning challenge.

For example, one manufacturing company studied was in Phase 4 in terms of its ability to conceptualize and deal with enhancements to its on-line MRP-II production scheduling system. At the same time, it was in Phase 3 in terms of driving its new CAD system across the entire engineering and product development functions. Finally, the company had just made an investment in several local-area word-processing networks as well as in two quite different approaches to the graphic user interface. It was clearly in Phase 1 with respect to these technologies. The firm's plans for the MRP-II system were detailed and crisp, whereas the local-area network was essentially a research project, and no coherent view existed as to where it was going.

In summary, "planned clutter" (as opposed to consistency) is desirable in a firm's approach to IT planning. Similarly, the approach to IT planning for different organizational units within a company should vary, since each often has quite different familiarity with specific technologies.

LIMITATIONS ON IT PLANNING RESULTS

As new products appear, as the competitive environment shifts, as laws and corporate strategies change, and as mergers and spin-offs take place, the priorities a company assigns to its various applications appropriately evolve. Some previous low-priority or unconceived applications may become critically important, while others that were once seen as vital will diminish in significance. This volatility places a real premium on building a flexible management framework that permits orderly and consistent change to meet evolving business requirements.

In a similar vein, every IT planning process must make some very specific assumptions about the nature and role of technological evolution. If this evolution occurs at a different rate from the one forecasted (as is often the case), then major segments of the plan may have to be reworked in terms of both scope and thrust. Suppose, for example, the present speed of access to a one-billion-character file were suddenly increased in the coming year by an order of magnitude beyond current expectations with no change in cost. Many organizations' plans would require careful reexamination, not just of the priority of applications but, more important, of their very structure as completely new application areas would become possible. Some individuals have used this as a reason not to plan but, rather, to "remain creatively opportunistic" on a year-to-year basis. On balance, we have found the evidence supporting this viewpoint to be unconvincing.

Planning as a Resource Drain

Every person and every dollar assigned to IT planning represent resources that are diverted away from such activities as new systems development. The extent to which human and financial resources should be devoted to planning is always in question. Just as the style of planning changes over time as parts of the organization pass through different phases with different technologies, the commitment of resources to planning also should change. This too suggests that the instability in an IT planning process relates positively to its role of stimulating a creative view of the future. If not carefully managed, IT planning can evolve into a mind-numbing, noncreative process of routinely changing the numbers, as opposed to a sensitive focus on the company's real opportunities and problems.

Fit to Corporate Culture

An important aspect of IT planning is implementation within the realities of the corporate culture. For example, in organizations with a very formal corporate planning process that is actively supported by senior management, the internal user–management climate typically supports formal approaches to IT planning. In middle management's eyes, IT planning is a legitimate activity, and devoting time to it is an appropriate thing to do. Other organizations, however, have quite different cultures and approaches to corporate planning. These factors significantly alter both the form and the degree of commitment that can be expected from users to an IT planning process. This is discussed further later in the chapter.

Strategic Impact of IT Activities

As discussed in earlier chapters, for some organizations IT activities are an area of great strategic importance, while for other organizations they play (and appropriately will continue to play) a cost-effective, useful, but distinctly supportive role. It is inappropriate for organizations in which IT plays a distinctly support role to expect the same amount of senior management thinking to be devoted to IT items as in organizations of the former type. Making the issue more complicated, the IT function that in the past did not have strategic importance may, because of its new-technology-enabled applications portfolio, have great significance in the future. Thus, IT planning may become very important to the firm at some time, and in the process it must face and surmount the challenge of breaking the habits and molds of the past.

In an environment of management turmoil, high turnover, and re-assessment, it is unlikely that there can be the same intensity and commitment to IT planning that is possible in a stable environment in which individuals have a strong emotional attachment to the organization. Although such negative factors limit the benefits of planning and make the process more complex, they do not eliminate the *need* for it. Rather, they increase the multidimensional complexity of the planning task and they diminish reasonable expectations of the output's quality.

For other organizations, the opposite is true. While IT now plays an important operational role, future applications may not offer great payoff or significance. In that event, a less intensive focus on IT strategic planning will be in order, and different people will be involved than in the past when it was more significant.

These ideas (discussed first in Chapter 2) are illustrated here within four quite different IT environments. (Also see Figure 13–1.)

Strategic.   "Strategic" companies are critically dependent on the smooth functioning of the IT activity. Appropriately managed, such firms require considerable IT planning, and IT planning is closely integrated with corporate planning in a two-way dialogue because IT can open new operational capabilities for the firms. Not only does IT need the guidance of corporate goals, but the achievement of corporate goals can be severely impacted by IT performance and capabilities or lack thereof. In short, the impact of IT on the firm's performance requires significant general management involvement in IT planning.

Comments by the chief executive officer of a large financial institution to his senior staff captured this perspective:

> Most of our customer services and much of our office support for those services involve some kind of systematic information processing. Without the computer hardware and software supporting these processing efforts, we would undoubtedly drown in a sea of paper—unless we were first eliminated from the market because our costs were so high and our services so inefficient that we had no customers to generate the paper. Either way, it is abundantly clear that information systems are critical to our survival and our success.
>
> In our businesses, the critical resources that ultimately determine our marketing and our operating performance are people and systems.

Turnaround.   Similarly to "strategic" companies, "turnaround" firms also need a substantial IT planning effort, and it is closely linked to corporate planning. Corporate long-term performance can be severely impacted by shortfalls in IT performance and capabilities, with crucial initiatives being missed. Here also, the impact of IT on the

FIGURE 13–1 Information Technology Strategic Grid

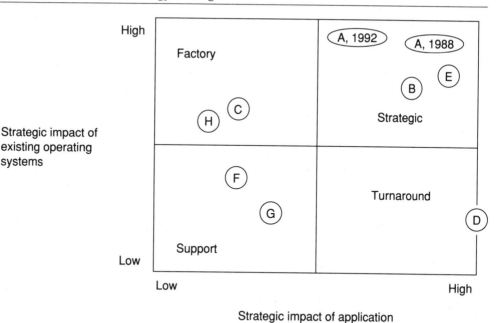

Key:

A. Major Bank 1988-1992
B. Major Insurance Company
C. Medium-size Grocery Chain
D. $100 Million Distributor
E. Major Airline
F. Major Chemical Company
G. Major Process Industry Manufacturers
H. Insurance Broker

firm's future is such that significant general management involvement in IT planning is appropriate.

These firms may receive considerable amounts of IT operational support, but the company is not absolutely dependent on the uninterrupted cost-effective functioning of this support for achieving its short-term or long-term objectives. Successful implementation of the applications under development, however, are absolutely vital for the firm's reaching its strategic objectives.

A good example of this was a rapidly growing manufacturing firm. The IT embedded in its factories and accounting processes, although important, did not require instantaneous reliability for the firm to operate effectively. However, the rapid growth of the firm's domestic and international installations—in number of products, number of sites, number of staff, and so forth—had severely strained its management control systems. This had made improving its global IT systems strategically important. The company enhanced the IT leadership, gave IT new organizational placement, and increased its commitment to IT planning in order to resolve the situation. As this example illustrates, improved IT planning is very frequently only one of the changes that must be implemented to enhance senior management's overview of IT in a "turnaround" company.

Factory. Strategic goal setting for IT and linkage to long-term corporate strategy are not nearly as critical for "factory" firms. Whereas good IT planning requires appropriate guidance regarding the corporation's direction, only limited feedback about IT constraints and capabilities need to be fed into corporate planning. Senior management involvement in IT planning appropriately is much less in this environment, but detailed year-to-year operational IT planning is absolutely critical. The 1987 flood in the computer room of a major New York investment bank (described earlier) with its massive dislocation of operating procedures, gives vivid testimony to what can happen when management fails to focus appropriately on operational issues when they really matter.

Support. For companies in the "support" quadrant strategic goal setting for IT and its linkage to long-term corporate strategy is not nearly as important as it is in "turnaround" and "strategic" environments. IT constraints are not critical to corporate success, and overachievement or underachievement of IT departmental performance do not significantly impact the firm's performance. Senior management involvement in the IT planning process can be much less here. The key danger, however, is that new opportunities may arise in the world of evolving technology, and the firm will be so "stuck" in "support" procedures that it will completely miss the opportunities.

Mismatches: Using the Strategic Grid

Selecting the appropriate planning approach is further complicated when a mismatch exists between where an organization is on the grid (see Figure 13–1) and where senior management believes it *should* be. In such a case more planning is needed for energizing the firm to make appropriate adjustments. An example illustrates the complexity of this problem.

A large financial institution's senior management was very comfortable with the company's IT performance, although it appeared on their agenda only infrequently. The IT management team, however, was deeply concerned that their senior IT managers lacked a thorough understanding of the firm's goals, what its products would be four to five years hence, and the types of organization structures and controls that would be needed. IT management knew that senior IT managers needed this input so that IT could provide the necessary support for achieving the firm's goals.

The institution was a large international one with a very sophisticated but closely held corporate planning activity. Appropriately in a world of major shifts in what financial institutions can and should do, there was great concern at the top about the confidentiality of this information, and only a handful of individuals (four or five) knew the full scope of this direction. Since neither the IT manager nor his boss was among this handful, IT was substantially in the dark about the plans of the organization and could only crudely assess it by trying to guess why some projects were funded and others were not.

The company had a full-time IT planning manager, who had three assistants and reported to the IT manager. For the last two years the IT planners had worked closely with middle-management users and the information technologists to develop strategies and applications portfolios that were seen by both sides as relevant to their needs. Because there was little formal or informal linkage between the IT planning activity and the corporate planning department (repeatedly corporate planning had communicated, "Don't call us, we'll call you"), the IT staff had two overriding concerns:

1. The plans and strategies developed for IT might be technically sound and might meet the needs of user management as they understand them today, but they may be unproductive or indeed counterproductive if they do not support the corporate thrust.
2. Corporate plans are developed "at the top" by four or five executives who are completely isolated from IT and its issues. This could unwittingly place onerous or unworkable support requests on IT in the future.

At this stage senior management perceived IT as a "factory," believed it was being staffed and managed appropriately, and had no concerns about the IT planning process. IT saw itself as "strategic" but could not sell the concept to anyone.

This frustration was resolved when an outside review of the institution's overall strategy (initiated by the chairman) noted in its conclusions that IT, a strategic force in similar firms, was not being treated as such in this firm and was moving in an unproductive direction. The outside reviewer's credibility was such that senior management readily accepted that they had misunderstood the role of IT and that IT should indeed be treated as strategic. Unfortunately, they perceived IT management as inadequate for this newly defined (newly *recognized*) challenge, and many senior IT staff did not survive the transition.

On the surface, when one read the written plan, IT planning had looked good. In fact, it had failed to come to grips with the realities of the corporate environment. Consequently, an organization for which IT activities were of significant strategic importance had been left in a state of potential unpreparedness and risk. This was fatal for the IT planners when IT activities were belatedly recognized as critical to the organization's achievement of its

---

FIGURE 13-2 Portfolio Analysis Questionnaire

	Percentage of Development Budget	Strategic Weight[a]
1. Projects involved in research impact of new technologies or anticipated new applications where generation of expertise, insight, and knowledge is the main benefit.	0–5 5–15 Over 15	1 2 3
2. Projects involved in cost-displacement or cost-avoidance productivity improvement.	Over 70 40–70 Under 40	3 2 1
3. Do estimated aggregate improvements of these projects exceed 10% of firm's after-tax profits or 1% of sales?	Yes No	2 0
4. Projects focused on routine maintenance to meet evolving business needs (processing new union contract payroll data) or new regulatory or legal requirements.	Over 70 40–70 Under 40	1 2 3
5. Projects focused on existing system enhancements that do not have identifiable hard benefits.	Under 10 10–40 Over 40	3 2 1
6. Projects whose primary benefit is new decision support information to top three levels of management. No tangible identifiable benefits.	0–5 5–15 Over 15	0 2 4
7. Projects whose primary benefit is new decision support information to middle management or clerical staff.	0–5 5–15 Over 15	0 1 2
8. Projects that allow the firm to develop and offer new products or services for sale or that	Over 20 10–20	4 3

[a]Larger numbers denote greater strategic importance.

---

product and productivity goals, because they were unfairly held accountable for this state of affairs.

Assessing the extent to which IT is strategic is useful for the company as a whole and for the individual business units and functions. IT's impact typically varies widely by unit and function, and thus the IT planning process must be adapted to deal with these differences. Those units where IT is of high impact require much more intense IT planning than those units for which it is of low impact, of course. This makes the planning more complex, but it also makes it more useful.

Figure 13–2 presents the questionnaire one firm uses to analyze the strategic thrust of the development portfolio for each of its organiza-

FIGURE 13–2 *(continued)*

	Percentage of Development Budget	Strategic Weight[a]
enable additional significant new features to be added to existing product line.	5–10	2
	Under 5	1
9. Projects that enable development of new administrative control and planning processes. No tangible benefit.	Over 20	4
	10–20	3
	5–10	2
	0–5	1
10. Projects that offer significant tangible benefits through improved operational efficiencies (reduce inventory, direct reduction in operating costs, improved credit collection, etc.).	Over 20	4
	10–20	3
	5–10	2
	0–5	1
11. Do tangible benefits amount to 10% of after-tax profit or 1% of gross sales?	Yes	2
	No	1
12. Projects that appear to offer new ways for the company to compete (faster delivery, higher quality, broader array of support services).	Over 20	4
	10–20	3
	5–10	2
	Under 5	1
13. Size of development budget as a percent of value added.	Over 4	3
	3–4	2
	2–3	1
	2	0

[a]Larger numbers denote greater strategic importance.

tional units. The questions were designed to uncover whether, on balance, the developmental work being done is critical to the firm's future competitive posture, or whether it is useful but not strategic to competitive success. Similarly, Figure 13–3 presents the questionnaire the firm uses to analyze how critical the existing systems are to an organizational unit's achieving its basic operating objectives. The firm uses these questionnaires as rough diagnostic tools.

Table 13–1 suggests that a firm's position on the strategic grid not only influences its IT planning needs, but has numerous other implications, including the role of the executive steering committee, the placement of IT in the organization, the appropriate IT management control system, and so on. Further, since organizational units within a company may be in different quadrants of the grid, the planning, organization, and control approaches suitable for one unit may be inappropriate for another. Finally, an IT planning approach that is suitable at one time may be totally wrong if the firm's position on the grid changes.

FIGURE 13–3 Operational Dependence Questionnaire[a]

1. Impact of a one-hour shutdown at main center
    Major operational disruption in customer service, plant shutdown, groups of staff totally idle.
    Inconvenient, but core business activities continue unimpaired.
    Essentially negligible.
2. Impact of two-to three-week total shutdown at main center
    Almost fatal; no ready source of backup.
    Major external visibility; major revenue shortfall or additional costs.
    Expensive; core processes can be preserved at some cost and at reduced quality levels.
    Minimal; fully acceptable tested backup procedures exist; incremental costs manageable;
        transition costs acceptable.
3. Costs of IT as percent of total corporate costs
    Over 10%.
    2%–10%.
    Under 2%.
4. Operating systems
    Operating system software totally customized and maintained internally.
    Major reliance on vendor-supplied software but significant internal enhancements.
    Almost total reliance on standard vendor package.
5. Labor
    Data center work force organized; history of strikes.
    Nonunionized work force; either inexperienced and/or low morale.
    Unorganized work force; high morale.
6. Quality control—criticalness of processing errors
    Major external exposure.
    Modest external exposure.
    Irritating; modest consequence.
7. Number of operationally critical on-line systems or batch systems
    10 or more.
    3–5.
    0–2.
8. Dispersion of critical systems
    One location.
    Two to three installations.
    Run by multiple departments; geographic dispersion of processing.
9. Ease of recovery after six-hour failure
    Three to four days; heavy workload, critical system.
    12–24 hours; critical systems.
    Negligible; almost instantaneous.
10. Recovery after quality control failure
    Time-consuming, expensive; many interrelated systems.
    Some disruption and expense.
    Relatively quick; damage well contained.
11. Feasibility of coping manually, 80%–20% basis (i.e., handling 20% of the transactions that
    have 80% of the value)
    Impossible.
    Somewhat possible.
    Relatively easy.

[a]First answer to each question indicates great operational vulnerability; last answer indicates low operational
vulnerability.

TABLE 13–1 Managerial Strategies for "Support" and "Strategic" Companies

Factor	*"Support" Company*	*"Strategic" Company*
Steering committee	Middle-level management membership. Existence of committee is less critical.	Active senior management involvement. Committee is key.
Planning	Less urgent. Mistakes in resource allocation not fatal.	Critical. Must link to corporate strategy. Careful attention to resource allocation is vital.
Project portfolio risk profile	Avoid high-risk projects because of constrained benefits. A poor place for corporate strategic gambles.	Some high-risk, high-potential-benefit projects are appropriate if possibility exists to gain strategic advantage.
IT capacity management	Can be managed in a looser way. Operational headaches are less severe.	Critical to manage. Must leave slack.
IT management reporting level	Can be low.	Should be very high.
Technical innovation	A conservative posture one to two years behind state of art is appropriate.	Critical to stay current and fund R&D. Competitor can gain advantage.
User involvement and control over system	Lower priority. Less heated debate.	Very high priority. Often emotional.
Charge-out system	Managed cost center is viable. Charge-out is less critical and less emotional.	Critical that it be sensitively designed.
Expense control	System modernization and development expenses are postponable in time of crisis.	Effectiveness is key. Must keep applications up to date; save money other places.
Uneven performance of IT management	Time is available to resolve it.	Serious and immediately actionable.

IT PLANNING AND CORPORATE STRATEGY

As noted in earlier chapters, IT has been a very sharp competitive weapon for a number of organizations and has significantly altered the firms' competitive postures. The extent to which it can be used competitively influences how a firm should think about and plan IT. Of particular importance is the firm's *underlying basis of competitive strength*.

Generic Competitive Strategies and IT Role

Michael Porter's book *Competitive Strategy*[3] provides a framework for thinking about this. Porter suggests that there are three generic strategies a firm can adopt. We mentioned them briefly in Chapter 3 and describe them here in more detail as they relate to IT as a component of corporate strategy.

Strategy 1: Be the Low-Cost Producer. This strategy is appropriate for a standardized product. Significant profit and market-share increases come from driving operating costs significantly below those of the competition. IT offers strategic value in this environment *if* it can:

1. Permit reductions in production and clerical staffs. This will reduce the cost per unit by lowering labor costs.
2. Permit fuller utilization of manufacturing facilities by better scheduling and other means. Less fixed-asset expense will be attached to the cost per unit.
3. Allow significant reductions in inventory, accounts receivable, and so forth. That is, reduce interest costs and facilities costs.
4. Provide better utilization of materials and lower overall costs by reducing waste. Use of lower-grade materials is possible in settings where quality degradation is not an issue.
5. Permit customer-perceived value-added differentiation along one or more aspects of the value chain, thus changing the rules of competition.

If the firm's manufacturing and distribution technologies do not permit these types of savings or offer the opportunity to create the customer-perceived value-added differentiation that can transform the rules of competition, IT is probably not of strategic importance to the firm's long-term competitive posture. Consequently, close, sustained linkage between the IT and corporate planning processes would not be essential. However, in this world of fast-moving technology an intense study should be undertaken every four to five years to revalidate this.

Strategy 2: Produce a Unique, Differentiated Product. This differentiation can occur along a number of dimensions such as quality, special design features, availability, and special services that offer end-consumer value. IT offers strategic value to this corporate environment *if* it:

1. Is a significant component of either the product or key aspects of the firm's value chain—hence an important, distinguishable fea-

---

[3]Michael Porter, *Competitive Strategy: Techniques for Analyzing Industries and Competitors* (New York: Free Press, 1985).

ture. Banks, brokerage houses, and credit card operations all compete on IT-based service differentiation; operations, inbound logistics, outbound logistics, and after-sales service each have strong IT components.

2. Can significantly reduce the lead time for product development, customization, and delivery. In many industries today computer-aided design/computer-aided manufacturing (CAD/CAM) provides this advantage.

3. Can permit customization of a product to the customer's specific needs in a way not possible before. This is seen in the use of CAD/CAM in producing such made-to-order specialized-textile items as men's suits.

4. Can provide a visibly higher and unique level of customer service and need satisfaction that can be built into the end price. An example of this is special-order inquiry status for key items.

If IT cannot produce unique features for firms and business units competing in this way (or deliver such massive cost reductions as to change the rules of competition), it is unlikely to have strategic impact on the firm's ability to achieve long-term competitive position. Accordingly, a close linkage between IT planning and corporate planning will not be essential on an ongoing basis. Again, a study should be undertaken every several years to validate this.

Strategy 3: Identify and Fill the Needs of Specialized Markets. Such a market might be a geographic region or a cluster of very specialized end-user needs. IT plays a strategic role for this type of firm *if:*

1. IT permits better identification of special areas of customer need and unevenness in the market through collection and analyses of company or industry sales databases to spot unusual trends. Micro-marketing in a variety of industries such as food, credit cards, and clothing has enabled firms to gain significant advantage by tailoring product performance and mix features to very specific submarkets with great success. Firms that have not reacted have felt considerable pain.

2. The firm's outputs are IT-intensive products or products whose end features can be modified by IT customization to specialized needs.

Again, this analysis gives important insight into how close the link between corporate planning and IT should be.

Summary. These paragraphs suggest that:

1. The competitive position of a business unit and its generic business strategy profoundly influence how intensely the firm should engage in planning for potential IT investments. Key inputs to the strate-

gic/turnaround/factory/support categorizations flow from analysis of the firm's competitive position and underlying bases of advantage.

2. The business units within a firm may have very different competitive positions in their sector and thus have quite different generic competitive strategies. Consequently, no single approach is likely to be appropriate for planning IT's contribution and role in each business unit.

3. Since competitive position, competitive strategy, and technology all change over time, a long-term approach to IT planning that does not vary in response to such changes is almost always inappropriate.

Corporate Environmental Factors that Influence Planning

Research has identified four corporate environmental factors that influence how IT planning must be structured in order to improve the likelihood of success.[4]

Perceived Importance and Status of the Systems Manager. The IT manager's status must align with the role that IT plays, or *should* play, in the overall operation and strategy-formulating process of the company. In an environment where IT has strategic or turnaround importance, a low-status IT manager (low status in reporting level and/or compensation) has difficulty getting the necessary information from general management in the planning process. If the corporate communication culture (style) at the top is informal, this low status can be fatal, as the IT manager will be outside the key communication loop. If the corporate culture is more formal, development and management of appropriate committees and other formal processes can significantly alleviate this potential problem.

In a company where IT is and should be serving a support function, lower status is appropriate for the IT director, and less effort needs to be made to assure alignment of IT and corporate strategy. A lower level of investment (in dollars and type of staff) in IT planning is also appropriate for such situations. These factors are apparent in the comments of a director of strategic planning for a large process-manufacturing company: "We relate to IT by giving them insight on the corporate goals and the elements and forms of a good planning system. Because of their role in the company, we do not solicit feedback from them as to 'the art of the possible.' The nature of their operation is such that they can provide no useful input to decisions of corporate strategy."

---

[4]Pyburn, "Information Systems Planning" (see footnote 1).

Physical Proximity of the Systems Group and the General Management Team.   In an organization where many important decisions are made informally in ad hoc sessions and where IT has strategic or turnaround importance, key IT management staff should be physically close to the senior line manager. (Their offices should be nearby.) Regardless of the systems manager's status, being an active member of the team in this type of organization is difficult when one is geographically distant from the other members of the team. According to a manager in one such company, "The people who are around when a problem surfaces are the ones who solve it. We don't wait to round up the missing bodies." When the prevailing management culture is more formal, physical proximity is less important. In these situations formal written communications and scheduled formal meetings largely replace the informal give-and-take.

In informal organizations in which IT is "strategic" or "turnaround," it is critical that the IT managers, and preferably a small staff, be at corporate headquarters, even if their systems development groups must be located many miles away. For "support" and "factory" organizations with informal cultures, location at corporate headquarters is much less critical.

Corporate Culture and Management Style.   In an organization where the management culture is characterized as "low key and informal" and the relationship between the IT manager and senior management is informal and personal, formal IT planning procedures do not appear to be critical to effective planning. Development of this relationship is typically assisted by geographic proximity and the IT manager's status. As an organization becomes more formal, however, disciplined IT planning becomes more significant, even in a systems environment that is not highly strategic.

Organizational Size and Complexity.   As organizations increase in size and complexity and as IT applications grow larger and more complex, formal planning processes help to ensure the kind of broad-based dialogue that is essential to the development of an integrated vision of IT. This relates to the previous comments concerning management culture and style, because greater size and complexity typically necessitate more formal practices. If the business unit size is small and relatively simple, formal planning approaches are less critical, irrespective of other factors. Similarly, for a smaller business unit where the systems environment is primarily "support," IT planning can safely be more informal. However, as the portfolio of work increases in size and integration across user areas, planning must be more disciplined and formal.

In aggregate these corporate environmental items explain why recommendations on how to do IT planning "in general" almost always are too inflexible for a specific firm. Even within a firm, these issues often force considerable diversity of practice between organization units.

An Example.   Here is an example that illustrates how these issues have shaped the planning process in a billion-dollar manufacturing organization.

Key aspects of the corporate IT environment include:

1. The company has a medium-sized corporate IT facility and stand-alone IT facilities of some significant size in its six U.S. divisions. The divisional IT facilities report "straight-line" to their respective divisions and "dotted-line" to the corporate IT function. The corporate IT group is part of a cluster of corporate staff activities, and considerable power has traditionally been located at the corporate level.
2. The corporate planning activity reports to the vice president of corporate IT. In addition, this officer has enjoyed a long personal and professional relationship with both the chairman of the board and the CEO, and the management culture of the company is informal. Responsibility for IT was initially given to him because the number of operational and developmental problems had reached crisis proportions. Under normal circumstances IT has had a "support" role, but these difficulties had pushed the firm into the "turnaround" category.
3. The closeness of relationships between the division general managers and their IT managers varies widely. The size of the divisions' application portfolios in relation to their overall size also varies considerably, with IT activities playing a more significant role in some divisions than in others.

IT planning at the divisional level begins when the corporate IT group gives them some rather loose guidelines concerning technological direction. It culminates in the preparation of a division IT plan. The planning processes and dialogues vary widely from division to division in terms of line manager involvement. In some divisions the line managers are intimately involved in the process of developing the plan, and the division general manager invests considerable time in final review and modification. In other divisions the relationship is not so close. IT plans are developed almost entirely by the IT organization, and review by general management is very limited. These differences seem to reflect the respective contributions of IT to the strategic functioning of the individual divisions.

Critical to the IT planning process is an annual three-day meeting of the vice president of corporate IT and his key staff, where the divisional IT managers present their plans. The vice president of corporate IT plays a major role in these sessions, as he critiques and suggests modifications to the plans to ensure their fit with corporate objectives. His thorough understanding of the corporation's plans, the thinking of the divisional general managers, and the thinking of the chairman and president enable him to immediately spot shortfalls in IT plans, especially in those of divisions with weak IT–line management relationships.

As a result, IT plans emerge that fit the real business needs of the organization, and the IT activity is well regarded. A set of planning processes that might lead to disaster in other settings has worked well here because of the special qualities of the vice president of corporate IT and style of communication between him and general management that is appropriate for this firm's culture.

SUMMARY

Research evidence continues to show a correlation between effective IT planning and user perception of effective IT activity. Effective execution of IT planning, however, has been found to be far more subtle and complex than envisioned by earlier authors. In addition to generating new ideas, a major role of the IT planning process is to stimulate discussion and exchange of insights between the specialists and the users. Effectively managed, it is an important element in averting potential conflicts in the firm.

The absence of this planning process can lead to enormous communication problems. A financial institution that we studied, for example, attempted at least four different approaches to IT planning over a six-year period. Each was started with great fanfare and with different staffs and organizations, and each limped to a halt. However, when the firm abandoned its planning efforts, deep and ultimately irreconcilable differences arose between IT and the user organization. Communicating viewpoints and discussing problems and potential opportunities may be as important as selecting appropriate projects.

In this context we conclude that:

1. Organizations in which IT activity is integral to corporate strategy implementation have a special need to build links between IT and the corporate strategy formulation process. Complex to implement, this requires dialogue and resolution along many dimensions. Key aspects of the dialogue are:
   a. Testing elements of corporate strategy to ensure that they are possible within the existing IT resource constraints and capabilities. On some occasions the resources needed are obtainable; in

other settings resources are unavailable, and painful readjustments must be made. Conversely, it is important that the potentials of new technologies are well understood by the formulators of corporate strategy, because they may suggest new ways of operating.

    b. Transfer of planning and strategy-formulation skills to the IT function.

    c. Ensuring long-term availability of appropriate IT resources.

In "support" and "factory" settings such linkage is less critical. Over time the nature of this linkage may appropriately change as the firm's strategic IT mission evolves.

2. As an organization grows in size, systems complexity, and formality, IT planning must be directly assigned to someone in order to retain focus and avoid the risk of significant pieces "dropping between the cracks." The job is subtle and complex. A strong set of enabling and communication skills is critical if the planner is to relate to all individuals and units affected by this technology and cope with their differing familiarity with it. Ensuring the involvement of IT staff and users for both inputs and conclusions is key. The great danger is that planners will define the task with more of a *doing* orientation than an *enabling* one and inappropriately interpose their own priorities and understandings. To overcome this problem, many organizations define this job as a transitional one, rather than a career one.

3. "Planned clutter" in the planning approach is appropriate, because the company's applications portfolio should contain *technologies* in different *phases* with different *strategic payouts* to different *units* of the firm at different *times*. While it may seem superficially attractive and orderly to plan all technologies for all business units at the same level of detail and schedule, in reality this would be inappropriate.

4. IT planning must be tailored to the realities of the organization's environment. Importance and status of the IT manager, physical placement of senior IT staff in relation to general management, corporate culture and management style, and organization size and complexity all influence how IT planning should be carried out.

5. The planning process must incorporate and integrate a broad range of technologies—internal and external electronic communications, data processing, image processing, personal computers, ...

Chapter 14

The IT Business

Previous chapters have presented frameworks for viewing the information technology activity and the functions of IT management. Taken together, the chapters of this book specify in detail how to conduct an IT management audit. This final chapter concludes the book by highlighting the impact of its six major themes:

- Information technology has different strategic importance to different organizations.
- The merging of the computing, telecommunication, and office support technologies into a single whole.
- The importance of organization learning to technology assimilation.
- The shift of make-or-buy decisions toward greater reliance on external sources of software and computing support.
- The continuing validity of the systems life cycle concept.
- The need to balance continuously the pressures of the three constituencies: IT management, user management, and general management.

"THE IT BUSINESS" ANALOGY

We have chosen to view an organization's IT activity as a stand-alone "business within a business" and, in particular, to apply the concepts of marketing-mix analysis. This permits us to develop a synthesis of the concepts of organization, planning, control, and strategy formulation for IT. Within this analogy we will speak of the business's strategy formulation as its "marketing mix," its steering committee as "the board of directors," and its IT director as "the chief executive officer." These items are particularly relevant to the interface between the IT business and its host, or parent, organization—the firm.[1] We will not explain the details of operating strategy, since the general aspects of IT operations management are covered in Chapter 11. Nor do we discuss here the issues of internal accounting and control within the IT organization, as they do not impact directly on the interface between the two businesses. For similar reasons we discuss only those IT organizational issues that deal with external relations of the IT business.

IT is a high-technology, fast-changing industry. A particular "IT business" in this industry may be growing rapidly, remaining more or less steady, or declining. Its "territory" encompasses the development, maintenance, and operation of all information technologies within a firm, regardless of where they are located and to whom they report.

The scope of technologies to be coordinated by the IT business has expanded tremendously as computers, telecommunications, and office support have merged, and its product offerings are exploding into such new consumer areas as electronic mail, editing, and computer-aided design/computer-aided manufacturing. The complexity of implementing projects, the magnitude of work to be done, and the scarcity of human resources have forced it to change from a business that primarily *produced* things to one that *distributes* things; a significant percentage of its work now involves coordinating the acquisition of outside services for use by its customers. This shift has forced major changes in its approach to planning and controls in order to deal effectively with these new products and new sources of supply.

Implicit in this view of the IT business is that, at least at a *policy* level, the overwhelming majority of firms require an integrated perspective and approach to IT. The IT activities include not just the corporate IT center and its directly linked networks, but also standalone PCs, distributed systems development activities, outside software company contracts, computer service bureaus, and so on. Many users of IT services—its customers—possess options to buy services from providers other than the central IT organization—the business within the business.

We believe this analogy is useful for applying management principles and theories to the IT function in a way that generates important insights. Similarly we believe that the analogy we draw between general management and a board of directors is useful in conceptualizing a realistic role for an executive steering committee.

Like all analogies, this one can be pushed too far, and some caution is in order. For example, the financing of the IT business is not analogous to the corporate capital markets, since its capital support comes

---

[1]Throughout this chapter the term *firm* refers to the parent holding company of the IT business.

directly from the firm (with no debt analogy), and its revenues— exclusively in many cases—also come directly from the firm. In many respects, the customer bases of the IT business and the firm are dependent on common files, et cetera, so the customers cannot be treated as entirely independent. Similarly, the IT business is free from many of the legal and governmental constraints on the firm. Other legal and governmental constraints—such as the Equal Employment Opportunity Commission (EEOC), for instance—are placed on it in the context of the firm's total corporate posture, and there is little possibility or need for the IT business to strike an independent posture.

The rest of this chapter is devoted to three topics related to managing the IT business:

- The IT marketing mix.
- The role of the IT board of directors.
- The role of the IT chief executive officer.

THE IT MARKETING MIX

The Products

The IT product line is continuously evolving. Table 14–1 summarizes the key aspects of change. Some of the dynamism of the product line is due to the enormous proliferation of opportunities afforded by the economics of new technology. Other dynamic elements are changing customer needs as a result of ordinary shifts in business and new insights (Phase-2 learning) into how technology can be applied to specific operations.

IT products range in size from very small to enormous in terms of development time and complexity to operate. A large product can have such a lengthy development period that significant uncertainty exists whether it will meet the current customers' needs when it is completed. (Four years—the time needed to rebuild some automobile manufacturing processes—is not uncommon.) The introduction of some products can be delayed with only limited damage. If delays of any magnitude occur in the development of other products, severe damage to consumers (users) will occur. In terms of day-to-day operations, the importance of cost, good response time, quality control, and so on, varies widely.

Product Obsolescence. Product obsolescence is a major headache in the IT business. Products eventually become clumsy, and introducing the necessary enhancements—styling changes—to keep them relevant is increasingly expensive. Eventually major factory retooling is

TABLE 14-1 Changes in IT Product Line

	Focus	
Factor	The Past	The Future
Product obsolescence	Developing new products.	Heavy maintenance of old products to meet challenges of obsolescence.
Source	Most products manufactured inside.	Significant percent sourced from outside.
Dominant economic constraint	Capital intensive (hardware; economy of scale).	Personnel intensive (economy of skill).
Product mix	Many large, few medium, many small products.	Some large, many medium, thousands of small products.
Profits/benefits	Good return on investment.	Many projects have intangible benefits.
New-product technologies	New technologies.	New technologies and re-groupings of old ones.
Services	Structured, such as auto-mated accounting and in-ventory control.	Unstructured, such as execu-tive decision support sys-tems and query systems.

necessary. Consumer needs (which can be satisfied by new technologies) and new manufacturing technologies offer significant opportunities for systems enhancements.

Sources, Marketplace Climate.   The method of delivering IT products is shifting as the IT customer makes sourcing decisions. An increasing percentage of IT development expenditures are going to software houses and time-sharing vendors, while production expenditures are being devoted to stand-alone minicomputers and personal computers. Formerly IT was primarily a *developer* and *manufacturer* of products; now it is becoming a significant *distributor* of products manufactured by others, including being a complete distributor in outsourcing situations, such as, the previously mentioned Eastman Kodak and General Dynamics cases. The distributor role involves identifying and evaluating products and professionally evaluating those identified by customers.

IT products run the gamut from those for which the need is clearly, correctly understood by customers (such as point-of-sale terminals) to those for which there is no perceived need and considerable, extended sales efforts must precede a sale. They range from those that are absolutely essential and critical to the customer (inventory control systems, for instance) to those that are desirable but whose purchase is essentially postponable (such as standard databases for spreadsheet files). Obviously, products at the two extremes require quite different sales approaches.

Sourcing decisions are complicated by differences in maturity of IT suppliers. For example, a relatively stable competitive pattern exists among suppliers of large mainframe computers. Conversely, there is much turbulence in the personal computer and office support markets. In fact, there is considerable uncertainty as to which companies will survive and what form their products will have five years from now. A competitive pattern is emerging here, but the AT&T divestiture and cellular innovations will confound the nature of competition for the foreseeable future in telecommunications.

Further, in the past, monopoly control over product delivery gave IT businesses considerable discretion in timing their introductions of new products. The changed climate of competition among suppliers means that IT has lost control over the marketing of new products in many organizations.

Profits/Benefits.   In terms of benefits the products range from those that can be crisply summarized in a return-on-investment (ROI) framework for the customer to those whose benefits are more qualitative and intangible in nature. Again, products at the ends of the spectrum require different marketing approaches. Some products are absolutely structured (certain types of accounting data), while others are tailored to individual tastes and preferences. Further, in many instances a product's complexity and inherent factors that influence quality are not easily comprehended by purchasers. Finally, some products require tailoring during installation. These products need specific field support and distribution staffs.

Implications for Marketing.   This description of IT product characteristics points to the complexity of the IT marketing task by showing that the IT business distributes evolving products distinguished by a wide range of characteristics. In other businesses a strong effort is often made to streamline the product line in order to facilitate economy and efficiency in manufacturing and distribution. The inability to accomplish this in many IT businesses has contributed to turbulence in their management. Too often they are trying to deliver too many products from their traditional monopoly-supplier position with weak promotion, surly sales, and fixation on manufacturing—as opposed to distributing. What works for one set of products may not work for another. Recognizing the need for and implementing a differentiated marketing approach is very difficult, particularly for a medium-sized IT business.

The IT Consumer

Description of the Consumer. The IT consumer is changing in terms of needs and sophistication. Table 14–2 summarizes important aspects of these changes. After 20 years of working with mature technologies, older consumers have developed a sensitivity to the problems of working within constraints. Many of them are quite unaware of the newer technologies and the enormous behavioral modifications they must make in order to use them properly. They bring their old purchasing habits to the new environment without understanding that it is new. Younger consumers, on the other hand, have close familiarity with personal computing and tend to be intolerant when they are unable to get immediate access to it. They also tend to be naive about the problems of designing and maintaining IT systems that must run on a regular basis. In general, both classes of consumers have major educational needs if they are to become responsible consumers.

The new user-friendly technologies have made the problem more complicated, because many consumers see the opportunity to withdraw from reliance on the IT business and set up their own small business. They are often propelled in this direction by their own entrepreneurs

TABLE 14–2 Changes in IT Consumer Profile

Factor	Consumers	
	Older	*Younger*
Experience with older technologies	Experienced.	Inexperienced.
Attitude toward newer technologies	Leery.	Enthusiastic and unsophisticated (but they do not recognize their lack of sophistication).
Visibility	Identifiable as consumers.	Often unidentifiable as consumers; numerous at all levels in organizations.
Attitude toward IT unit	Willing to accept IT staff as experts.	Many are hostile because they want to develop their own solutions.
Self-confidence	Low confidence in their own abilities (often cautious because of cost).	High confidence in their abilities and judgment (often unwarranted).
Turnover rate	High.	High.

or purchasing agents (that is, decentralized systems analysts) who are long on optimism and short on practical, firsthand expertise and realistic risk assessment.

In this environment, the IT marketing force needs to target new consumers and reach them before they make independent decisions. New application clusters and groups of consumers keep surfacing. The ever changing composition of consumer groups sustains the need for a field sales force. An effective job of educating people does no good if they move on to other assignments and are replaced by people who are unaware of current technologies and the sequence of decisions that led to the present status of the organization.

Firsthand personal computing experience and a barrage of advertising have substantially raised consumers' expectations and their general level of self-confidence in making IT decisions. Unfortunately, this confidence is often misplaced; there seems to be a lack of appreciation for subtle but important nuances and for the IT control practices necessary for a significant probability of success. This also increases the need for sustained direct sales and follow-up.

In today's environment there is an explosion in the number of service alternatives for customers, some of them with very low prices. It is confusing to the end consumers when products essentially similar to those available in-house appear to be available at much lower prices out of house. Great consumer sophistication is needed to identify a *real* IT bargain.

Implications for Marketing. These factors have substantially complicated the IT marketing effort. An unstable group of consumers with diversified, rapidly changing needs requires a far higher level of direct-selling effort than do consumers without this cluster of characteristics. The need to spend promotion money on a difficult group has been intensified by a low regard for corporate IT in many settings. Consumers who are hostile about the quality of IT support welcome solutions that will carry them as far away as possible from reliance on the central IT business unit. Trained to respond correctly to many of yesterday's technologies, they are inappropriately trained for today's. Underinvestment in the marketing that is necessary for dealing with these realities has been a major cause of dissatisfaction among users.

Costs

Cost Factors. From a marketing viewpoint, significant changes are occurring in the costs of producing and delivering systems. Table 14–3 identifies some of these changes. On the one hand, the cost of many elements of IT hardware has decreased dramatically and is likely to

TABLE 14–3 Changes in Consumer Costs

	Cost to the Consumer	
Cost Factor	The Past	The Future
Hardware	Very expensive.	Very expensive.
Economies of scale	Major in large systems; user stand-alones not feasible in most cases.	Limited in large systems; user stand-alones very attractive.
Software systems development	Expensive.	Less expensive in some cases.
Software acquisitions	Limited cost-effective outside opportunities.	Attractive cost-effective opportunites.
Development and production	Hard to estimate.	Hard to estimate.
Maintenance	Underestimated.	Soaring.

continue to drop significantly. On the other hand, progress in reducing the cost of software development is likely to continue to be slow for some time. On top of this, the ability to accurately estimate the development, production, and maintenance costs for large, high-technology, low-structure systems continues to be disappointing.

A critical component of cost explosion has been the steady increase in the cost of maintaining installed software. These expenses are usually not factored in carefully at the time of purchase, and they tend to grow exponentially as the business grows and changes over the years. In the short term these costs can be deferred with apparently little damage. In the long term, however, neglecting them can cause a virtual collapse of the product.

The proliferation of software houses and packages and the cost changes have accelerated the movement of the IT business into the distributor role. It is now cost-effective to purchase specialized databases and software that are useful to many users and that would be utterly uneconomic if developed by single users for their own purposes. Not all efforts in developing shared software have been successful, however. For example, a consortium of 25 regional banks funded a joint $13 million software development project (in areas such as demand deposit accounting and savings accounts). The consortium's inability to manage the project doomed it to failure. Another change is the growing number of users who have their own computer capacity. At some business schools 100 percent of the students and over 90 percent of the faculty own personal computers. The schools no longer own this equipment but facilitate its acquisition by the students and faculty.

As will be discussed in the section on pricing, it is difficult to identify potential or actual total costs for a particular product or service. In part this is because a particular data or software development may support multiple products and consumers. This generates concern as to whether costs should be treated as joint costs or by-product costs. Another complicating issue is the extent to which previously spent R&D costs (to get to today's skill levels) should be treated as part of a product's cost.

While cost management and control are a critical component of the IT business strategy, how they are executed varies significantly among IT settings. In high-growth, product-competitive environments there is less emphasis on IT efficiency and cost control than in environments where the IT products are more stable and competition is cost-based.

Implications for Marketing.   In summary, the changing cost structure of IT *products* has forced the IT *business* to reconsider its sourcing decisions and has pushed it to assume a much stronger distribution role. The relative emphases an IT business places on cost control, product-line growth, quality, and service depend on its business strategy. Thus wide variances exist.

Channels of Distribution

As described in Chapters 2, 7, and 8, the number of channels of distribution (to users) and their relative importance have been shifting rapidly. Table 14–4 shows some of the important changes in this domain. Historically, the major channel for both manufacturing and delivering the IT product has been the IT business itself; in most firms it has had a complete monopoly. Changing cost factors and shifts in user preferences have placed great pressure on this channel and have caused deep concern inside the IT business as it has tried to adapt to the new challenges of a competitive market—which it cannot totally serve in a cost-effective fashion from its manufacturing facility. Adapting to a new mission, the IT business is now *not* the sole channel but, rather, one of many sources of manufacturing, and it has assumed the major new role of identifying products in other channels and assessing their cost, quality, and other aspects. Adapting to this new role has made many IT businesses very uncomfortable psychologically as they have struggled with such incorrect notions of loss of power.

Risks in Using New Channels.   Successful, rapid adaptation by the IT business is critical to the health of its present and future consumers. The new channels, while offering very attractive products and cost structures, introduce sizable risks in many cases. The most important of these risks include:

TABLE 14-4   Changes in the IT Channels of Distribution

Distribution Factor	The Past	The Future
Development by central IT	Heavy.	Significant but smaller percent of total.
Direct purchase of hardware/software by user	Limited.	Major.
Service source for individual user	Limited to service from large, shared system.	Can obtain powerful independent system.
Service bureaus	Sell time.	Sell products and time bundled together.
Use of external databases via time-sharing	Limited.	Major.
Number of software and processing services	A few; crude.	Many.
Software development by users	Limited.	Major (facilitated by packages and user-friendly languages).
Reliance on external contract analysts/programmers	Very significant.	More significant; full outsourcing is a real alternative.

1. Misassessment of the real development and operations costs of the products in the channel. Important short-term and, more important, long-term cost factors may be completely overlooked.
2. Consumer vulnerability to abuse of data by failure to control access, install documentation procedures, and implement data disciplines.
3. Financial vulnerability of the supplier. If there is a possibility of failure, the consumer's fundamental interests need to be protected in some way.
4. Obsolescence of products. If the supplier is not likely to keep the products modernized (at some suitable cost) for the consumer over the years, alternatives (if they are important) should be available. (Obviously, a financial-transaction processing system may be more vulnerable to obsolescence than a decision support model.)

Considerable marketing and internal adjustment of perspectives are needed by the IT business if its consumers are to feel that they can rely on the IT staff to evaluate alternate channels objectively—instead of pushing their own manufacturing facility at every opportunity. A long-term solution will develop knowledgeable consumers. Failure to execute this mission will ultimately cripple the IT business's effectiveness in servicing its customers' needs. This will occur through fragmentation of data needed by many consumers, redundant development efforts, and an increase in poorly conceived and managed local factories.

Competition

The IT-marketing-mix analogy is weakest in describing administrative practice and problems in the area of competition. The IT business faces two principal competitive obstacles:

1. Potential consumers independently seeking solutions without engaging the IT business in either its manufacturing or its distribution capacity.
2. Potential consumers failing to recognize that they have problems or opportunities that can be addressed by IT.

In the first case, competition arises because of poor performance of the IT business. Its inability to formulate and implement sensible, useful guidelines to assist consumers in their purchase decisions is a failure of IT to adapt its product line to meet the needs of the changing times. For the broad purposes of the firm it may be useful to run this aspect of the IT business as a loss leader. Loss of manufacturing business to other channels in a planned or managed way should not be seen as a competitive loss to the IT business, but simply as a restructuring of its product line to meet changing consumer needs. One of the most successful IT businesses the authors have seen has recently halved its central IT manufacturing capacity. It has created in its place a series of small manufacturing centers near major clusters of users (at divisional headquarters). These systems include an explosion of stand-alone office support systems with all phases of the systems life cycle except the construction phase under user control.

With regard to the second case, competition—really the cost of delayed market opportunity—arises as a result of ineffective management of price, product, or distribution policies and results in consumers in an imperfect market allocating funds to projects that may have less payoff than IT products. The IT business has a monopoly responsibility: sometimes it produces a product; other times it stimulates consumer awareness of appropriate external sources of supply. The notion of aggressive external competition hurting the IT business through pricing, product innovation, and creative distribution is not appropriate in this setting.

Promotion

The rapid changes in information technology and the turnover in consumers make promotion one of the most important elements of the marketing mix to manage. This is because, unlike the previously discussed elements, it is largely within the control of IT management. Phase-2 learning by consumers is at the core of a successful IT business. Even as today's mature technologies are being delivered to consumers, a strong need exists to cultivate tomorrow's consumers by exposing them to tomorrow's products. Price discounts (introductory offers), branch offices (decentralized analysts), and a central IT sales force are key to making this happen.

A multinational electronics company, for example, has a 400-person central IT manufacturing facility near its corporate headquarters. Included in this staff are five international marketing representatives who constantly promote new IT products and services. Their job consists of preparing promotional material, organizing educational seminars, and making frequent trips to overseas units so as to develop and maintain close professional relationships with IT consumers. These relationships permit them to effectively disseminate services and to acquire insight into the performance of the existing products and the need for new products. This level of effort is regarded as absolutely essential to the IT business.

In large part the need to adapt is due to the recent shift in the industry. From the beginning of the industry to the late 1970s, the large information systems suppliers sold primarily to the IT managers. Most vendors that initially had a strong industrial marketing approach have now added a retail marketing one. Office-support and computer suppliers have not only opened retail stores; they also now sell directly to end users. This has forced the IT business to promote the validity of its guidelines within the firm to protect its firm's users from disasters.

A number of IT businesses have organized both their development and production control activities around market structure, as opposed to manufacturing technology. In other words, rather than a traditional development group, a programming group, and a maintenance group, they have assigned development staffs to specific clusters of consumers. This structure promotes close, long-term relationships and better understanding and action on operation problems as they arise.

The extreme of this approach was McGraw-Hill's 1984 corporate reorganization away from a media-oriented structure (newspaper, television, etc.) toward an end-customer structure, each unit of which can be served by a mix of media. Within these market units it is appropriate to fund specific integrating and liaison positions, as opposed to purely technical positions. This approach is critical, since as a result of past performance and poor marketing, the IT business may be in a weak competitive position compared to outside software companies with large marketing staffs. This large investment in promotion is often among the IT unit's most important expenditures and should be the last to be cut back.

IT newsletters containing announcements of new services and products—that is, advertising and promotional material—should be sent to key present and potential business consumers regularly. Similarly, IT can conduct a program of consumer educational seminars or classes and publicize appropriate external educational programs to assist the marketing effort. Complemented by appropriate sales calls, this can accelerate Phase-2 learning.

The ideal mix of these promotional tools varies widely by organizational setting. Just as industrial and consumer companies have very different promotion programs, so also should different IT units. The strategic relevance of products to consumers and the consumers' sophistication level and geographic location are some factors that affect appropriate promotion.

Price

The setting of IT prices—an emotional and rapidly changing process, as noted in Chapter 9—is a very important element in establishing a businesslike, professional relationship between the IT business and its consumers. Indeed, aggressive, marketing-oriented pricing policies legitimize the concept of the stand-alone IT business. Issues that make pricing complicated are discussed here.

Inefficient Market.   Establishing rational, competitive criteria is complicated by several factors:

1. Product quality is largely hidden and is very elusive to all but the most sophisticated and meticulous consumer. Prices that on the surface appear to be widely disparate may actually be quite comparable.
2. Vendors differ in their goals, product mixes, and stability. A small vendor that is trying to buy into a market may offer a very attractive price in order to defuse questions about its financial viability.
3. Vendors may price a service as a by-product of some other necessary business. This can produce a more attractive price than a pricing system that attempts to charge each user a proportionate share of the full cost of the manufacturing operation. This explains the bargains available when in-house operations try to dispose of excess capacity in return for some "financial contribution." Long-term sta-

bility should be a concern to the consumer. (What if my output were to become the main product and the other consumer's output the by-product?)

4. Excess-capacity considerations may allow attractive short-term marginal prices. A variant of this is a bargain entry-level price to attract the consumer. Once captured, the customer is subjected to significantly higher prices. This pricing practice is particularly prevalent for large, internally developed telecommunications systems.

Introductory Offers. To stimulate Phase-2 learning and long-term demand, deep discounts on early business are often appropriate. This can generate access to long-term profits at quite different price or cost structures.

Monopoly Issues. Review and regulation of pricing decisions by senior management is sometimes needed because of IT's de facto monopoly position. Highly confidential data and databases needed by multiple users in geographically remote locations are examples of IT products that cannot be supplied by providers other than the firm's IT business. It is important that the prices of these services be appropriately regulated to prevent abuses.

"Unbundling." The pricing strategy should incorporate two practices that are not widely used. The first is "unbundling" development, maintenance, operations, and special turnaround requirements into separate packages, each with its own price. Establishing these prices "at arm's length" in advance is critical in maintaining a professional relationship with the consumers. The IT business must negotiate the prices with as much care as outside software companies exercise in their negotiations with these consumers. This negotiation can be useful in educating users on the true costs of service.

The second desirable practice is making prices understandable to the consumers. This is accomplished by stating prices in *consumer* units such as price per number of report pages, per number of customer records, per invoice, and so on, rather than as utilization of such IT-resource units as CPU cycles and MIPS. The added risk (if any) of shocking a potential consumer with the facts of economic life tends to be more than offset by much better communication between the IT business and the consumer.

Profit. A final pricing issue, which also strains the independent-business analogy, is the amount of emphasis that should be placed on showing a profit. In the short term (in some cases even for the long term), *should* an IT business make a profit, or even break even in some settings? IT businesses in firms where consumers need a lot of education and where much Phase-1 and -2 experimentation is needed may appropriately run at a deficit for a long time. This issue must be resolved before the pricing policy is established.

Establishing an appropriate IT pricing policy is one of the most complex pricing decisions made in industry. An appropriate resolution, critical to a healthy relationship with the IT consumer, weaves a course between monopolistic and genuine competitive issues, deals with imperfect markets, and resolves ambiguities concerning the role of profits.

THE ROLE OF THE BOARD OF DIRECTORS

A subject of general interest that first surfaced in Chapter 1 is the appropriate relationship of the firm's general management to the IT business. We find it useful to think of it as similar to the role of a board of directors in any business. (Many firms give this de facto recognition by creating an executive steering committee.) Viewing its role in this way, the key tasks of general management can be summarized as follows:

1. Appoint and continually assess the performance of the IT chief executive officer (normally a function of the nominating committee).
2. Assure that appropriate standards are in place and being adhered to. This includes the receipt and review of detailed reports on the subject from the IT auditor and a more cursory review by the firm's external auditors (normally a function of the audit committee).
3. Ensure that the board is constructed to provide overall guidance to the IT business from its various constituencies. Unlike the board of a publicly held firm, the IT board does not need a representation of lawyers, bankers, investment bankers, and so forth. It does need senior user managers who can and are willing to provide user perspective. (As the strategic importance of the IT business to the firm decreases, the level of these managers should also decrease.) At the same time, people from R&D and technology planning and production (people who have IT development and operations backgrounds) need to be present to ensure feasibility of suggestions.
4. Provide broad guidance for the strategic direction of the IT business, ensuring that comprehensive planning processes are present within the IT business and that the outputs of the planning processes fit the firm's strategic direction. Practically, the board will carry out this surveillance through a combination of:
   a. IT management presentations on market development, product planning, and financial plans.
   b. Review of summary documentation of overall direction.
   c. Formal and informal briefings by selected board members on how the IT business is supporting the firm's business needs.
   d. Request for and receipt of internal and external reviews of these issues as appropriate.

This definition of the board's role addresses the realities of the members' backgrounds and available time for this kind of work. Focusing on operational or technical detail is unlikely to be suitable or effective. In many settings periodic (every one to two years) education sessions for the board members have been useful for making them more comfortable in their responsibilities and for bringing them up to date on trends within the particular IT business and the IT industry in general.

THE ROLE OF THE IT CHIEF EXECUTIVE OFFICER

Historically a high-turnover job, the IT chief executive position is difficult and demanding, requiring a steadily shifting mix of skills over time. It is critical that the IT CEO:

1. Maintain board relationships personally. This includes keeping the board appropriately informed about major policy issues and problems and being fully responsive to their needs and concerns. A need for a strong link between the board and the customers exists that is not present in many other settings.
2. Ensure that the strategy-formulation processes evolves adequately and that appropriate detailed action programs are developed. As in any high-technology business, high-quality technical review of potential new technologies is absolutely essential. Its interpretation is crucial and may well lead to major changes in organization, product mix, and marketing strategy. Without aggressive CEO leadership, the forces of cultural inertia may cause the IT business to delay far too long.
3. Pay close attention to salary, personnel practices, and employee quality-of-life issues. The IT work force is far more mobile and difficult to replace than the firm's other employees.
4. Give high priority to manufacturing security, which is more important in an IT business than in most other businesses. A single, disgruntled employee can do a vast amount of damage that may go undetected for a long time.
5. Assure an appropriate management balance between the marketing, manufacturing, and control parts of the IT business. Of the three, marketing—in its broadest sense—is the one most often neglected. CEOs who have begun their careers in manufacturing and dealt with operating difficulties tend to be most sensitive to manufacturing issues. However, since their manufacturing experience was at a particular time with a particular mix of technology assimilation problems and a particular set of control responses, even their perspectives in these areas may not be appropriate for today's manufacturing challenges.

6. Develop an IT esprit de corps. A key factor of success in the IT business is the belief in IT's value to the firm. Senior IT managers must develop team spirit and lead their organizations into new ventures with enthusiasm. At the same time, they must earn the confidence of the board by exhibiting good judgment—not only taking risks but also making wise decisions on how to limit the market and when to forgo a useful technology. They must balance keeping abreast with reading the market's receptiveness accurately.

SUMMARY

This chapter has discussed several important complicating aspects of the IT business. Complex and shifting products, changing consumers, new channels of distribution, and evolving cost structures have forced a major reanalysis and redirection of IT's product offerings and marketing efforts. The changed marketing environment has forced significant changes in IT manufacturing, organization, control systems, and most fundamentally, in its perception of its strategic mission.

Ted Levitt's classic article, "Marketing Myopia"[2] best captures this idea. Levitt noted that the great growth industry of the 19th century— the railroads—languished because the owners and managers saw themselves in the *railroad* business, rather than the *transportation* business. The point here is that IT is not in the electronic-based computer, telecommunications, and office support business. Rather, it is in *the business of bringing a sustained stream of innovation in information technology to companies' operations and*, in many cases, *products*. Far too many people in the IT business myopically believe they are running a computer center! Failure to perceive and act on their broader role can lead to a collapse of their operations, loss of jobs, and great disservice to the customer base.

When IT is defined in this way, the dynamic, successful marketing mix for the 1990s suddenly snaps into focus. To rely on an existing product structure and attempt to devise more efficient ways to deliver the old technology within old organizational structures will certainly lead to dissolution of the IT business. The IT organization has been an agent of change for its customers for 30 years. The change agent itself also must change if it is to remain relevant.

---

[2]Theodore Levitt, "Marketing Myopia," *Harvard Business Review*, September–October 1975.

Annotated Bibliography

GENERAL MANAGEMENT LIBRARY FOR THE
IT MANAGER

Ackoff, Russell L. *Creating the Corporate Future: Plan or Be Planned For.* New York: John Wiley & Sons, 1981.

An important book that provides a broad context for IT planning.

Anthony, Robert N. *The Management Control Function.* Boston, Mass.: Harvard Business School Press, 1988.

This book introduces the framework of operational control, management control, and strategic planning and has been a major contributor to thinking about the different areas of IT application and their different management problems.

Badaracco, Joseph L., Jr. *The Knowledge Link.* Boston, Mass.: Harvard Business School Press, 1991.

How firms cooperate to exchange information in order to capitalize on each other's knowledge.

Barabba, Vincent P., and Gerald Zaltman. *Hearing the Voice of the Market.* Boston, Mass.: Harvard Business School Press, 1991.

How to develop an inquisitive market program that develops competence in utilizing information.

Bartlett, Christopher A., and Sumantra Ghoshal. *Managing across Borders: The Transnational Solution.* Boston, Mass.: Harvard Business School Press, 1991.

A succinct and mind-expanding discussion of the impact, true costs, and strategic value of computer systems and their notable future influence.

Bower, Joseph L. *Managing the Resource Allocation Process: A Study of Corporate Planning and Investment.* Boston, Mass.: Division of Research, Harvard Business School Classics, 1986.

This in-depth analysis of corporate planning and capital budgeting provides critical insights relevant to both the role of steering committees and how IT planning can be done effectively.

Buzzell, Robert D., ed. *Marketing in an Electronic Age.* Boston, Mass.: Harvard Business School Press, 1985.
A series of essays on how information technology will impact the marketing function.

Clark, Kim B., and Takahiro Fujimoto. *Product Development Performance.* Boston, Mass.: Harvard Business School Press, 1991.
A descriptive analysis of European, Japanese, and U.S. automobile manufacturing to demonstrate the salient aspects of quality and timely manufacturing management.

Foulkes, Fred K. *Executive Compensation.* Boston, Mass.: Harvard Business School Press, 1991.
Thirty leading compensation consultants advise on effective programs.

Heskett, James L. *Managing in the Service Economy.* Boston, Mass.: Harvard Business School Press, 1986.
Practical advice on the issues in managing a service organization. Much of this advice translates directly to the IT resource.

Kimberly Miles and Associates. *The Organizational Life Cycle.* San Francisco: Jossey–Bass, 1981.
Reports, findings, and analyses of key issues concerning the creation, transformation, and decline of organizations.

Lawrence, Paul R., and Jay W. Lorsch. *Organization and Environment: Managing Integration and Differentiation.* Boston, Mass.: Harvard Business School Classics, 1986.
This classic presents the underlying thinking of the need for specialized departments and how they should interface with the rest of the organization. It is relevant for all IT organizational decisions.

Merchant, Kenneth A. *Control in Business Organizations.* Marshfield, Mass.: Pitman Publishing, 1986.
An excellent framework for thinking about contemporary management control issues.

Porter, Michael E. *Competitive Advantage: Creating and Sustaining Superior Performance.* New York: Free Press, 1985.
The comprehensive text on how to identify and achieve competitive advantage.

Porter, Michael E., ed. *Competition in Global Industries.* Boston, Mass.: Harvard Business School Press, 1986.
A series of articles relating to competitive issues in the international environment.

Schein, Edgar H. *Organizational Psychology,* 3rd ed. Englewood Cliffs, N.J.: Prentice-Hall, 1980.

This classic book on the field focuses on how to manage the tension between the individual and the organization.

IT LIBRARY FOR THE GENERAL MANAGER

Anderla, Georges, and Anthony Dunning. *Computer Strategies: 1990–9.* New York: John Wiley & Sons, 1987.

A description of the Japanese chip maker strategy, the economic implications of chip development, and the true "costs" of computing in the 1990s.

Bradley, Stephen P., and Jerry A. Hausman, eds. *Future Competition in Telecommunications.* Boston, Mass.: Harvard Business School Press, 1989.

A symposium of industry suppliers, customers, and regulators discussing the future impacts of deregulation.

Itami, Hiroyuki, with Thomas W. Roehl. *Mobilizing Invisible Assets.* Cambridge, Mass.: Harvard University Press, 1987.

A description of how the Japanese organization brings experience and analysis to bear in developing and implementing strategy.

Keen, Peter G. W. *Every Manager's Guide to Information Technology.* Boston, Mass.: Harvard Business School Press, 1991.

A glossary of key terms and concepts of computer and planning procedures.

Keen, Peter G. W. *Shaping the Future: Business Design through Information Technology.* Boston, Mass.: Harvard Business School Press, 1991.

A succinct and mind-expanding discussion of the impact, true costs, and strategic value of computer systems and their notable future influence.

Leebaert, Derek, ed. *Technology 2001: The Future of Computing and Communications.* Cambridge, Mass.: MIT Press, 1991.

A set of articles by research scientists from every major player in the business, e.g., IBM, DEC, Cray, Apple, etc. A sound view of the future.

Rochester, Jack B., and John Gantz. *The Naked Computer.* New York: William Morrow and Company, Inc., 1983.

An interesting and broad compendium of computer lore that has shaped the myths and realities of developing and using computer systems.

Walton, Richard E. *Technology and the Organization.* Boston, Mass.: Harvard Business School Press, 1989.

A thoughtful perspective on how to develop and maintain congruence between the organization and systems in the implementation of an IT-based strategy by a leading organizational scholar/consultant.

Zuboff, Shoshana. *In the Age of the Smart Machine.* New York: Basic Books, 1988.
An insightful integration of the dual nature of the influence of computer-based systems on a working group and discussion of how best to create a learning organization.

Index

A

ACORD, 100
Action controls, 159
Adaptation
  to change, 87-88
  technological, 29,
    250-51
Advantage, maintaining,
  22
Aetna Insurance, 70
After-sale service, 52,
  55-56
Airlines, 19, 20, 21, 22,
  23, 42, 54, 61, 62, 63,
  72, 76, 80, 93, 95, 96,
  98, 99, 104-5, 198,
  233-34
Allegis Corporation,
  95-96
Alliances. *See*
  Information-enabled
  alliances
Allocated cost center,
  161-66
Allocation
  priorities of, 68
  problems of, 162-64
Alternative organiza-
  tions, 195-96
Amadeus Coalition, 98
Amdahl, 155
American Airlines, 19,
  21, 22, 54, 61, 62, 63,
  72, 76, 80, 93, 98, 99,
  105, 198
American Express/Shear-
  son Lehman, 70

American Gem Market
  System, 100
American Hospital Sup-
  ply Corporation, 62,
  99, 101
American President
  Lines, 234
Analogy, and IT busi-
  ness, 269-71
Analysis
  cost. *See* Cost analysis
  ICA. *See* Industry and
    competitive analy-
    sis (ICA)
  of impact, 43-51
  and portfolio analysis
    questionnaire,
    258-59
  and value chain oppor-
    tunity, 51-58
Annotated bibliography,
  286-89
Anthony, Robert, 251
APOLLO, 72, 76, 80
Apple Corporation, 128
Applications, Orwellian,
  232
Applications develop-
  ment portfolio, 24
Applications develop-
  ment process, 33-37
Appraisal program, of
  technology, 243-44
Appropriateness, 9
Architectural alterna-
  tives, 107-32
  and assimilation
    phases, 115

  and evolving IT envi-
    ronment, 107-10
  and managing infor-
    mation technology,
    114-23
  and merging informa-
    tion technology,
    111-14
  and patterns of hard-
    ware/data distribu-
    tion, 123-30
  See also Architecture
Architecture
  alternatives. *See* Ar-
    chitectural alter-
    natives
  of control. *See* Control
  guidance on, 237-38
  and operations strat-
    egy, 197-99
Argyris, Chris, 28, 115
Arthur Andersen, 177
Artifacts, 122
ASAP, of American Air-
  lines, 62, 63
Assessment, of risk of
  individual projects,
  178-82
Asset investment levels,
  91-92
Assimilation, 115-19
AT&T, 25, 96, 111, 113,
  114, 206
ATM. *See* Automatic
  teller machines
  (ATM)
Audit, management, 17
Audit function, 172-73